LYING

SISSELA BOK

LYING

Moral Choice in Public and Private Life

VINTAGE BOOKS
A Division of Random House, Inc.
New York

VINTAGE BOOKS EDITION, December 1989

Copyright © 1978, 1989 by Sissela Bok

All rights reserved under International and Pan-American Copyright
Conventions. Published in the United States by Vintage Books, a
division of Random House, Inc., New York, and in Canada by
Random House of Canada Limited, Toronto. Originally published
by Pantheon Books, a division of Random House, Inc., in May 1978.

Library of Congress Cataloging in Publication Data
Bok, Sissela.
    Lying.
    Bibliography: p.
    Includes index.
    1.   Truthfulness and falsehood.   I.   Title.
BJ1421.B64   1979   177'.3   78-21949
    ISBN 0-679-72470-2 (pbk.)

Since this copyright page cannot accommodate all acknowledgments,
they have been placed on the following pages.

Manufactured in the United States of America

10   9   8   7   6   5   4

Grateful acknowledgment is made to the following for permission to reprint previously published material:

Lewis White Beck: Excerpt from "On a Supposed Right to Lie from Altruistic Motives" in *The Critique of Practical Reason and Other Writings in Moral Philosophy* by Immanuel Kant, ed. and trans. by Lewis White Beck.

Basil Blackwell, Publisher: Excerpt from "Utilitarianism Revised" by R. F. Harrod. Reprinted from *Mind* 45 (1936): 137–56.

The Bobbs-Merrill Co., Inc.: Excerpt from *On the Law of War and Peace* by Hugo Grotius, trans. by Francis W. Kelsey.

Burns & Oates: Excerpt from *Summa Theologica* 2, 2, ques. 110, art. 2, by Thomas Aquinas, literally trans. by the Fathers of the English Dominican Province. Copyright Burns & Oates 1953, 1977.

The Catholic University of America Press: Excerpts from "Lying" and "Against Lying" in *Treatises on Various Subjects*, vols. 14, 16, by St. Augustine, ed. by R. J. Deferrari, in *Fathers of the Church series*.

Harvard University Press: Excerpt from *The Poems of Emily Dickinson*, ed. by Thomas H. Johnson. Reprinted by permission of the publishers and the Trustees of Amherst College. Copyright © 1951, 1955 by the President and Fellows of Harvard College.

Alfred A. Knopf, Inc.: Excerpt from *Three Plays* by Jean-Paul Sartre. Copyright 1948, 1949 by Alfred A. Knopf, Inc. Reprinted by permission of Alfred A. Knopf, Inc.

MacMillan & Co., London: Excerpt from "Classification of Duties—Veracity" in *The Method of Ethics*, 7th ed., by H. Sidgwick.

Macmillan Publishing Co. and SCM Press: Excerpt from "What Is Meant by 'Telling the Truth'?" by Dietrich Bonhoeffer in *Ethics*, ed. by Eberhard Berthge. Copyright © 1955 by Macmillan Publishing Co. Inc. © SCM Press, Ltd., 1955

Methuen & Co. Ltd.: Excerpt from *The Object of Morality* by G. J. Warnock.

Ward, Lock, Ltd.: Excerpt from "Of Truth" in *Essays Civil and Moral* by Francis Bacon.

For Derek

CONTENTS

ACKNOWLEDGMENTS

I am happy to thank those many friends who shared with me the thoughts that the subject of lying inevitably brings to mind; and to thank especially those who read all or part of the manuscript: Graham Allison, Barbara Barss, John Blum, Hilary Bok, Harold Bursztajn, Ann Cohen, Burton Dreben, Neva and Walter Kaiser, Margaret Kiskadden, Melvin Levine, Alva Myrdal, Bertha Neustadt, John Noonan, Jr., Brita Stendahl, Judith Thomson, and Ruth and Lloyd Weinreb. Their criticisms meant a great deal at every stage of writing; if I did not always take their advice, I alone am to blame.

My gratitude goes also to John Coakley and Deborah Narcini for locating and translating theological texts; and to Deborah Lipman for most expert assistance in preparing the manuscript. I thank James Peck, moreover, for his most welcome help in editing this book.

Finally, I dedicate this book to my husband, in recognition of all that his interest, criticism, and support have meant.

PREFACE

Over ten years have passed since this book was first published, in 1978. During that period, the issues of truthfulness and deceit have received considerable debate. I can no longer subscribe, therefore, to the claim I made in the Introduction, that those issues have received extraordinarily little contemporary analysis. Questions of truthfulness and deception are now taken up in classrooms as in the media and in scholarly literature. Codes of ethics, such as the 1980 "Principles of Medical Ethics" of the American Medical Association, have incorporated clauses stressing honesty.

More than debate, however, will be needed to press for changes in actual practices of lying, especially as those most tempted to engage in such practices find it easiest to ignore all hard questions about what they are doing. New examples have come to supplement those of Watergate and Vietnam and others mentioned in this book. In Wall Street investment firms, as among TV evangelists, in political campaigns, and in the interlocking schemes of the Iran-Contra scandal, we have seen how pervasive the resulting damage can be to those who lie, equivocate, and resort to innuendo as well as to their dupes. We have also seen the erosion of public trust as lies build up into vast institutional practices.

Rather than updating *Lying* to take these new developments into account, I have chosen to consider many of them in two books published in the intervening years: *Secrets: On the Ethics of Concealment and Revelation* (1982) and *A Strategy for Peace: Human Values and the Threat of War* (1989). In the first, I could do so while pursuing issues, such as that of self-deception and secrecy, that I had explicitly set aside in writing *Lying* in order to be able to concentrate on clear-cut lies. And in the second, I have incorporated constraints on lying and on excessive secrecy into a moral framework that can be shared by religious and secular traditions alike, and that is applicable both within and between nations.

—Sissela Bok
June 1989

INTRODUCTION

When regard for truth has been broken down or even slightly weakened, all things will remain doubtful.

—St. Augustine, "On Lying"

Doth any man doubt, that if there were taken out of men's minds vain opinions, flattering hopes, false valuations, imaginations as one would, and the like, but it would leave the minds of a number of men poor shrunken things, full of melancholy and indisposition, and unpleasing to themselves?

—Bacon, "Of Truth"

After prolonged research on myself, I brought out the fundamental duplicity of the human being. Then I realized that modesty helped me to shine, humility to conquer, and virtue to oppress.

—Camus, *The Fall*

Should physicians lie to dying patients so as to delay the fear and anxiety which the truth might bring them? Should professors exaggerate the excellence of their students on recommendations in order to give them a better chance in a tight job market? Should parents conceal from children the fact that they were adopted? Should social scientists send investigators masquerading as patients to physicians in order to learn about racial and sexual biases in diagnosis and treatment? Should government lawyers lie to members of Congress who might otherwise oppose a much-needed welfare bill? And should journalists lie to those from whom they seek information in order to expose corruption?

We sense differences among such choices; but whether to lie, equivocate, be silent, or tell the truth in any given situation is often a hard decision. Hard because duplicity can take so many forms, be present to such different degrees, and have such different purposes and results. Hard also because we know how questions of truth and lying inevitably pervade all that is said or left unspoken within our families, our communities, our working relationships. Lines seem most difficult to draw, and a consistent policy out of reach.

I have grappled with these problems in my personal life as everyone must. But I have also seen them at close hand in my professional experience in teaching applied ethics. I have had the chance to explore particular moral quandaries encountered at work, with nurses, doctors, lawyers, civil servants, and many others. I first came to look closely at problems of professional truth-telling and deception in preparing to write about the giving of placebos.[1] And I grew more and more puzzled by a discrepancy in perspectives: many physicians talk about such deception in a cavalier, often condescending and joking way, whereas patients often have an acute sense of injury and of loss of trust at learning that they have been duped.

I learned that this discrepancy is reflected in an odd state of affairs in medicine more generally. Honesty from health professionals matters more to patients than almost everything else that they experience when ill. Yet the requirement to be honest with patients has been left out altogether from medical oaths and codes of ethics, and is often ignored, if not actually disparaged, in the teaching of medicine.

As I widened my search, I came to realize that the same

discrepancy was present in many other professional contexts as well. In law and in journalism, in government and in the social sciences, deception is taken for granted when it is felt to be excusable by those who tell the lies and who tend also to make the rules. Government officials and those who run for elections often deceive when they can get away with it and when they assume that the true state of affairs is beyond the comprehension of citizens. Social scientists condone deceptive experimentation on the ground that the knowledge gained will be worth having. Lawyers manipulate the truth in court on behalf of their clients. Those in selling, advertising, or any form of advocacy may mislead the public and their competitors in order to achieve their goals. Psychiatrists may distort information about their former patients to preserve confidentiality or to keep them out of military service. And journalists, police investigators, and so-called intelligence operators often have little compunction in using falsehoods to gain the knowledge they seek.

Yet the casual approach of professionals is wholly out of joint with the view taken by those who have to cope with the consequences of deception. For them, to be given false information about important choices in their lives is to be rendered powerless. For them, their very autonomy may be at stake.

There is little help to be found in the codes and writings on professional ethics. A number of professions and fields, such as economics, have no code of ethics in the first place. And the existing codes say little about when deception is and is not justified.*

The fact is that reasons to lie occur to most people

---

*Scholars in many fields have had no reason in the past to adopt a code of ethics. But some are now exerting so much influence on social choice and human welfare that they should be required to work out codes similar to those that have long existed in professions like medicine or law.

quite often. Not many stop to examine the choices confronting them; existing deceptive practices and competitive stresses can make it difficult not to conform. Guidance is hard to come by, and few are encouraged to consider such choices in schools and colleges or in their working life.

As I thought about the many opportunities for deception and about the absence of a real debate on the subject, I came to associate these with the striking recent decline in public confidence not only in the American government, but in lawyers, bankers, businessmen, and doctors. In 1960, many Americans were genuinely astonished to learn that President Eisenhower had lied when asked about the U-2 incident, in which an American spy plane and pilot had been forced down in the Soviet Union. But only fifteen years later, battered by revelations about Vietnam and Watergate, 69 percent of the respondents to a national poll agreed that "over the last ten years, this country's leaders have consistently lied to the people."[2]

The loss of confidence reaches far beyond government leadership. From 1966 to 1976, the proportion of the public answering yes to whether they had a great deal of confidence in people in charge of running major institutions dropped from 73 percent to 42 percent for medicine; for major companies from 55 percent to 16 percent; for law firms from 24 percent (1973) to 12 percent; and for advertising agencies from 21 percent to 7 percent.[3]

Suspicions of widespread professional duplicity cannot alone account for the loss of trust. But surely they aggravate it. We have a great deal at stake, I believe, in becoming more clear about matters of truth-telling, both for our personal choices and for the social decisions which foster or discourage deceptive practices. And when we think about these matters, it is the reasons given for deceiving which must be examined. Sometimes there *may* be sufficient reason to lie—but when? Most often there is not —and why? Describing how things are is not enough.

Choice requires the formulation of criteria. To lie to the dying, for example, or to tell them the truth—which is the best policy? Under what circumstances? And for what reasons? What kinds of arguments support these reasons or defeat them?

Since I was trained in philosophy, it is natural for me to look to moral philosophers for guidance in answering such questions and providing the needed analysis; for the choices of standards, of action, of goals, and ways of life, as well as of social systems, are the essential concerns of moral philosophy.* Is there, then, a theory of moral choice which can help in quandaries of truth-telling and lying?

Once again, the paucity of what I found was astonishing. The striking fact is that, though no moral choices are more common or more troubling than those which have to do with deception in its many guises, they have received extraordinarily little contemporary analysis. The major works of moral philosophy of this century, so illuminating in other respects, are silent on this subject. The index to the eight-volume *Encyclopedia of Philosophy* contains not one reference to lying or to deception, much less an entire article devoted to such questions.[4] Even if one looks back over the last few centuries, the little discussion which is to be found is brief and peremptory. And works in other disciplines—in psychology, for example, or in political science—most often approach problems of deception in a merely descriptive or strategic manner.

It is difficult to understand all the reasons why so few efforts have been made to analyze our everyday dilemmas

---

*One of the simplest and, in my opinion, best definitions of ethics is that of Epicurus, quoted by Diogenes Laertius, *Lives of Eminent Philosophers* (Cambridge, Mass.: Harvard University Press, 1925), Book 10, Ch. 30: "Ethics deals with things to be sought and things to be avoided, with ways of life and with the *telos*." ("*Telos*" is the chief good, the aim, or the end of life.)

of truth-telling. The great distance which so often separates philosophers from applied concerns of any kind provides a partial answer. In philosophy, as elsewhere, professionalization has brought in its wake a vocabulary, a theoretical apparatus, and academic boundaries forbidding to outsiders and confining for those within. In part, also, the very background of truth and falsity against which lying must be seen has led many thinkers to set ever greater preliminaries to the moral questioning of situations where truth seems to be at issue. How can we even begin to probe such situations, they ask, unless we first know what "truth" means? In ethics, finally, attention has gone primarily to questions of meaning and theory quite remote from problems of concrete moral choice.

I have often had to go back, therefore, to the classical period and the Middle Ages for a more direct grasp of the questions central to this book: What *actual choices* should we make when we are wondering whether to lie or to tell the truth? And why? Issues such as whether to perjure oneself to protect a political refugee, or whether to feign worship of a hated deity in order to escape persecution, were once hotly debated among theologians and philosophers.* What remains of their debate may be fragmentary, at times unsystematic. But their writings are alive to us still; I have drawn on them often.

Some now look back with derision or impatience at the Stoics, the Muslim mystics, the Early Christian fathers, or the rabbis for their passionate pursuit of minute distinctions. Nevertheless, we have much to learn from these traditions. Without such groundwork, larger distinctions often blur, as they now have.

It is high time to take up once more this debate, set forth its contours, and try to bring to it a comprehensive treatment that is still lacking—one that will try to examine all the plausible factors and all the reasons given for

*Some of these writings are gathered in the Appendix to this book.

lying, and see whether they can be made to shed light on the choices we make, as individuals and in society. And it is important to see the debate in the contexts in which human beings confront such choices. I have tried, therefore, to use examples from literature, from private life, and from work. They are merely examples; many others will spring to mind. While completeness is obviously out of the question, the cases selected may shed light on the major kinds of lies, ways in which they vary, and excuses used for telling them. And the juxtaposition of examples from very different walks of life may help to remove them from the customary narrowly professional or personal perspectives.

These purposes are best served by concentrating on choices between truth-telling and clear-cut lying, rather than on other forms of deception such as evasion or the suppression of relevant information. If some clarity can be brought to questions about actual lying, then the vaster problems of deception will seem less defeating.

The main task will not be to produce a sordid catalogue of falsehoods and corrupt dealings, nor to go over once again what each day's newspaper reveals about deception in high places. Rather, I want to stress the more vexing dilemmas of ordinary life; dilemmas which beset those who think that their lies are too insignificant to matter much, and others who believe that lying can protect someone or benefit society. We need to look most searchingly, not at what we would all reject as unconscionable, but at those cases where many see *good reasons* to lie.

Chapters I to IV examine the nature of lying, how it affects human choice, and basic approaches to evaluating lies. Chapter V examines white lies to show why those approaches are inadequate. Chapters VI and VII consider in detail what circumstances help to excuse lies, and whether some can actually be justified in advance. Chapters VIII to XV take up in greater detail certain kinds of lies commonly thought justifiable: lies in wartime, for example, or to children; lies told to protect confidentiality or to conduct research.

If I can show that we have all been poorly served by the dominant practices, then the most important remaining questions are: What are the alternatives, for society and for each of us individually, to merely going along with such practices? And how can we act so as to *change* them? What institutional and personal incentives may be needed? And what real risks might dissuade would-be liars? In the conclusion, I have begun—but no more than begun—to raise these questions. I recognize that the alternatives I have envisaged are directed primarily at less coercive societies. But I hope that the study of the problems of truth-telling will shed light also on the relation between coercion and deception, whether in a family, an institution, or a society.

This book is a personal exploration rather than an effort to dictate conclusions. It aims to narrow the gap between the worlds of the moral philosopher and those confronting urgent practical moral choices. In showing the path that I have taken, the work I have found helpful, and the tentative results I have reached, I hope to invite others to take up the debate.

LYING

IS THE "WHOLE TRUTH"
ATTAINABLE?

"I was born for this, I came into the world for this: to bear witness to the truth; and all who are on the side of truth listen to my voice."

"Truth?" said Pilate, "what is that?"

—John 18.37

If, like truth, the lie had but one face, we would be on better terms. For we would accept as certain the opposite of what the liar would say. But the reverse of truth has a hundred thousand faces and an infinite field.

—Montaigne, *Essays*

Like freedom, truth is a bare minimum or an illusory ideal (the truth, the whole truth, and nothing but the truth about, say, the battle of Waterloo or the *Primavera*).

—J. L. Austin, "Truth," *Philosophical Papers*

The "Whole Truth"

Is it not naïve to set forth on a general exploration of lying and truth-telling? Some will argue that the task is impossible. Life is too complex, they will say, and societies too diverse. How can one compare the bargaining in an Eastern bazaar, the white lies of everyday life, the lie for national defense, and that to spare a dying child? Is it not arrogant and myopic to conceive of doing so?

And even if these variations could somehow be encompassed, the argument continues, how can we ever attain the truth about any complex matter—the battle of Waterloo, in Austin's example—or even a single circumstance? How can one, in fact, do full justice to the words used in court: "The truth, the whole truth, and nothing but the truth"?

These words mock our clumsy efforts to remember and convey our experiences. The "whole truth" has seemed so obviously unattainable to some as to cause them to despair of human communication in general. They see so many barriers to prevent us from obtaining truthful knowledge, let alone communicating it; so many pitfalls in conveying what we mean.

How can a physician, for example, tell the "whole truth" to a patient about a set of symptoms and their causes and likely effects? He certainly does not know all there is to know himself. Even all he does know that might have a bearing—incomplete, erroneous, and tentative though it be—could not be conveyed in less than weeks or even months. Add to these difficulties the awareness that everything in life and experience connects, that all is a "seamless web" so that nothing can be said without qualifications and elaborations in infinite regress, and a sense of lassitude begins to steal over even the most intrepid.

This book is intended as a reply to such arguments. The whole truth *is* out of reach. But this fact has very little to do with our choices about whether to lie or to speak honestly, about what to say and what to hold back. These choices can be set forth, compared, evaluated. And when they are, even rudimentary distinctions can give guidance.

If arrogance there be, it lies rather in the immobilizing

impatience with all that falls short of the "whole truth." This impatience helps explain why the contemporary debate about deception is so barren. Paradoxically, the reluctance to come to grips with *deception* can stem from an exalted and all-absorbing preoccupation with *truth*.

"Truth"—no concept intimidates and yet draws thinkers so powerfully. From the beginnings of human speculation about the world, the questions of what truth is and whether we can attain it have loomed large. Every philosopher has had to grapple with them.* Every religion seeks to answer them.

One pre-Socratic Greek tradition saw truth—*aletheia* —as encompassing all that we remember: singled out through memory from everything that is destined for Lethe, "the river of forgetfulness." The oral tradition required that information be memorized and repeated, often in song, so as not to be forgotten. Everything thus memorized—stories about the creation of the world, genealogies of gods and heroes, advice about health—all partook of truth, even if in another sense completely fabricated or erroneous. In this early tradition, repeating the songs meant keeping the material alive and thus "true," just as creating works of art could be thought of as making an object true, bringing it to life.[1]

Only gradually did the opposition between truth and error come to be thought central to philosophy, and the nature of verification itself spotlighted. The immense preoccupation with epistemology took hold with Plato and has never diminished since. In logic, in epistemology, in theology, and in metaphysics, the topic of "truth" has continued to absorb almost limitless energies.[2] And since the strands from these diverse disciplines are not always

*A glance at the Index of the recently published *Encyclopedia of Philosophy* reveals the contrast. As mentioned in the Introduction, it has no reference to "lying" or "deception." "Truth," on the other hand, receives over 100 references.

disentangled, a great many references to "truth" remain of unsurpassed vagueness.[3]

Truth and Truthfulness

In all such speculation, there is great risk of a conceptual muddle, of not seeing the crucial differences between two domains: the *moral* domain of intended truthfulness and deception, and the much vaster domain of truth and falsity in general. The moral question of whether you are lying or not is not *settled* by establishing the truth or falsity of what you say. In order to settle this question, we must know whether you *intend your statement to mislead*.

The two domains often overlap, and up to a point each is indispensable to the other. But truth and truthfulness are not identical, any more than falsity and falsehood.[4] Until the differences are seen, and the areas of overlap and confusion spotlighted, little progress can be made in coping with the moral quandaries of lying.

The two domains are sometimes taken to be identical. This can happen whenever some believe that they have access to a truth so complete that all else must pale by comparison. Many religious documents or revelations claim to convey what is true. Those who do not accept such a belief are thought to live in error, in ignorance, even in blindness. At times, the refusal of nonbelievers to accept the dogma or truth revealed to the faithful is called, not merely an error, but a lie. The battle is seen as one between upholders of the faith and the forces of deception and guile.* Thus Bonhoeffer writes that:

---

* The confusion between "error" and "lie" underlying such a belief occasionally gives rise to the conclusion that those who are in possession of the truth—and thus not liars—are both infallible and incapable of lying. In order to sort out just what is meant by any one such claim, it is necessary to ask: Is the person believed infallible incapable of

Jesus calls Satan "the father of the lie." (John 8.44) The lie is primarily the denial of God as He has evidenced Himself to the world. "Who is a liar but he that denieth that Jesus is the Christ?" (I John 2.22)[5]

Convinced that they know the truth—whether in religion or in politics—enthusiasts may regard lies for the sake of this truth as justifiable. They may perpetrate so-called pious frauds to convert the unbelieving or strengthen the conviction of the faithful. They see nothing wrong in telling untruths for what they regard as a much "higher" truth.

In the history of human thought, we find again and again such a confusion of the two domains. It is not unrelated to the traditions which claim that truth exists, that it can be revealed, that one can hope to come face to face with it. Even Nietzsche, at war with such traditions, perpetuates the confusion:

> There is only *one* world, and that world is false, cruel, contradictory, misleading, senseless. [. . .] We need lies to vanquish this reality, this "truth," we need lies in order to live. [. . .] That lying is a necessity of life is itself a part of the terrifying and problematic character of existence.[6]

The several meanings of the word "false" only add to the ease of confusing the two domains. For whereas "false" normally has the larger sense which includes all that is wrong or incorrect, it takes on the narrower, moral sense when applied to persons. A false person is not one merely wrong or mistaken or incorrect; it is one who is intentionally deceitful or treacherous or disloyal. Compare, to see the difference, a "false note" and a

---

lying? of other forms of deceit? of being wrong? of being deceived? and with respect to what forms of knowledge? *Cf.* a Sufi saying: "The pious would not deceive and the intelligent man cannot be deceived." *A Sufi Rule for Novices*, ed. Menahem Wilson (Cambridge, Mass.: Harvard University Press, 1975), p. 41.

"false friend"; a "false economy" and a "false witness."*

Any number of appearances and words can mislead us; but only a fraction of them are *intended* to do so. A mirage may deceive us, through no one's fault. Our eyes deceive us all the time. We are beset by self-delusion and bias of every kind. Yet we often know when we mean to be honest or dishonest. Whatever the essence of truth and falsity, and whatever the sources of error in our lives, *one* such source is surely the human agent, receiving and giving out information, intentionally deflecting, withholding, even distorting it at times.† Human beings, after all, provide for each other the most ingenious obstacles to what partial knowledge and minimal rationality they can hope to command.

We must single out, therefore, from the countless ways in which we blunder misinformed through life, that which is done with the *intention to mislead;* and from the countless partial stabs at truth, those which are intended to be truthful. Only if this distinction is clear will it be possible to ask the moral question with rigor. And it is to this question alone—the intentional manipulation of information—that the court addresses itself in its request for "the truth, the whole truth, and nothing but the truth."

* To further complicate matters, there are, of course, many uses of "false" to mean "deceitful" or "treacherous" which do not apply directly to persons, but rather to what persons have intended to be misleading. A "false trail," a "false ceiling," or a "false clue" carry different overtones of deceptiveness.

†Messages between human beings can suffer from a number of unintended distortions or interferences, originating either at the source, en route, or at the reception. The speaker, for example, may be mistaken, inarticulate, or using a language unknown to the listener. En route, the message may be deflected by outside noise, by atmospheric conditions, by interruption. At the receiving end, deafness, fatigue, language problems, or mental retardation may affect the reception of the message.

But one obstacle remains. Even after the two domains of the ethical and the epistemological are set apart, some argue that the latter should have priority. It is useless to be overly concerned with truthfulness, they claim, so long as one cannot know whether human beings are capable of knowing and conveying the truth in the first place. Such a claim, if taken seriously, would obviously make the study of truth-telling and deception seem pointless and flat. Once again, the exalted and all-absorbing preoccupation with "truth" then comes to nourish the reluctance to confront falsehood.

Skeptics have questioned the easy certitudes of their fellows from the earliest times. The most extreme among them have held that nothing can be known at all; sometimes they have gone very far in living out such a belief. Cratylus, a contemporary of Socrates, is said to have refused discussion of any kind. He held that the speakers and the words in any conversation would be changing and uncertain. He therefore merely wiggled his finger in response to any words to show that he had heard them but that a reply would be pointless. And Pyrrho, in the third century B.C., denied that anything could be known and concluded that nothing could therefore be said to be honorable or dishonorable, just or unjust.[7]

For these radical skeptics, just as for those who believe that complete and absolute truth can be theirs, ethical matters of truth-telling and deception melt into insignificance by comparison with the illumination of truth and the dark void of its absence. As a result, both groups largely ignore the distinctions between truthfulness and falsehood in their intense quest for certainty regarding truth.[8]

But the example of Cratylus shows how difficult it is to live up to thoroughgoing skepticism. Most thinkers who confuse intentional deception and falsity nevertheless manage to distinguish between the two in their ordinary lives. And those who consider the study of "truth" to be prior to any use of information put such concerns aside in their daily routines.⁹ They make informed choices of books in libraries; of subway connections and tools and food; they take some messages to be more truthful than others, and some persons as more worthy of their trust than others.¹⁰

Ordinary decisions can no doubt be made in spite of theoretical beliefs which confuse truth and truth-telling, or which set epistemological certainty ahead of ethical analysis. But the fact remains that moral choice is often harmed thereby; for to the extent that one has radical doubts about the reliability of all knowledge, to that extent the moral aspects of how human beings treat one another, how they act, and what they say to each other, may lose importance. Worst of all, this loss is especially likely to afflict one's own moral choices. For whereas it is only prudent to support morality in others, we are more hospitable to doubts about the possibility of moral choice when it comes to our own decisions.

The most important reason why philosophers have done so little to analyze the problems of deception goes beyond particular views about truth and truthfulness, and is more general. In most fields, theory is more congenial, less frustrating, than application. Ethics is no different. Many hesitate to grapple with concrete ethical problems, intertwined as they are with psychological and political strands rendering choice so difficult. Why tackle such choice when there are so many abstract questions of meaning and definition, of classification and structure, which remain to challenge the imagination?

As philosophy has become an increasingly academic and specialized enterprise, this hesitation has grown. But it was always there. Thus Epictetus, in the first century A.D., refers to it as follows, using the "principle not to speak falsely" as his example:

The primary and most necessary part of philosophy is the application of principles, as for instance the principle not to speak falsely.

The second part is that of the arguments, as in "Wherefore ought one not to speak falsely?"

The third confirms these, and distinguishes between them, as in "Wherefore is that an argument?" For what is an argument, what a consequence, what a contradiction [conflict], what truth, what falsehood?

Therefore, the third part is necessary because of the second, and the second because of the first; while the first is the most necessary, and is where we ought to remain. But we do the reverse; we squander our time in the third part, and to it goes all our zeal, while we utterly neglect the first. And thus we do lie, but are ready with the arguments which prove that one ought not to lie.[11]

Applied ethics, then, has seemed uncongenial and lacking in theoretical challenge to many moral philosophers even apart from any belief in epistemological priority and from muddles about the meaning of "truth." As a result, practical moral choice comes to be given short shrift, and never more so than in the case of lies. To be sure, many do make some mention of lying. It is often used as an example, or ruled out in some summary manner. But such analysis cannot help but seem inadequate to those confronting difficult problems in their lives—wondering, perhaps, whether to lie to protect a client's confidences, or to keep shattering news from a sick man.

For all these reasons, deception commands little notice. This absence of real analysis is reflected also in teaching and in codes of professional ethics. As a result, those who confront difficult moral choices between truthfulness and deception often make up their own rules. They think up their own excuses and evaluate their own arguments. I shall take these up in the chapters to come. But one deserves mention here, for it results from a misuse of skepticism by those who wish to justify their lies, giving rise to a clearly fallacious argument. It holds that since we can never know the truth or falsity of anything anyway, it does not matter whether or not we lie when we have a good reason for doing so. Some have used this argument to explain why they and their entire profession must regretfully forego the virtue of veracity in dealing with clients. Such a view is stated, for example, by an eminent physician in an article frequently referred to in medical literature:

> Above all, remember that it is meaningless to speak of telling the truth, the whole truth, and nothing but the truth to a patient. It is meaningless because it is impossible—a sheer impossibility. [. . .] Since telling the truth is impossible, there can be no sharp distinction between what is true and what is false.
>
> [. . .] Far older than the precept, "the truth, the whole truth, and nothing but the truth," is another that originates within our profession, that has always been the guide of the best physicians, and, if I may venture a prophecy, will always remain so: So far as possible, do no harm. You can do harm by the process that is quaintly called telling the truth. You can do harm by lying. [. . .] But try to do as little harm as possible.[12]

The same argument is often used by biomedical investigators who claim that asking subjects for their informed consent to be used in research is meaningless because it is impossible to obtain a *genuinely* informed consent. It is used by government officials who decide not to inform citizens of a planned war or emergency measure. And very often, it is then supplemented by a second argument: Since there is an infinite gradation between what is truthful and what is deceitful, no lines can be drawn and one must do what one considers best on other grounds.

Such arguments draw on our concerns with the adequacy of information to reach a completely unwarranted conclusion: one that gives *carte blanche* to what those who lie take to be well-meant lies. The difference in perspectives is striking. These arguments are made by the liar but never by those lied to. One has only to imagine how the professionals who argue in this way would respond if their dentists, their lawyers, or their insurance agents used similar arguments for deceiving *them*. As dupes we know what as liars we tend to blur—that information can be more or less adequate; that even where no clear lines are drawn, rules and distinctions may, in fact, be made; and that truthfulness can be required even where full "truth" is out of reach.

The fact that the "whole truth" can never be reached in its entirety should not, therefore, be a stumbling block in the much more limited inquiry into questions of truth-telling and falsehood. It *is* possible to go beyond the notion that epistemology is somehow prior to ethics. The two nourish one another, but neither can claim priority. It is equally possible to avoid the fallacies which arise from the confusion of "truth" and "truthfulness," and to draw distinctions with respect to the adequacy and relevance of the information reaching us. It is therefore legitimate to go on to define deception and to analyze the moral dilemmas it raises.

Defining Intentional Deception and Lying

When we undertake to deceive others intentionally, we communicate messages meant to mislead them, meant to make them believe what we ourselves do not believe. We can do so through gesture, through disguise, by means of action or inaction, even through silence. Which of these innumerable deceptive messages are also lies? I shall define as a lie any intentionally deceptive message which is *stated*. Such statements are most often made verbally or in writing, but can of course also be conveyed via smoke signals, Morse code, sign language, and the like. Deception, then, is the larger category, and lying forms part of it.*

This definition resembles some of those given by philosophers and theologians, but not all.[13] For it turns out that the very choice of definition has often presented a moral dilemma all its own. Certain religious and moral traditions were rigorously opposed to all lying. Yet many adherents wanted to recognize at least a few circumstances when intentionally misleading statements could be allowed. The only way out for them was, then, to define lies in such a way that some falsehoods did not count as lies. Thus Grotius, followed by a long line of primarily Protestant thinkers, argued that speaking falsely to those—like thieves—to whom truthfulness is not owed cannot be called lying.[14] Sometimes the rigorous tradition was felt to be so confining that a large opening to allowable misstatements was needed. In this way, casuist thinkers developed the notion of the "mental reservation," which, in some extreme formulations, can allow you to make a completely misleading statement, so long as you add something in your own mind to make it true.[15] Thus, if you are asked whether you broke somebody's vase, you could answer "No," adding in your own mind the mental reservation "not last year" to make the statement a true one.

Such definitions serve the special purpose of allowing persons to subscribe to a strict tradition yet have the leeway in actual practice which they desire. When the strict traditions were at their strongest, as with certain forms of Catholicism and Calvinism, such "definitional" ways out often flourished. Whenever a law or rule is so strict that

*It is perfectly possible to define "lie" so that it is identical with "deception." This is how expressions like "living a lie" can be interpreted. For the purposes of this book, however, it is best to stay with the primary distinction between deceptive *statements*—lies—and all the other forms of deception.

most people cannot live by it, efforts to find loopholes will usually ensue; the rules about lying are no exception.

I see nothing wrong with either a narrow or a wider definition of lying, so long as one retains the prerogative of morally evaluating the intentionally misleading statements, no matter whether they fall within the category of lying or outside it.* But a narrower definition often smuggles in a moral term which in itself needs evaluation. To say, for instance, that it is *not* lying to speak falsely to those with no right to your information glides over the vast question of what it means to have such a right to information. In order to avoid this difficulty, I shall use instead a more neutral, and therefore wider, <u>definition of a lie</u>: an <u>intentionally deceptive message in the form of a</u> <u>statement</u>.

All deceptive messages, whether or not they are lies, can also be more or less affected by self-deception,[16] by error, and by variations in the actual intention to deceive. These three factors can be looked at as filters of irregular thickness, distortion, and color that alter the ways in which a message is experienced by both deceived and deceivers. To complicate matters further, someone who intends to deceive can work *with* these filters and manipulate them; he can play on the biases of some persons, the imagination of others, and on errors and confusion throughout the system.

The interaction of these filters through which communication passes and is perceived is immensely complex. Each year we learn more about the complexity of communication, and about the role of the brain in sending and

---

*Consider the analogy with defining "hitting people." Say that you have religious texts which proscribe all "hitting" of people absolutely. Then, if you still want to be allowed to hit another, perhaps in self-defense or in play, you will find it useful to define "hitting" so as not to include the kinds you wish to allow. You may say, then, that "hitting" people is to be defined as striking them when you have no right to do so.

receiving messages. We see the intricate capacities of each person for denial, deflection, distortion, and loss of memory; but also for accuracy, regeneration, and invention. Add the fact that communication takes place over a period of time, sometimes long, and often between more than two persons. The many experiments on rumors show how information can be distorted, added to, partially lost, when passed from one person to another, until it is almost unrecognizable even though no one may have intended to deceive.[17]

Merely trying to encompass these factors in our minds can lead to discouragement about the ethics of deception. It is for this reason that I propose that we remove the filters in the chapters that follow, so as to look primarily at clear-cut lies—lies where the intention to mislead is obvious, where the liar knows that what he is communicating is not what he believes, and where he has not deluded himself into believing his own deceits. We must, of course, always keep the filters in mind and never forget the underlying complexity. But with clear-cut lies we can make much sharper distinctions than if we look first at all the subtler variations. And it is important to try to resolve some of the problems these lies pose. After all, many of the most searing moral choices involve deciding whether or not to tell an outright lie.

If we could gain greater clarity for these choices and thereby narrow the margin of remaining doubt, we might then return to all the borderline difficulties with firmer ground under our feet. In the pages to come, therefore, clear-cut lies will often be singled out and considered separately. What do such lies do to our perception and our choices? And when might they be justified?

TRUTHFULNESS, DECEIT, AND TRUST

Suppose men imagined there was no obligation to veracity, and acted accordingly; speaking as often against their own opinion as according to it; would not all pleasure of conversation be destroyed, and all confidence in narration? Men would only speak in bargaining, and in this too would soon lose all mutual confidence.

—Francis Hutcheson, *A System of Moral Philosophy*

A great man—what is he? . . . He rather lies than tells the truth; it requires more spirit and *will*. There is a solitude within him that is inaccessible to praise or blame, his own justice that is beyond appeal.

—Friedrich Nietzsche, *The Will to Power*

Lying, after all, is suggestive of game theory. It involves at least two people, a liar and someone who is lied to; it transmits information, the credibility and veracity of which are important; it influences some choice another is to make that the liar anticipates; the choice to lie or not to lie is part of the liar's choice of strategy; and the possibility of a lie presumably occurs to the second party, and may be judged against some *a priori* expectations; and the payoff configurations are rich in their possibilities . . .

—Thomas Schelling, "Game Theory and the Study of Ethical Systems"

Lying and Choice

Deceit and violence—these are the two forms of deliberate assault on human beings.[1] Both can coerce people into acting against their will. Most harm that can befall victims through violence can come to them also through deceit. But deceit controls more subtly, for it works on belief as well as action. Even Othello, whom few would have dared to try to subdue by force, could be brought to destroy himself and Desdemona through falsehood.

The knowledge of this coercive element in deception, and of our vulnerability to it, underlies our sense of the *centrality* of truthfulness. Of course, deception—again like violence—can be used also in self-defense, even for sheer survival. Its use can also be quite trivial, as in white lies. Yet its potential for coercion and for destruction is such that society could scarcely function without some degree of truthfulness in speech and action.*

Imagine a society, no matter how ideal in other respects, where word and gesture could never be counted upon. Questions asked, answers given, information exchanged—all would be worthless. Were all statements randomly truthful or deceptive, action and choice would be undermined from the outset. There must be a minimal degree of trust in communication for language and action to be more than stabs in the dark. This is why some level of truthfulness has always been seen as essential to human society, no matter how deficient the observance of other moral principles. Even the devils themselves, as Samuel Johnson said, do not lie to one another, since the society of Hell could not

---

* But truthful statements, though they are not meant to deceive, can, of course, themselves be coercive and destructive; they can be used as weapons, to wound and do violence.

subsist without truth any more than others.[2]

A society, then, whose members were unable to distinguish truthful messages from deceptive ones, would collapse. But even before such a general collapse, individual choice and survival would be imperiled. The search for food and shelter could depend on no expectations from others. A warning that a well was poisoned or a plea for help in an accident would come to be ignored unless independent confirmation could be found.

All our choices depend on our estimates of what is the case; these estimates must in turn often rely on information from others. Lies distort this information and therefore our situation as we perceive it, as well as our choices. A lie, in Hartmann's words, "injures the deceived person in his life; it leads him astray."[3]

To the extent that knowledge gives power, to that extent do lies affect the distribution of power; they add to that of the liar, and diminish that of the deceived, altering his choices at different levels.[4] A lie, first, may misinform, so as to obscure some *objective*, something the deceived person wanted to do or obtain. It may make the objective seem unattainable or no longer desirable. It may even create a new one, as when Iago deceived Othello into wanting to kill Desdemona.

Lies may also eliminate or obscure relevant *alternatives*, as when a traveler is falsely told a bridge has collapsed. At times, lies foster the belief that there are more alternatives than is really the case; at other times, a lie may lead to the unnecessary loss of confidence in the best alternative. Similarly, the estimates of *costs and benefits* of any action can be endlessly varied through successful deception. The immense toll of life and human welfare from the United States' intervention in Vietnam came at least in part from the deception (mingled with self-deception) by those who channeled overly optimistic information to the decision-makers.

Finally, the degree of *uncertainty* in how we look at our

choices can be manipulated through deception. Deception can make a situation falsely uncertain as well as falsely certain. It can affect the objectives seen, the alternatives believed possible, the estimates made of risks and benefits. Such a manipulation of the dimension of certainty is one of the main ways to gain power over the choices of those deceived. And just as deception can initiate actions a person would otherwise never have chosen, so it can prevent action by obscuring the necessity for choice. This is the essence of camouflage and of the cover-up—the creation of apparent normality to avert suspicion.

Everyone depends on deception to get out of a scrape, to save face, to avoid hurting the feelings of others. Some use it much more consciously to manipulate and gain ascendancy. Yet all are intimately aware of the threat lies can pose, the suffering they can bring. This two-sided experience which we all share makes the singleness with which either side is advocated in action all the more puzzling. Why are such radically different evaluations given to the effects of deception, depending on whether the point of view is that of the liar or the one lied to?

The Perspective of the Deceived

Those who learn that they have been lied to in an important matter—say, the identity of their parents, the affection of their spouse, or the integrity of their government —are resentful, disappointed, and suspicious. They feel wronged; they are wary of new overtures. And they look back on their past beliefs and actions in the new light of the discovered lies. They see that they were manipulated, that the deceit made them unable to make choices for themselves according to the most adequate information available, unable to act as they would have wanted to act had they known all along.

It is true, of course, that personal, informed choice is

not the only kind available to them. They may *decide* to abandon choosing for themselves and let others decide for them—as guardians, financial advisors, or political representatives. They may even decide to abandon choice based upon information of a conventional nature altogether and trust instead to the stars or to throws of the dice or to soothsayers.

But such alternatives ought to be personally chosen and not surreptitiously imposed by lies or other forms of manipulation. Most of us would resist loss of control over which choices we want to delegate to others and which ones we want to make ourselves, aided by the best information we can obtain. We resist because experience has taught us the consequences when others choose to deceive us, even "for our own good." Of course, we know that many lies are trivial. But since we, when lied to, have no way to judge which lies are the trivial ones, and since we have no confidence that liars will restrict themselves to just such trivial lies, the perspective of the deceived leads us to be wary of *all* deception.

Nor is this perspective restricted to those who are actually deceived in any given situation. Though only a single person may be deceived, many others may be harmed as a result. If a mayor is deceived about the need for new taxes, the entire city will bear the consequences. Accordingly, the perspective of the deceived is shared by all those who feel the consequences of a lie, whether or not they are themselves lied to. When, for instance, the American public and world opinion were falsely led to believe that bombing in Cambodia had not begun, the Cambodians themselves bore the heaviest consequences, though they can hardly be said to have been deceived about the bombing itself.

An interesting parallel between skepticism and determinism exists here. Just as skepticism denies the possibility of *knowledge,* so determinism denies the possibility of *freedom.* Yet both knowledge and freedom to act on it are required for reasonable choice. Such choice would be denied to someone genuinely convinced—to the very core of his being—of both skepticism and determinism. He would be cast about like a dry leaf in the wind. Few go so far. But more may adopt such views selectively, as when they need convenient excuses for lying. Lies, they may then claim, do not add to or subtract from the general misinformation or "unfreedom" of those lied to. Yet were they to adopt the perspective of the deceived, such excuses for lying to them would seem hollow indeed. Both skepticism and determinism have to be bracketed—set aside— if moral choice is to retain the significance for liars that we, as deceived, know it has in our lives.

Deception, then, can be coercive. When it succeeds, it can give power to the deceiver—power that all who suffer the consequences of lies would not wish to abdicate. From this perspective, it is clearly unreasonable to assert that people should be able to lie with impunity whenever they want to do so. It would be unreasonable, as well, to assert such a right even in the more restricted circumstances where the liars claim a good reason for lying. This is especially true because lying so often accompanies every *other* form of wrongdoing, from murder and bribery to tax fraud and theft. In refusing to condone such a right to decide when to lie and when not to, we are therefore trying to protect ourselves against lies which help to execute or cover up all other wrongful acts.

For this reason, the perspective of the deceived supports the statement by Aristotle:

> Falsehood is in itself mean and culpable, and truth noble and full of praise.[5]

There is an initial imbalance in the evaluation of truthtelling and lying. Lying requires a *reason*, while truthtelling does not. It must be excused; reasons must be produced, in any one case, to show why a particular lie is not "mean and culpable."

Those who adopt the perspective of would-be liars, on the other hand, have different concerns. For them, the choice is often a difficult one. They may believe, with Machiavelli, that "great things" have been done by those who have "little regard for good faith." They may trust that they can make wise use of the power that lies bring. And they may have confidence in their own ability to distinguish the times when good reasons support their decision to lie.

Liars share with those they deceive the desire not to *be* deceived. As a result, their choice to lie is one which they would like to reserve for themselves while insisting that others be honest. They would prefer, in other words, a "free-rider" status, giving them the benefits of lying without the risks of being lied to. Some think of this free-rider status as for them alone. Others extend it to their friends, social group, or profession. This category of persons can be narrow or broad; but it does require as a necessary backdrop the ordinary assumptions about the honesty of most persons. The free rider trades upon being an exception, and could not exist in a world where everybody chose to exercise the same prerogatives.

At times, liars operate as if they believed that such a free-rider status is theirs and that it excuses them. At other times, on the contrary, it is the very fact that others *do* lie that excuses their deceptive stance in their own eyes. It is crucial to see the distinction between the free-loading liar and the liar whose deception is a strategy for survival in a corrupt society.*

All want to avoid being deceived by *others* as much as possible. But many would like to be able to weigh the

---

* While different, the two are closely linked. If enough persons adopt the free-rider strategy for lying, the time will come when all will feel pressed to lie to survive.

advantages and disadvantages in a more nuanced way whenever they are themselves in the position of choosing whether or not to deceive. They may invoke special reasons to lie—such as the need to protect confidentiality or to spare someone's feelings. They are then much more willing, in particular, to exonerate a well-intentioned lie on their own part; dupes tend to be less sanguine about the good intentions of those who deceive them.

But in this benevolent self-evaluation by the liar of the lies he might tell, certain kinds of disadvantage and harm are almost always overlooked. Liars usually weigh only the immediate harm to others from the lie against the benefits they want to achieve. The flaw in such an outlook is that it ignores or underestimates two additional kinds of harm—the harm that lying does to the liars themselves and the harm done to the general level of trust and social cooperation. Both are cumulative; both are hard to reverse.

How is the liar affected by his own lies? The very fact that he *knows* he has lied, first of all, affects him. He may regard the lie as an inroad on his integrity; he certainly looks at those he has lied to with a new caution. And if they find out that he has lied, he knows that his credibility and the respect for his word have been damaged. When Adlai Stevenson had to go before the United Nations in 1961 to tell falsehoods about the United States' role in the Bay of Pigs invasion, he changed the course of his life. He may not have known beforehand that the message he was asked to convey was untrue; but merely to carry the burden of being the means of such deceit must have been difficult. To lose the confidence of his peers in such a public way was harder still.

Granted that a public lie on an important matter, once revealed, hurts the speaker, must we therefore conclude that *every* lie has this effect? What of those who tell a few white lies once in a while? Does lying hurt them in the same way? It is hard to defend such a notion. No one trivial lie undermines the liar's integrity. But the problem for liars is that they tend to see *most* of their lies in this benevolent light and thus vastly underestimate the risks they run. While no one lie always carries harm for the liar, then, there is *risk* of such harm in most.

These risks are increased by the fact that so few lies are solitary ones. It is easy, a wit observed, to tell a lie, but hard to tell only one. The first lie "must be thatched with another or it will rain through." More and more lies may come to be needed; the liar always has more mending to do. And the strains on him become greater each time—many have noted that it takes an excellent memory to keep one's untruths in good repair and disentangled.[6] The sheer energy the liar has to devote to shoring them up is energy the honest man can dispose of freely.

After the first lies, moreover, others can come more easily. Psychological barriers wear down; lies seem more necessary, less reprehensible; the ability to make moral distinctions can coarsen; the liar's perception of his chances of being caught may warp. These changes can affect his behavior in subtle ways; even if he is not found out he will then be less trusted than those of unquestioned honesty. And it is inevitable that more frequent lies *do* increase the chance that some will be discovered. At that time, even if the liar has no personal sense of loss of integrity* from his deceitful practices, he will surely re-

---

*The word "integrity" comes from the same roots which have formed "intact" and "untouched." It is used especially often in relation to truthfulness and fair dealing and reflects, I believe, the view that by lying one hurts oneself. The notion of the self-destructive aspects of doing wrong is part of many traditions. See, for example, the *Book of Mencius:* "Every man has within himself these four beginnings [of humanity, righteousness, decorum, wisdom]. The man who considers himself incapable of exercising them is destroying himself." See Merle Severy, ed., *Great Religions of the World* (Washington, D.C.: National Geographic Society, 1971), p. 167; and W.A.C.H. Dobson trans., *Mencius* (Toronto: University of Toronto Press, 1963), p. 132.

gret the damage to his credibility which their discovery brings about. Paradoxically, once his word is no longer trusted, he will be left with greatly *decreased* power—even though a lie often does bring at least a short-term gain in power over those deceived.

Even if the liar cares little about the risks to others from his deception, therefore, all these risks to himself argue in favor of at least weighing any decision to lie quite seriously. Yet such risks rarely enter his calculations. Bias skews all judgment, but never more so than in the search for good reasons to deceive. Not only does it combine with ignorance and uncertainty so that liars are apt to overestimate their own good will, high motives, and chances to escape detection; it leads also to overconfidence in their own imperviousness to the personal entanglements, worries, and loss of integrity which might so easily beset them.[7]

The liar's self-bestowed free-rider status, then, can be as corrupting as all other unchecked exercises of power. There are, in fact, very few "free rides" to be had through lying. I hope to examine, in this book, those exceptional circumstances where harm to self and others from lying is less likely, and procedures which can isolate and contain them. But the chance of harm to liars can rarely be ruled out altogether.

Bias causes liars often to ignore the second type of harm as well. For even if they make the effort to estimate the consequences to *individuals*—themselves and others— of their lies, they often fail to consider the many ways in which deception can spread and give rise to practices very damaging to human communities. These practices clearly do not affect only isolated individuals. The veneer of social trust is often thin. As lies spread—by imitation, or in retaliation, or to forestall suspected deception—trust is damaged. Yet trust is a social good to be protected just as much as the air we breathe or the water we drink. When it is damaged, the community as a whole suffers; and when it is destroyed, societies falter and collapse.

We live at a time when the harm done to trust can be seen first-hand. Confidence in public officials and in professionals has been seriously eroded. This, in turn, is a most natural response to the uncovering of practices of deceit for high-sounding aims such as "national security" or the "adversary system of justice." It will take time to rebuild confidence in government pronouncements that the CIA did not participate in a Latin American coup, or that new figures show an economic upturn around the corner. The practices engendering such distrust were entered upon, not just by the officials now so familiar to us, but by countless others, high and low, in the government and outside it, each time for a reason that seemed overriding.

Take the example of a government official hoping to see Congress enact a crucial piece of antipoverty legislation. Should he lie to a Congressman he believes unable to understand the importance and urgency of the legislation, yet powerful enough to block its passage? Should he tell him that, unless the proposed bill is enacted, the government will push for a much more extensive measure?

In answering, shift the focus from this case taken in isolation to the vast practices of which it forms a part. What is the effect on colleagues and subordinates who witness the deception so often resulting from such a choice? What is the effect on the members of Congress as they inevitably learn of a proportion of these lies? And what is the effect on the electorate as it learns of these and similar practices? Then shift back to the narrower world of the official troubled about the legislation he believes in, and hoping by a small deception to change a crucial vote.

It is the fear of the harm lies bring that explains statements such as the following from Revelations (22.15), which might otherwise seem strangely out of proportion:

These others must stay outside [the Heavenly City]: dogs, medicine-men, and fornicators, and murderers, and idolaters, and everyone of false life and false speech.[8]

It is the deep-seated concern of the multitude which speaks here; there could be few contrasts greater than that between this statement and the self-confident, individualistic view by Machiavelli:

> Men are so simple and so ready to obey present necessities, that one who deceives will always find those who allow themselves to be deceived.

Discrepant Perspectives

The discrepancy of perspectives explains the ambiguity toward lying which most of us experience. While we know the risks of lying, and would prefer a world where others abstained from it, we know also that there are times when it would be helpful, perhaps even necessary, if we ourselves could deceive with impunity. By itself, each perspective is incomplete. Each can bias moral judgments and render them shallow. Even the perspective of the deceived can lead to unfounded, discriminatory suspicions about persons thought to be untrustworthy.

We need to learn to shift back and forth between the two perspectives, and even to focus on both at once, as in straining to see both aspects of an optical illusion. In ethics, such a double focus leads to applying the Golden Rule: to strain to experience one's acts not only as subject and agent but as recipient, sometimes victim. And while it is not always easy to put oneself in the place of someone affected by a fate one will never share, there is no such difficulty with lying. We all know what it is to lie, to be told lies, to be correctly or falsely suspected of having lied. In principle, we can all readily share both perspectives. What is important is to make that effort as we consider the lies we would like to be able to tell. It is at such times of choice and judgment that the Golden Rule is hardest to follow. The Muslim mystic Al-Ghazali recommended the shift in perspectives in the following words:

> If you want to know the foulness of lying for yourself, consider the lying of someone else and how you shun it and despise the man who lies and regard his communication as foul. Do the same with regard to all your own vices, for you do not realize the foulness of your vices from your own case, but from someone else's.[9]

The parallel between deception and violence as seen from these two perspectives is, once again, striking. For both violence and deception are means not only to unjust coercion, but also to self-defense and survival. They have been feared and circumscribed by law and custom, when seen from the perspective of those affected by lies and by assaults. In religion and in ethics alike, they have been proscribed, and advice has been given on how to cope with the oppression in their wake.

But they have also been celebrated through the ages when seen from the perspective of the agent, the liar, the forceful man. The hero uses deceit to survive and to conquer. When looked at from this point of view, both violence and deceit are portrayed with bravado and exultation. Nietzsche and Machiavelli are their advocates, epic poetry their home. See, for example, how Athena, smiling, addresses Odysseus in the *Odyssey:*

> Whoever gets around you must be sharp
> and guileful as a snake; even a god
> might bow to you in ways of dissimulation.
> You! You chameleon!
> Bottomless bag of tricks! Here in your own country
> would you not give your stratagems a rest
> or stop spellbinding for an instant?
>
> You play a part as if it were your own tough skin.

No more of this, though. Two of a kind, we are,
contrivers, both. Of all men now alive
you are the best in plots and story telling.
My own fame is for wisdom among the gods—
deceptions, too.[10]

The Principle of Veracity

The perspective of the deceived, then, reveals several reasons why lies are undesirable. Those who share it have
cause to fear the effects of undiscovered lies on the choices
of liars and dupes. They are all too aware of the impact
of discovered and suspected lies on trust and social cooperation. And they consider not only the individual lie but
the practice of which it forms a part, and the long-term
results which it can have.

For these reasons, I believe that we must at the very
least accept as an initial premise Aristotle's view that
lying is "mean and culpable" and that truthful statements
are preferable to lies in the absence of special considerations. This premise gives an initial negative weight to lies.
It holds that they are not neutral from the point of view
of our choices; that lying requires explanation, whereas
truth ordinarily does not. It provides a counterbalance to
the crude evaluation by liars of their own motives and of
the consequences of their lies. And it places the burden of
proof squarely on those who assume the liar's perspective.

This presumption against lying can also be stated so as
to stress the positive worth of truthfulness or veracity.[11]
I would like, in the chapters to come, to refer to the
"principle of veracity" as an expression of this initial imbalance in our weighing of truthfulness and lying.

It is not necessarily a principle that overrides all others, nor even the one most frequently appealed to. Nor is
it, obviously, sufficient by itself—witness the brutal but

honest regime or the tormentor who prides himself on his frankness. Rather, trust in some degree of veracity functions as a *foundation* of relations among human beings; when this trust shatters or wears away, institutions collapse.*

Such a principle need not indicate that all lies should be ruled out by the initial negative weight given to them, nor does it even suggest what kinds of lies should be prohibited. But it does make at least one immediate limitation on lying: in any situation where a lie is a possible choice, one must first seek truthful alternatives.[12] If lies and truthful statements appear to achieve the same result or appear to be as desirable to the person contemplating lying the lies should be ruled out. And only where a lie is a *last resort* can one even begin to consider whether or not it is morally justified. Mild as this initial stipulation sounds, it would, if taken seriously, eliminate a great many lies told out of carelessness or habit or unexamined good intentions.

When we try to move beyond this agreement on such an initial premise, the first fork in the road is presented by those who believe that *all* lies should be categorically ruled out. Such a position not only assigns a negative weight to lies; it sees this weight as so overwhelming that no circumstances can outweigh it. If we choose to follow that path, the quest for circumstances when lying is justified is obviously over.

*The function of the principle of veracity as a foundation is evident when we think of trust. I can have different kinds of trust: that you will treat me fairly, that you will have my interests at heart, that you will do me no harm. But if I do not trust your word, can I have genuine trust in the first three? If there is no confidence in the truthfulness of others, is there any way to assess their fairness, their intentions to help or to harm? How, then, can they be trusted? *Whatever* matters to human beings, trust is the atmosphere in which it thrives.

NEVER TO LIE?

But every liar says the opposite of what he thinks in his heart, with purpose to deceive. Now it is evident that speech was given to man, not that men might therewith deceive one another, but that one man might make known his thoughts to another. To use speech, then, for the purpose of deception, and not for its appointed end, is a sin. Nor are we to suppose that there is any lie that is not a sin, because it is sometimes possible, by telling a lie, to do service to another.

—St. Augustine, *The Enchiridion*

If any, in fact, do this: either teach men to do evil that good may come or do so themselves, their damnation is just. This is particularly applicable to those who tell lies in order to do good thereby. It follows, that officious lies, as well as all others, are an abomination to the God of Truth. Therefore there is no absurdity, however strange it may sound, in that saying of the ancient Father "I would not tell a wilful lie to save the souls of the whole world."

—John Wesley, *Sermon*

By a lie a man throws away and, as it were, annihilates his dignity as a man.

—Immanuel Kant, *Doctrine of Virtue*

The simplest answer to the problems of lying, at least in principle, is to rule out all lies. Many theologians have chosen such a position; foremost among them is St. Augustine. He cut a clear swath through all the earlier opinions holding that some lies might be justified. He claimed that God forbids all lies and that liars therefore endanger their immortal souls.[1]

He defined lying as having one thing in one's heart and uttering another with the intention to deceive,[2] thereby subverting the God-given purposes of human speech. His definition left no room at all for justifiable falsehood. And he confessed that this troubled him: he worried about lies to ailing persons, for instance, and lies to protect those threatened by assault or defilement. He allowed, therefore, that there are great differences among lies and that some are much more abhorrent than others. He set up an eightfold distinction, beginning with lies uttered in the teaching of religion, the worst ones of all, and ending with lies which harm no one and yet save someone from physical defilement.[3] These last are still sins and cannot be justified or advised to anyone, yet they can much more easily be pardoned. And he concluded that:

> It cannot be denied that they have attained a very high standard of goodness who never lie except to save a man from injury; but in the case of men who have reached this standard, it is not the deceit, but their good intention, that is justly praised, and sometimes even rewarded. It is quite enough that the deception should be pardoned, without its being made an object of laudation.[4]

The impact of Augustine's thinking on this subject was immense. Up to the time that he wrote, many different opinions had held sway. Even for Christians, the Bible had seemed to give examples of dissimulation and lying which made it difficult to object categorically to all lies. But Augustine explained these in such a way that he could continue to maintain that God forbade all lies, while distinguishing among lies according to the intention behind them and the harmfulness of their effects. These distinctions reappear in the penitentials of the early Middle Ages and are fully treated and worked out in the systematic works of the high Middle Ages, culminating in the treatment given to lying in the *Summa Theologica* by Thomas Aquinas.[5]

Throughout, Augustine's prohibition of all lies as sinful held sway. But such a doctrine turned out to be very difficult to live by. Many ways were tried to soften the prohibition, to work around it, and to allow at least a few lies. Three different paths were taken: to allow for pardoning of some lies; to claim that some deceptive statements are not falsehoods, merely misinterpreted by the listener; and finally to claim that certain falsehoods do not *count* as lies.

The first built upon Augustine's eightfold hierarchy, going from the most grievous lies to those most easily pardoned. Aquinas set a pattern which is still followed by Catholic theologians. He distinguished three kinds of lies: the officious, or helpful, lies; the jocose lies, told in jest; and the mischievous, or malicious, lies, told to harm someone. Only the latter constitute mortal sins for Aquinas. He agreed with Augustine that all lies are sins, but regarded the officious and jocose lies as less serious. The pardoning function came to grow more and more important and ultimately created great discord within the Church. Should one be able to tell lies and then have them wiped from one's conscience? Ought it to be possible to do so repeatedly, perhaps even to plan the lies with the pardon in mind? And by what means should the pardon be sought?

To arrive at reliable answers to such questions was a

tormenting task when views differed so sharply and when error might result in punishment after death. The two other paths around Augustine's strict prohibition occasioned similar disputes. They assumed, in effect, that certain intentionally deceptive statements are not lies in the first place. They might then be used in good conscience.

One such was the "mental reservation" or "mental restraint." It took its lead from Augustine's definition of lying as having one thing in one's heart and uttering another, but it *left out* the speaker's intention to deceive as part of the definition.[6] It thereby allowed the following argument: If you say something misleading to another and merely add a qualification to it in your mind so as to make it true, you cannot be responsible for the "misinterpretation" made by the listener. Some argued that such mental reservation could be used only for a just cause and when there was a chance for the deceived to make the correct inference.[7] Others went very far in expanding its usage—to the point where a clever person could always find the convenient mental reservation for any falsehood he wanted to convey. Needless to say, this doctrine aroused intense controversy, both within and outside Catholic circles. This is how Pascal begins his polemic against it in his *Provincial Letters*:

> "One of the most embarrassing of these cases is how to avoid telling lies, especially when one wants to induce a belief in a false thing. This purpose is admirably served by our doctrine of equivocation, according to which, as Sanchez has it, 'it is permitted to use ambiguous terms, leading people to understand them in another sense from that in which we understand them ourselves.'"
>
> "I know that, father," said I.
>
> "We have published it so often," continued he, "that at length everyone has learned about it. But do you know what is to be done when one finds no equivocal words?"
>
> "No, father."
>
> "I thought as much," said he; "this is something new: it

is the doctrine of mental reservations. 'A man may swear', as Sanchez says in the same place, 'that he never did such a thing (though he actually did it), meaning within himself that he did not do it on a certain day, or before he was born, or understanding any other such circumstance, while the words which he employs have no such sense as would discover his meaning; and this is very convenient in many encounters, and always very justified when necessary for health, honor, or the good.' "

"Indeed, father! is that not a lie, and perjury to boot?"[8]

The mental reservation turned out to have a long history, especially in court proceedings. Since oaths in court were originally sworn in the name of God with the fear that He might strike down those who took his name in order to support falsehoods,[9] some argued that a silent reservation, audible to God but not to the court, might avoid this fate. Thus, an adulterous woman might swear that she had not wronged her husband, adding silently that at least she had not done so that week, or at a certain house, thereby escaping her husband's wrath and a certain death, while not believing herself perjured in the eyes of God.

Resorting to mental reservations and other internal disclaimers to outward acts has been a matter of life and death in those many periods when religious persecution has raged. In the sixteenth century, for example, the so-called Nicodemites, who had converted to Lutheranism or Calvinism, tried to escape persecution by concealing their religious views and by participating in the Mass. They sought to justify this behavior on religious grounds, but Calvin condemned them in the harshest terms, advising them to emigrate from Catholic areas rather than to take part in "papist ceremonies."[10]

Nor is the mental reservation altogether a thing of the past. We still swear to omit it in many official oaths of citizenship and public office. And some still recommend it. A well-known Catholic textbook[11] advises doctors and nurses to deceive patients by this method when they see fit to do so. If a feverish patient, for example, asks what his temperature is, the doctor is advised to answer: "Your temperature is normal today," while making the mental reservation that it is normal for someone in the patient's precise physical condition.

The final way to avoid Augustine's across-the-board prohibition of all lies seeks to argue that not all intentionally false statements ought to count as lies from a moral point of view. This view found powerful expression in Grotius.[12] He argued that a falsehood is a lie in the strict sense of the word only if it conflicts with a right of the person to whom it is addressed. A robber, for instance, has no right to the information he tries to extort; to speak falsely to him is therefore not to lie in the strict sense of the word. The right in question is that of liberty of judgment, which is implied in all speech; but it can be lost if the listener has evil intentions; or not yet acquired, as in the case of children; or else freely given up, as when two persons agree to deceive one another. Grotius was a lawyer, and views such as his brought many to believe that if lies were not actually unlawful, they were morally acceptable, bringing no blame to the liar.[13] Such an argument oversimplifies his thinking, but it is a fact that Grotius helped to bring back into the discourse on lying the notion, common in antiquity but so nearly snuffed out by St. Augustine, that falsehood is at times justifiable.

Among those who discussed such doctrines with their students in ethics was Kant. Between 1775 and 1781, long before he had published his own works of moral philosophy, he gave yearly lectures on ethics at the University of Königsberg and used the required textbook, which discussed the familiar distinctions from Aquinas and Grotius.[14] To judge from notes taken by students, edited in this century, Kant expounded on this material in a lively way, using cases as illustrations.[15]

It is all the more striking, then, that when Kant finally published his own works on moral philosophy, his treatment of lying should expressly have taken a distance from all such subtleties.[16] His views set forth the strongest arguments we have against all lying.

Kant takes issue, first, with the idea that any generous motive, any threat to life, could excuse a lie. He argues that:

> Truthfulness in statements which cannot be avoided is the formal duty of an individual to everyone, however great may be the disadvantage accruing to himself or to another.[17]

This is the absolutist position, prohibiting all lies, even those told for the best of purposes or to avoid the most horrible of fates. For someone holding such a position, to be called a liar was a mortal insult—perhaps cause even for legal action or a duel; to be *proved* a liar could lead to self-exile out of shame.

Kant's view, if correct, would eliminate any effort to distinguish among lies, since he rejects them all. He takes the duty of truthfulness to be an "unconditional duty which holds in all circumstances";[18] a lie, even if it does not wrong any particular individual, always harms mankind generally, "for it vitiates the source of law." It harms the liar himself, moreover, by destroying his human dignity and making him more worthless even than a mere thing.[19]

Kant also rejects the way around Augustine's prohibition that consists in defining certain falsehoods as not being lies. He defines a lie as "merely an intentional untruthful declaration to another person" and dismisses the idea that we owe the duty of speaking the truth only to those who have a right to the truth.[20] On the contrary, truthfulness is a duty which no circumstances can abrogate. Whatever else may be said about Kant's position, it seems to have the virtue of clarity and simplicity. Others may argue about when to lie, but he makes a clean sweep.

Conflicts of Duty

But can we agree with Kant? His position has seemed too sweeping to nearly all his readers, even obsessive to some. For although veracity is undoubtedly an important duty, most assume that it leaves room for exceptions. It can clash with other duties, such as that of averting harm to innocent persons. Yet Kant holds[21] that "a conflict of duties and obligations is inconceivable," that if one does one's duty, one will turn out to have had no conflicting obligations. It is this refusal to consider conflicts of duty which drives Kant into such inflexible positions.

Most have held the contrary view—that there are times when truthfulness causes or fails to avert such great harm that a lie is clearly justifiable. One such time is where a life is threatened and where a lie might avert the danger. The traditional testing case advanced against the absolutist position is that discussed by Kant himself, where a would-be murderer inquires whether "our friend who is pursued by him had taken refuge in our house."[22] Should one lie in order to save one's friend? Or should one tell the truth?

This is a standard case, familiar from Biblical times, used by the Scholastics in many variations, and taken up by most commentators on deception. It assumes, of course, that mere silence or evasion will not satisfy the assailant. If this case does not weaken your resistance to all lies, it is hard to think of another that will.

In nineteenth-century England, the same case was taken up once more by Cardinal Newman. He was defending himself and Catholic scholars against charges of immorality and laxity regarding truthfulness. He argued that men of great rectitude, no matter what their faith, might resort to a lie in extreme circumstances. He quoted Samuel Johnson as stating:

> The General Rule is, that truth should never be violated; there must, however, be some exceptions. If, for instance, a murderer should ask you which way a man has gone.

Even so, Cardinal Newman added, Johnson might well have acted quite differently had he been put to the test:

> As to Johnson's case of a murderer asking which way a man has gone, I should have anticipated that, had such a difficulty happened to him, his first act would have been to knock the man down, and to call out for the police; and next, if he was worsted in the conflict, he would not have given the ruffian the information he asked at whatever risk to himself. I think he would have let himself be killed first.[23]

Cardinal Newman's supposition might well have astounded Johnson! Depending on the physical strength of the murderer, resistance by force might seem a very implausible alternative to deception. Kant evidently does not even consider it; confronted with this test case, he takes his stand squarely with those objecting even to lies under such extreme circumstances.

Most others have argued that, in such cases, where innocent lives are at stake, lies are morally justified, if indeed they are lies in the first place. Kant believes that to lie is to annihilate one's human dignity; yet for these others, to reply honestly, and thereby betray one's friend, would in itself constitute a compromise of that dignity. In such an isolated case, they would argue, the costs of lying are small and those of telling the truth catastrophic.

Similarly, a captain of a ship transporting fugitives from Nazi Germany, if asked by a patrolling vessel whether there were any Jews on board would, for Kant's critics, have been justified in answering No. His duty to the fugitives, they claim, would then have conflicted with the duty to speak the truth and would have far outweighed it. In fact, in times of such crisis, those who share Kant's opposition to lying clearly put innocent persons at the mercy of wrongdoers.[24]

Furthermore, force has been thought justifiable in all such cases of wrongful threat to life. If to use force in self-defense or in defending those at risk of murder is right, why then should a lie in self-defense be ruled out? Surely if force is allowed, a lie should be equally, perhaps at times more, permissible. Both words and force, as I mentioned in Chapter II, can be used coercively, so as to alter behavior. And even though we need the strongest protection against such coercion, there are times when it must be allowed. Kant's single-minded upholding of truthfulness above all else nullifies the use of falsehoods in self-defense. Can the principle of veracity reasonably be made to carry such a burden?

This burden would clearly create guilt for many: guilt at having allowed the killing of a fellow human rather than lie to a murderer. Kant attempts to assuage this guilt by arguing as follows: If one stays close to the truth, one cannot, strictly speaking, be responsible for the murderous acts another commits. The murderer will have to take the whole blame for his act. In speaking to him truthfully, one has done nothing blameworthy. If, on the other hand, one tells him a lie, Kant argues, one becomes responsible for all the bad consequences which might befall the victim and anyone else.[25] One may, for instance, point the murderer in what one believes to be the wrong direction, only to discover with horror that that is exactly where the victim has gone to hide.

There is much truth in saying that one is responsible for what happens after one has done something wrong or questionable. But it is a very narrow view of responsibility which does not also take some blame for a disaster one could easily have averted, no matter how much others are also to blame. A world where it is improper even to tell a lie to a murderer pursuing an innocent victim is not a world that many would find safe to inhabit.

It may even be that, in less rigorous moments, doubts beset Wesley and Kant and those who hold the most extreme views. A curious form of internal evidence for such a supposition is that they so often preface their most surprisingly intransigeant remarks with phrases such as "however strange it may sound."[26] They know that their stance is highly counterintuitive; yet something forces them to adopt it.

Religious Prohibitions

Stronger than intuition or common sense for moralists as stern as Augustine or Wesley is their belief that there is unimpeachable evidence to show that lies must be unconditionally ruled out. This evidence is almost always of a religious nature. It may be based on revelation, on an interpretation of the Bible, or on some other document regarded as irrefutable. Thus Paul included lying in his catalogue of grave departures from sound doctrine:

> Knowing this, that the law is not made for a righteous man, but for the lawless and disobedient, for the ungodly and for sinners, for unholy and profane, for murderers of fathers and murderers of mothers, for manslayers, for whoremongers, for them that defile themselves with mankind, for menstealers, for liars, for perjured persons and if there be any other thing that is contrary to sound doctrine;[27]

And Augustine, among many others, cited as support this passage from Psalms 5.7:

> Thou hatest all the workers of iniquity; thou wilt destroy all that speak a lie.

In Dante's *Inferno*, deceivers are tormented in the eighth circle of Hell, lowest of all except for that inhabited by traitors. Why such severe treatment? Because:

> Of every malice that gains hatred in Heaven the end is injustice; and every such end, either by force or by fraud, afflicts another. But because fraud is an evil peculiar to man, it more displeases God, and therefore the fraudulent are the lower, and more pain assails them.[28]

Even Kant, who claimed that his moral principles were quite independent of his religious beliefs, was profoundly influenced by his faith when he derived conclusions to human problems from his moral principles.* He grew up in a deeply pietistic family, with very strict views on matters of personal behavior. His positions on such questions as suicide parallel those which were religiously supported in the texts he knew. And he acknowledged that, without some assumption in his moral universe as to the existence of God, "the highest good" cannot be possible in the world.[29] The vehemence of his views on lying is in accord with his religious background.

Beneath the belief in the divine command to forgo all lying at all costs is yet another belief: that some grievous punishment will come to those who disobey such commands. Augustine stated the matter starkly: Death kills but the body, but a lie loses eternal life for the soul. To lie to save the life of another, then, is a foolish bargain:

---

*Sometimes Kant's views parallel religious views almost to the letter, but with the substitution of "natural purposiveness" for divine intention. Compare, for example, the quotation from Augustine at the beginning of this chapter with Kant in the *Doctrine of Virtue:* "the man who communicates his thoughts to someone in words which yet (intentionally) contain the contrary of what he thinks on the subject has a purpose directly opposed to the natural purposiveness of the power of communicating one's thoughts and therefore renounces his personality and makes himself a mere deceptive appearance of man, not man himself" (p.93).

Therefore, does he not speak most perversely who says that one person ought to die spiritually so that another may live corporeally? [. . .] Since, then, eternal life is lost by lying, a lie may never be told for the preservation of the temporal life of another.[30]

Such speculation obviously goes beyond the realm of ethics and belongs squarely in that of faith. To the degree that one believes in the immortality of the soul and in its "death" through lying, to that degree it does make sense to eschew lies, even when one might have saved a life by lying.* Any complete prohibition of lying, even in circumstances of threats to innocent lives, must, in order for it to be reasonable, rely on some belief that the lie is associated with a fate "worse than death."

The distinction, however, is not simply one between those with faith in divine retribution and those who lack it. For many who believe in such retribution do not agree that it will strike all who lie. Some hold that many lies may be forgiven; others argue that God never did rule out all lies; still others that not all we think of as lying is, in fact, lying.

And even among nonbelievers, there is no lack of disagreement about whether lies should be prohibited or not. True, fewer among them rule out *all* lies. But one can imagine some terror which might make any lie seem "worse than death": the fear, perhaps, of some authority figure who has outlawed lying and seems to have knowledge of any breach of the rules; or an exalted view of the injury to one's integrity which a lie might bring—an injury more grievous than any harm that might befall an innocent victim through one's forthrightness.

---

*However, it remains difficult to see why Wesley, in the quotation at the beginning of this chapter, would abjure a willful lie "to save the souls of the whole world." Why *not* lose one soul to save all the others?

To sum up, two beliefs often support the rigid rejection of all lies: that God rules out all lies and that He will punish those who lie. These beliefs cannot be proved or disproved. Many, including many Christians, refuse to accept one or both. Other religions, while condemning lying, rarely do so without exceptions. Thus the most frequent religious act of Buddhists is to recite each day five precepts, the fourth of which is an undertaking to abstain from telling lies. But certain lies are commonly regarded as not being sins, and thus not going against the precept.[31] Similarly, while Jewish texts regard lying as prohibited, certain lies, and especially those told to preserve the peace of the household, are regarded as exceptions.[32] All these traditions, therefore, leave room for a rejection of the absolutist prohibition of all lies.

I share their rejection. In the absence of some vast terror associated with lying, which goes far beyond the presumption against lying stated in Chapter II, I have to agree that there are at least *some* circumstances which warrant a lie. And foremost among them are those where innocent lives are at stake, and where only a lie can deflect the danger.

But, in taking such a position, it would be wrong to lose the profound concern which the absolutist theologians and philosophers express—the concern for the harm to trust and to oneself from lying, quite apart from any immediate effects from any one lie. Individuals, these thinkers claimed, have to consider the long-range effects of lying on human communities; and even if liars have no such forethought, the risks that they themselves run from lying ought to matter to them perhaps most of all. Over and over, penitentials and confessionals recommended penances for those who had lied—silence, fasting, prayer. These penances were harshest when the lie had harmed others; but the point is, they were occasioned primarily by the simple act of lying, even where no immediate harm had resulted.

Similarly, Kant stressed the injury to humankind from lying and dramatized this to the culprit by stating that "by a lie a man throws away and, as it were, annihilates his dignity as a man." It may seem exaggerated to apply this statement to any one small lie, but if one sees it instead as a warning against *practices* of lying, against biased calculations of pros and cons, and against assuming the character of a liar, it may be closer to the mark. For a liar often *does* diminish himself by lying, and the loss is precisely to his dignity, his integrity.

The more difficult task remains: that of drawing lines. In order to determine more carefully what kinds of lies can be told, it is necessary to look next at ways of comparing lies and at the excuses given for telling them. The method which comes first to mind is that of weighing the *consequences* of deceptive statements. In philosophy, the utilitarian tradition has been most prominently associated with such a procedure.

IV

WEIGHING THE CONSEQUENCES

What harm would it do, if a man told a good strong lie for the sake of the good and for the Christian church [. . .] a lie out of necessity, a useful lie, a helpful lie, such lies would not be against God, he would accept them.

—Martin Luther cited by his secretary, in a letter in Max Lenz, ed., *Briefwechsel Landgraf Phillips des Grossmüthigen von Hessen mit Bucer*, vol. I

Falsehood, take it by itself, consider it as not being accompanied by any other material circumstances, nor therefore productive of any material effects, can never, upon the principle of utility, constitute any offense at all. Combined with other circumstances, there is scarce any sort of pernicious effect which it may not be instrumental in producing.

—J. Bentham, *The Principles of Morals and Legislation*

I do not necessarily do you any harm at all if, by deed or word, I induce you to believe what is not in fact the case; I may even do you good, possibly by way, for example, of consolation or flattery. Nevertheless [. . .] it is easy to see how crucially important it is that the natural inclination to have recourse to it should be counteracted.

—G. J. Warnock, *The Object of Morality*

Erasmus, well-acquainted with zealots, observed that a rigid condemnation of all falsehood is simply unworkable. All falsehoods are not lies, he wrote, and the idea put forth by many theologians, that not even one harmless lie should be told to save the bodies and souls of the whole human race, runs counter to common sense.[1]

Chief among those who have relied on a common-sense stance in ethics are the utilitarian philosophers and their precursors in antiquity. They did not accept the premise that God has ruled out all lies. They brought a great sense of freedom to those whom they could convince that what ought to be done was not necessarily what the soothsayer or the ruler or the priests required, but rather, quite simply, what brought about the greatest balance of good over evil. For utilitarians, an act is more or less justifiable according to the goodness or badness of its consequences. Their procedure for weighing moral choice is very similar to ways in which most of us do in fact approach many situations of moral conflict— close, therefore, to the workings of common sense.

Sidgwick, using such a method, assumed that certain lies, such as those told to invalids and children for their own good, are necessary. His justification for this position is a consequentialist one—it compares the consequences of lying to those of not lying in particular cases:

> But if the lawfulness of benevolent deception in any case be admitted, I do not see how we can decide when and how far it is admissible, except by considerations of expediency; that is, by weighing the gain of any particular deception against the imperilment of mutual confidence involved in all violation of the truth.[2]

Unlike the theories discussed in the last chapter, utilitarianism generates no controversies over how to *define* lying. It requires no special leeway for mental reservations in order to acknowledge some deception as justified; it need not define some falsehoods as not being true lies, nor yet some truthful statements as not being duties. Utilitarianism simply requires an evaluation of courses of action, be they deceptive or not. For those, on the other hand, who claim that all lies are absolutely wrong, the precise definition of a lie is obviously crucial.

Utilitarians also differ from Kant (though not, as we have seen, from Augustine) in stressing the differences in seriousness between one lie and another. They are therefore much closer to our actual moral deliberation in many cases where we are perplexed. In choosing whether or not to lie, we *do* weigh benefits against harm and happiness against unhappiness. We judge differently the lie to cover up an embezzlement and the lie to camouflage a minor accounting error. And we judge both of those to be different in turn from a sympathetic lie told to avoid hurting a child's feelings. In making such judgments, the difference has to do precisely with the degree to which the lie may cause or avoid harm, increase or decrease happiness.

But, as soon as more complex questions of truthfulness and deception are raised, the utilitarian view turns out to be unsatisfactory as well. First of all, the more complex the acts, the more difficult it becomes to produce convincing comparisons of their consequences. It is hard enough to make estimates of utility for one person, keeping in mind all the different alternatives and their consequences. But to make such estimates for several persons is often well-nigh impossible, except, once again, in the starkest cases. The result is that, even apart from lying, those conflicts which are most difficult to resolve, such as questions of suicide or capital punishment, cause as much disagreement among utilitarians as among everyone else.

A second reason to be wary of a simple-seeming utilitarian calculation is that it often appears to imply that lies, apart from their resultant harm and benefits, are in themselves neutral. It seems to say that a lie and a truthful statement which achieve the same utility are *equivalent*. Is there not, then, a contradiction between such a view and the principle of veracity which I set forth in Chapter II? For this principle holds, in effect, that before we even begin to weigh the good and bad aspects of a lie, the falsehood itself is negatively weighted; while such a negative weight may be overridden, it is there at the outset. To go back to Bentham's statement about falsehood, quoted at the head of this chapter, must it be taken to disagree with the premise that lies are to be negatively weighted from the outset? Not really. For in ordinary life, as Bentham would be the first to agree, falsehood cannot be taken "by itself"; most lies *do* have negative consequences for liars, dupes, all those affected, and for social trust.[3] And when liars evaluate these consequences, they are peculiarly likely to be biased; their calculations frequently go astray. Therefore, even strict utilitarians might be willing to grant the premise that in making moral choices, we should allow an initial presumption against lies.[4] There would be no need to see this presumption as something mysterious or abstract, nor to say that lies are somehow bad "in themselves." Utilitarians could view the negative weight instead as a correction, endorsed by experience, of the inaccurate and biased calculations of consequences made by any one liar.

The common assumption that lies can be evaluated on a risk-benefit scale determined by the liar can therefore be set aside on utilitarian grounds. The risks are different from those ignored in the moral vacuum conjured up by Bentham. And the chances for the liar to arrive at rationalizations in secret are unlimited. The long-range results of an acceptance of such facile calculations, made by those most biased to favor their own interests and to disregard risks to others, would be severe.[5]

This stumbling block, though not fundamental to the utilitarian tradition, is deeply entrenched in much actual utilitarian writing on deception. The subject of lying appears there, as it does so frequently in moral philosophy, merely as an illustration. A brief example is given, followed by a quick calculation of pros and cons, with no weight accorded to the lie at the outset of the calculation.[6] The result, most often, is an equally quick intuitive conclusion.

The well-known desert island examples of lying and promise-breaking exhibit this type of quick calculation. They ask what we should do in circumstances where a lie or a broken promise could accomplish a great deal of good, harm no one, and never be discovered.

> I have promised a dying man on a desert island, from which subsequently I alone am rescued, to give his hoard of gold to the South Australian Jockey Club. On my return I give it to the Royal Adelaide Hospital, which, we may suppose, badly needs it for a new X-ray machine. Could anybody deny that I had done rightly without being open to the charge of heartlessness? (Remember that the promise was known only to me, and so my action will not in this case weaken the general confidence in the social institution of promising.)[7]

Such textbook examples are designed to measure resistance to lying and promise-breaking in their own right, quite apart from any harm to the dying man or to society, which can never know about the act. They facilitate clear thinking about whether or not we consider the breach of promise or the lie reprehensible. They also provide a vivid illustration of the profound disagreement which exists among us. For in most groups asked to consider the example, a substantial number will choose each of the two answers.

But those who see in this example a vacuum where no one can be harmed ignore the risks to the liar himself of personal discomfort and loss of integrity, of a greater likelihood, however slight, of having to lie again to shore up the first lie; and of a somewhat diminished resistance to lying for causes he may wish to further in the future. Whatever one may decide in the desert island case, then, one ought not to proceed on the assumption that the choice has no harmful consequences whatsoever.

Choices between lies and truthful statements, therefore, exhibit the difficulties often thought to beset utilitarianism as a method for coping with moral conflict. But the problems mentioned so far might in principle be counteracted within utilitarianism. They need not invalidate the general effort to weigh factors in a moral problem. The hard tasks of interpersonal utility estimates may even arise less often than is now thought, once the powerful reasons against most lies are taken into account. The presumption against lying before any consequences in a particular case are evaluated can be acknowledged and explored, and steps can be taken to diminish the bias with which liars judge their choices.

Systems

Utilitarians can argue, then, that a far-reaching consequentialist system can account for any objections raised. Those adhering to other systems of ethics claim to cope with such objections through principles erected in place of, or in addition to, that of utility. These principles may in turn be derived from some authority, such as God's will, or a holy text; they may also be worked out by using some method such as Kant's Categorical Imperative: "Act only on that maxim whereby thou canst at the same time will that it should become a universal law."

Many have labored to erect such systems: to find a

method by which to judge moral choice, or some single principle from which judgments can be derived, or some hierarchy among principles so as to resolve conflicts. In this way, methods, principles, and priority rules have sprung up, forming elaborate and hotly debated structures.

These structures are often elegant in operation, noble in design. They refine our moral perception and illuminate the intricacies of moral choice; they put a firm footing under our most indispensable moral judgments; and they help us make sense of human relationships, compare different levels of integrity, and shed light on models for how best to lead our lives or govern our societies.

But when we have to make difficult concrete moral choices, they give us little help. This need not be a criticism; many claim that systems of moral philosophy were not meant for such everyday tasks.[8] Yet it is natural to *try* to use them at those times when we are most bewildered, when it seems that in obeying one moral principle we are transgressing another.

Unfortunately, there is no evidence that systems, or overriding principles such as that of utility, or priority rules among principles, lead us to clear conclusions, much as the mind strains for such a result.[9] (I must stress here that I am talking about those concrete conflicts which conscientious persons find *hard;* needless to say, easier choices, such as the condemnation of torture, can be derived within any moral or religious system as well as through the use of common sense.[10])

For adherents of every moral system—be they Kantians, utilitarians, believers in God's will or in Natural Law—have been found on every conceivable side of the difficult moral issues that have divided mankind.[11] On the subjects of suicide and abortion, revolution and war, opposed positions have been conscientiously worked out within each of the competing systems.[12] Exactly the same is true of the hard choices raised with respect to lying.

A system of moral philosophy put to such uses is like a magician's hat—almost anything can be pulled out of it, wafted about, let fly. No one can be quite sure it was not in the hat all along. And the philosopher is often in the end his own most amazed spectator. He may not know how he did it—but the doves are aloft, the silk scarves in his hands!

Uncertainty and imprecision beset hard moral choices. The more the intervening steps are multiplied and the more we are told that one thing can be explained in terms of another or derived from another, the more room is left for bias, self-deception, even sleight of hand. The methods advocated within many moral systems, moreover, for those who wish to arrive at solutions to concrete problems, are often so rudimentary that any answer can emerge, depending on what values are introduced at the beginning.*

What paths, what means of inquiry into the troubling questions of truth-telling and lying remain if systems help so little? I believe that any method, to be of help, should originate with the actual choices people make. It should have to look at the actual excuses they give, to themselves and to others, the arguments by which they appeal to principles, and the means by which they evaluate such arguments when others make them. To take such a path will require a search for cases, examples, descriptions of

*This defect in method may be based in part on a semantic confusion. The word "method" has two meanings: the first comes from the Greek words *meta* and *hodos*, meaning a following after, a path, a means of inquiry. This is the sense in which we obviously need methods in moral philosophy. But a second sense, foreign to the Greek, was worked out in the sixteenth century in Latin by logicians: it is that of "systematic arrangement and order." Some thinkers have mistakenly assumed that they possess a method in the first sense as soon as they have perfected a systematic arrangement of their theory, giving them a method in the second sense only.

what happens. It will lead into working lives, family relationships, political practices.

Many have used such an approach to human problems. In every religious and legal tradition, individuals have labored to resolve difficult conflicts of conscience. The Roman Stoics were among the greatest practitioners of this form of applied ethics, with their thoughtful discussions of problems of suicide or slavery or even minor questions of politeness. Talmudic scholars and Early Christian thinkers pushed the discussion of concrete problems to great refinement.[13]

Cases of conscience cannot be examined in a moral vacuum. Traditionally, they have been discussed in a specific religious, moral, or legal framework. The religious and legal approaches illuminate important distinctions, and cannot be ignored in any inquiry into deception. But they are often influenced by considerations quite separate from those of ethics: considerations of faith, in religion, and of what it is appropriate and feasible to regulate, in law. The background for my inquiry will therefore be that of moral philosophy. And although I shall use no moral system from which to derive my conclusion, the questions which I shall ask of justifications advanced for different lies will, in the end, be questions of benefit and harm, questions asking why lying *matters* and what it *does* to individuals and to institutions.

By following such a path I hope to make more headway than by trusting to intuition or staying with the abstraction of a system. But certain intractable dilemmas will remain. There will be times when two alternatives, however different, present us with a near-equilibrium as we compare them. At other times there may even be alternatives which *are* quite equal, so far as our limited capacities can make out. At still other times so much uncertainty surrounds the moral alternatives that choice is difficult. At all such times, the question is not so much *what* the right choice might be, but rather *who* should make the choice and what are the appropriate *procedures* for choosing.

A good place to begin is with the large category of white lies. It demonstrates both the futility of trying to rule out lies altogether and the shallowness of the intuitive utilitarian approach, which has regarded them as harmless and therefore acceptable.

WHITE LIES

Never have I lied in my own interest; but often I have lied through shame in order to draw myself from embarrassment in indifferent matters [. . .] when, having to sustain discussion, the slowness of my ideas and the dryness of my conversation forced me to have recourse to fictions in order to say something.
——Jean-Jacques Rousseau, *Reveries of a Solitary*

When a man declares that he "has great pleasure in accepting" a vexatious invitation or is the "obedient servant" of one whom he regards as an inferior, he uses phrases which were probably once deceptive. If they are so no longer, Common Sense condemns as over-scrupulous the refusal to use them where it is customary to do so. But Common Sense seems doubtful and perplexed where the process of degradation is incomplete and there are still persons who may be deceived: as in the use of the reply that one is "not at home" to an inconvenient visitor from the country.
——Henry Sidgwick, *Methods of Ethics*

Harmless Lying

White lies are at the other end of the spectrum of deception from lies in a serious crisis. They are the most common and the most trivial forms that duplicity can take.

The fact that they are so common provides their protective coloring. And their very triviality, when compared to more threatening lies, makes it seem unnecessary or even absurd to condemn them. Some consider *all* well-intentioned lies, however momentous, to be white; in this book, I shall adhere to the narrower usage: a white lie, in this sense, is a falsehood not meant to injure anyone, and of little moral import. I want to ask whether there *are* such lies; and if there are, whether their cumulative consequences are still without harm; and, finally, whether many lies are not defended as "white" which are in fact harmful in their own right.

Many small subterfuges may not even be intended to mislead. They are only "white lies" in the most marginal sense. Take, for example, the many social exchanges: "How nice to see you!" or "Cordially Yours." These and a thousand other polite expressions are so much taken for granted that if someone decided, in the name of total honesty, not to employ them, he might well give the impression of an indifference he did not possess. The justification for continuing to use such accepted formulations is that they deceive no one, except possibly those unfamiliar with the language.

A social practice more clearly deceptive is that of giving a false excuse so as not to hurt the feelings of someone making an invitation or request: to say one "can't" do what in reality one may not *want* to do. Once again, the false excuse may prevent unwarranted inferences of greater hostility to the undertaking than one may well feel. Merely to say that one can't do something, moreover, is not deceptive in the sense that an elaborately concocted story can be.

Still other white lies are told in an effort to flatter, to throw a cheerful interpretation on depressing circumstances, or to show gratitude for unwanted gifts. In the eyes of many, such white lies do no harm, provide needed support and cheer, and help dispel gloom and boredom.

They preserve the equilibrium and often the humaneness of social relationships, and are usually accepted as excusable so long as they do not become excessive. Many argue, moreover, that such deception is so helpful and at times so necessary that it must be tolerated as an exception to a general policy against lying. Thus Bacon observed:

> Doth any man doubt, that if there were taken out of men's minds vain opinions, flattering hopes, false valuations, imaginations as one would, and the like, but it would leave the minds of a number of men poor shrunken things, full of melancholy and indisposition, and unpleasing to themselves?[1]

Another kind of lie may actually be advocated as bringing a more substantial benefit, or avoiding a real harm, while seeming quite innocuous to those who tell the lies. Such are the placebos given for innumerable common ailments, and the pervasive use of inflated grades and recommendations for employment and promotion.

A large number of lies without such redeeming features are nevertheless often regarded as so trivial that they should be grouped with white lies. They are the lies told on the spur of the moment, for want of reflection, or to get out of a scrape, or even simply to pass the time. Such are the lies told to boast or exaggerate, or on the contrary to deprecate and understate;[2] the many lies told or repeated in gossip; Rousseau's lies told simply "in order to say something"; the embroidering on facts that seem too tedious in their own right; and the substitution of a quick lie for the lengthy explanations one might otherwise have to provide for something not worth spending time on.

Utilitarians often cite white lies as the *kind* of deception where their theory shows the benefits of common sense and clear thinking. A white lie, they hold, is trivial; it is either completely harmless, or so marginally harmful that the cost of detecting and evaluating the harm is much greater than the minute harm itself. In addition, the white lie can often actually be beneficial, thus further tipping the scales of utility. In a world with so many difficult problems, utilitarians might ask: Why take the time to weigh the minute pros and cons in telling someone that his tie is attractive when it is an abomination, or of saying to a guest that a broken vase was worthless? Why bother even to define such insignificant distortions or make mountains out of molehills by seeking to justify them?

Triviality surely does set limits to when moral inquiry is reasonable. But when we look more closely at practices such as placebo-giving, it becomes clear that all lies defended as "white" cannot be so easily dismissed. In the first place, the harmlessness of lies is notoriously disputable. What the liar perceives as harmless or even beneficial may not be so in the eyes of the deceived. Second, the failure to look at an entire practice rather than at their own isolated case often blinds liars to cumulative harm and expanding deceptive activities. Those who begin with white lies can come to resort to more frequent and more serious ones. Where some tell a few white lies, others may tell more. Because lines are so hard to draw, the indiscriminate use of such lies can lead to other deceptive practices. The aggregate harm from a large number of marginally harmful instances may, therefore, be highly undesirable in the end—for liars, those deceived, and honesty and trust more generally.

Just as the life-threatening cases showed the Kantian analysis to be too rigid, so the cases of white lies show the casual utilitarian calculation to be inadequate. Such a criticism of utilitarianism does not attack its foundations, because it does not disprove the importance of weighing consequences. It merely shows that utilitarians most often do not weigh enough factors in their quick assumption that white lies are harmless. They often fail to look at *practices* of deception and the ways in which these multiply and reinforce one another. They tend to focus, rather, on the individual case, seen from the point of view of the individual liar.

In the post-Watergate period, no one need regard a concern with the combined and long-term effects of deception as far-fetched. But even apart from political life, with its peculiar and engrossing temptations, lies tend to spread. Disagreeable facts come to be sugar-coated, and sad news softened or denied altogether. Many lie to children and to those who are ill about matters no longer peripheral but quite central, such as birth, adoption, divorce, and death. Deceptive propaganda and misleading advertising abound. All these lies are often dismissed on the same grounds of harmlessness and triviality used for white lies in general.

It is worth taking a closer look at practices where lies believed trivial are common. Triviality in an isolated lie can then be more clearly seen to differ markedly from the costs of an entire practice—both to individuals and to communities. One such practice is that of giving placebos.

Placebos

The common practice of prescribing placebos to unwitting patients illustrates the two miscalculations so common to minor forms of deceit: ignoring possible harm and failing to see how gestures assumed to be trivial build up into collectively undesirable practices.[3] Placebos have been used since the beginning of medicine. They can be sugar pills, salt-water injections—in fact, any medical procedure which has no specific effect on a patient's condition, but which can have powerful psychological effects leading to relief from symptoms such as pain or depression.

Placebos are prescribed with great frequency. Exactly how often cannot be known, the less so as physicians do not ordinarily talk publicly about using them. At times, self-deception enters in on the part of physicians, so that they have unwarranted faith in the powers of what can work only as a placebo. As with salesmanship, medication often involves unjustified belief in the excellence of what is suggested to others. In the past, most remedies were of a kind that, unknown to the medical profession and their patients, could have only placebic benefits, if any.

The derivation of "placebo," from the Latin for "I shall please," gives the word a benevolent ring, somehow placing placebos beyond moral criticism and conjuring up images of hypochondriacs whose vague ailments are dispelled through adroit prescriptions of beneficent sugar pills. Physicians often give a humorous tinge to instructions for prescribing these substances, which helps to remove them from serious ethical concern. One authority wrote in a pharmacological journal that the placebo should be given a name previously unknown to the patient and preferably Latin and polysyllabic, and added:

> [I]t is wise if it be prescribed with some assurance and emphasis for psychotherapeutic effect. The older physicians each had his favorite placebic prescriptions—one chose tincture of Condurango, another the Fluidextract of *Cimicifuga nigra.*[4]

After all, health professionals argue, are not placebos far less dangerous than some genuine drugs? And more likely to produce a cure than if nothing at all is prescribed? Such a view was expressed in a letter to the *Lancet:*

> Whenever pain can be relieved with a ml of saline, why should we inject an opiate? Do anxieties or discomforts that are allayed with starch capsules require administration of a barbiturate, diazepam, or propoxyphene?[5]

Such a simplistic view conceals the real costs of placebos, both to individuals and to the practice of medicine.

First, the resort to placebos may actually prevent the treatment of an underlying, undiagnosed problem. And even if the placebo "works," the effect is often short-lived; the symptoms may recur, or crop up in other forms. Very often, the symptoms of which the patient complains are bound to go away by themselves, sometimes even from the mere contact with a health professional. In those cases, the placebo itself is unnecessary; having recourse to it merely reinforces a tendency to depend upon pills or treatments where none is needed.

In the aggregate, the costs of placebos are immense. Many millions of dollars are expended on drugs, diagnostic tests, and psychotherapies of a placebic nature. Even operations can be of this nature—a hysterectomy may thus be performed, not because the condition of the patient requires such surgery, but because she goes from one doctor to another seeking to have the surgery performed, or because she is judged to have a great fear of cancer which might be alleviated by the very fact of the operation.

Even apart from financial and emotional costs and the squandering of resources, the practice of giving placebos is wasteful of a very precious good: the trust on which so much in the medical relationship depends. The trust of those patients who find out they have been duped is lost, sometimes irretrievably. They may then lose confidence in physicians and even in bona fide medication which they may need in the future. They may obtain for themselves more harmful drugs or attach their hopes to debilitating fad cures.

The following description of a case[6] where a placebo was prescribed reflects a common approach:

> A seventeen-year-old girl visited her pediatrician, who had been taking care of her since infancy. She went to his office without her parents, although her mother had made the appointment for her over the telephone. She told the

pediatrician that she was very healthy, but that she thought she had some emotional problems. She stated that she was having trouble sleeping at night, that she was very nervous most of the day. She was a senior in high school and claimed she was doing quite poorly in most of her subjects. She was worried about what she was going to do next year. She was somewhat overweight. This, she felt, was part of her problem. She claimed she was not very attractive to the opposite sex and could not seem to "get boys interested in me." She had a few close friends of the same sex.

Her life at home was quite chaotic and stressful. There were frequent battles with her younger brother, who was fourteen, and with her parents. She claimed her parents were always "on my back." She described her mother as extremely rigid and her father as a disciplinarian, who was quite old-fashioned in his values.

In all, she spent about twenty minutes talking with her pediatrician. She told him that what she thought she really needed was tranquilizers, and that that was the reason she came. She felt that this was an extremely difficult year for her, and if she could have something to calm her nerves until she got over her current crises, everything would go better.

The pediatrician told her that he did not really believe in giving tranquilizers to a girl of her age. He said he thought it would be a bad precedent for her to establish. She was very insistent, however, and claimed that if he did not give her tranquilizers, she would "get them somehow." Finally, he agreed to call her pharmacy and order medication for her nerves. She accepted graciously. He suggested that she call him in a few days to let him know how things were going. He also called her parents to say that he had a talk with her and he was giving her some medicine that might help her nerves.

Five days later, the girl called the pediatrician back to say that the pills were really working well. She claimed that she had calmed down a great deal, that she was working things out better with her parents, and had a new outlook on life. He suggested that she keep taking them twice a day for the rest of the school year. She agreed.

A month later, the girl ran out of pills and called her pediatrician for a refill. She found that he was away on vacation. She was quite distraught at not having any medication left, so she called her uncle who was a surgeon in the next town. He called the pharmacy to renew her pills and, in speaking to the druggist, found out that they were only vitamins. He told the girl that the pills were only vitamins and that she could get them over the counter and didn't really need him to refill them. The girl became very distraught, feeling that she had been deceived and betrayed by her pediatrician. Her parents, when they heard, commented that they thought the pediatrician was "very clever."

The patients who do *not* discover the deception and are left believing that a placebic remedy has worked may continue to rely on it under the wrong circumstances. This is especially true with drugs such as antibiotics, which are sometimes used as placebos and sometimes for their specific action. Many parents, for example, come to believe that they must ask for the prescription of antibiotics every time their child has a fever or a cold. The fact that so many doctors accede to such requests perpetuates the dependence of these families on medical care they do not need and weakens their ability to cope with health problems. Worst of all, those children who cannot tolerate antibiotics may have severe reactions, sometimes fatal, to such unnecessary medication.[7]

Such deceptive practices, by their very nature, tend to escape the normal restraints of accountability and can therefore spread more easily than others. There are many instances in which an innocuous-seeming practice has grown to become a large-scale and more dangerous one. Although warnings against the "entering wedge" are often rhetorical devices, they can at times express justifiable caution; especially when there are great pressures to move along the undesirable path and when the safeguards are insufficient.

In this perspective, there is much reason for concern about placebos. The safeguards against this practice are few or nonexistent—both because it is secretive in nature and because it is condoned but rarely carefully discussed in the medical literature.[8] And the pressures are very great, and growing stronger, from drug companies, patients eager for cures, and busy physicians, for more medication, whether it is needed or not. Given this lack of safeguards and these strong pressures, the use of placebos can spread in a number of ways.

The clearest danger lies in the gradual shift from pharmacologically inert placebos to more active ones. It is not always easy to distinguish completely inert substances from somewhat active ones and these in turn from more active ones. It may be hard to distinguish between a quantity of an active substance so low that it has little or no effect and quantities that have some effect. It is not always clear to doctors whether patients require an inert placebo or possibly a more active one, and there can be the temptation to resort to an active one just in case it might also have a specific effect. It is also much easier to deceive a patient with a medication that is known to be "real" and to have power. One recent textbook in medicine goes so far as to advocate the use of small doses of effective compounds as placebos rather than inert substances—because it is important for both the doctor and the patient to believe in the treatment! This shift is made easier because the dangers and side effects of active agents are not always known or considered important by the physician.

Meanwhile, the number of patients receiving placebos increases as more and more people seek and receive medical care and as their desire for instant, push-button alleviation of symptoms is stimulated by drug advertising and by rising expectations of what science can do. The use of placebos for children grows as well, and the temptations to manipulate the truth are less easily resisted once such great inroads have already been made.

Deception by placebo can also spread from therapy and diagnosis to experimentation. Much experimentation with placebos is honest and consented to by the experimental subjects, especially since the advent of strict rules governing such experimentation. But grievous abuses have taken place where placebos were given to unsuspecting subjects who believed they had received another substance. In 1971, for example, a number of Mexican-American women applied to a family-planning clinic for contraceptives. Some of them were given oral contraceptives and others were given placebos, or dummy pills that looked like the real thing. Without fully informed consent, the women were being used in an experiment to explore the side effects of various contraceptive pills. Some of those who were given placebos experienced a predictable side effect—they became pregnant. The investigators neither assumed financial responsibility for the babies nor indicated any concern about having bypassed the "informed consent" that is required in ethical experiments with human beings. One contented himself with the observation that if only the law had permitted it, he could have aborted the pregnant women!

The failure to think about the ethical problems in such a case stems at least in part from the innocent-seeming white lies so often told in giving placebos. The spread from therapy to experimentation and from harmlessness to its opposite often goes unnoticed in part *because* of the triviality believed to be connected with placebos as white lies. This lack of foresight and concern is most frequent when the subjects in the experiment are least likely to object or defend themselves; as with the poor, the institutionalized, and the very young.

In view of all these ways in which placebo usage can spread, it is not enough to look at each incident of manipulation in isolation, no matter how benevolent it may be. When the costs and benefits are weighed, not only the individual consequences must be considered, but also the cumulative ones. Reports of deceptive practices inevitably leak out, and the resulting suspicion is heightened by the anxiety which threats to health always create. And so even the health professionals who do not mislead their patients are injured by those who do; the entire institution of medicine is threatened by practices lacking in candor, however harmless the results may appear in some individual cases.

This is not to say that all placebos must be ruled out; merely that they cannot be excused as innocuous. They should be prescribed but rarely, and only after a careful diagnosis and consideration of non-deceptive alternatives; they should be used in experimentation only after subjects have consented to their use.

Letters of Recommendation

Another deceptive practice where not much may seem to be at stake yet which has high accumulated costs is that of the inflated recommendation. It seems a harmless enough practice, and often an act of loyalty, to give extra praise to a friend, a colleague, a student, a relative. In the harsh competition for employment and advancement, such a gesture is natural. It helps someone, while injuring no one in particular, and balances out similar gestures on the part of many others. Yet the practice obviously injures those who do not benefit from this kind of assistance; and it injures them in a haphazard and inequitable way. Two applicants for work, who are equally capable, may be quite differently rated through no fault of their own.

The existing practices also pose many problems for the individuals caught up in them. Take, for instance, a system where all recommendations given to students are customarily exaggerated—where, say, 60 percent of all graduates are classified as belonging to the top 10 percent.

If a professor were to make the honest statement to an employer that a student is merely among the top 60 percent, he might severely injure that student's ability to find work, since the statement would not be taken at face value but would be wrongly interpreted to mean that his real standing was very near the bottom.

Or consider officer evaluation reports in the U.S. Army. Those who rate officers are asked to give them scores of "outstanding," "superior," "excellent," "effective," "marginal," and "inadequate." Raters know, however, that those who are ranked anything less than "outstanding" (say, "superior" or "excellent") are then at a great disadvantage,[9] and become likely candidates for discharge. Here, superficial verbal harmlessness combines with the harsh realities of the competition for advancement and job retention to produce an inflated set of standards to which most feel bound to conform.

In such cases, honesty might victimize innocent persons. At the same time, using the evaluations in the accepted manner is still burdensome or irritating to many. And the blurring of the meaning of words in these circumstances can make it seem easier, perhaps even necessary, not to be straightforward in others.

It is difficult for raters to know what to do in such cases. Some feel forced to say what they do not mean. Others adhere to a high standard of accuracy and thereby perhaps injure those who must have their recommendations.

To make choices on the basis of such inflated recommendations is equally difficult. This is especially true in large organizations, or at great distances, where those who receive the ratings never know who the raters are or by what standards they work.

The entire practice, then, is unjust for those rated and bewildering for those who give and make use of ratings. It also robs recommendations of whatever benefits they are intended to bring. No one can know what is meant by a particular rating. Such a practice is fraught with difficulties; the costs to deceivers and deceived alike are great.

For this reason, those who give ratings should make every effort to reduce the injustice and to come closer to the standard of accuracy which they would accept were it not for the inflated practice. But if one goes against such a practice, one does have the responsibility of indicating that one is doing so, in order to minimize the effect on those rated. To do so requires time, power, and consistency. A counselor at a school for highly sought-after students, for example, can make it clear to college recruiters that he means every word he uses in his recommendations of students. So can colleagues who know each other well, when they discuss job applicants. But many are caught up in practices where they are nearly anonymous, perhaps transient, and where they have no contact with those who ask them to make out ratings for students or staff members or military personnel. They are then quite powerless: while it may be demeaning to participate in the inflated practices, it is hard to resist them singlehandedly. In verbal inflation as with monetary inflation, more general measures are often necessary. It must, therefore, be more excusable for those individuals to cooperate with the general norm, who cannot establish a different verbal "currency" for what they say.

Institutions, on the other hand, do have more leverage. Some can seek to minimize the reliance on such reports altogether. Others can try to work at the verbal inflation itself. But it is very difficult to do so, especially for large organizations. The U.S. Army tried to scale down evaluations by publishing the evaluation report I have cited. It suggested mean scores for the different ranks, but few felt free to follow these means in individual cases, for fear of hurting the persons being rated. As a result, the suggested mean scores once again lost all value.

Truthfulness at What Price?

These examples show that one cannot dismiss lies merely by claiming that they don't matter. More often than not, they do matter, even where looked at in simple terms of harm and benefit. Any awareness of how lies spread must generate a real sensitivity to the fact that most lies believed to be "white" are unnecessary if not downright undesirable. Many are not as harmless as liars take them to be. And even those lies which would generally be accepted as harmless are not needed whenever their goals can be achieved through completely honest means. Why tell a flattering lie about someone's hat rather than a flattering truth about their flowers? Why tell a general white lie about a gift, a kind act, a newborn baby, rather than a more specific truthful statement? If the purpose is understood by both speaker and listener to be one of civility and support, the *full* truth in such cases is not called for.*

I would not wish to argue that all white lies should be ruled out. Individuals caught up in the practices of making inflated recommendations, for example, may have no other recourse. In a few cases, placebos may be the only reasonable alternative. And certain marginally deceptive social excuses and conventions are unavoidable if feelings are not to be needlessly injured.

But these are very few. And it is fallacious to argue that all white lies are right because a few are. As a result, those who undertake to tell white lies should look hard for alternatives. They should see even these lies as links in much wider practices and should know the ways in which

*If, on the other hand, one is asked for one's honest opinion, such partial answers no longer suffice. A flattering truth that conceals one's opinion is then as deceitful as a flattering lie. To avoid deception, one must then choose either to refuse to answer or to answer honestly. (See Chapter XI for a discussion of responses to intrusive questions.)

these practices can spread. If they do, white lies, where truly harmless and a last resort—told, for instance, to avoid hurting someone's feelings—can be accepted as policy, but *only* under such limited circumstances.

Most of us doubtless come into more frequent contact with white lies than with any other form of deception. To the extent that we train ourselves to see their ramifications and succeed in eliminating them from our speech, the need to resort to them will diminish. If we can then make it clear to others that we stand in no need of white lies from *them*, many needless complications will have been avoided.

A word of caution is needed here. To say that white lies should be kept at a minimum is *not* to endorse the telling of truths to all comers. Silence and discretion, respect for the privacy and for the feelings of others must naturally govern what is spoken. The gossip one conveys and the malicious reports one spreads may be true without therefore being excusable. And the truth told in such a way as to wound may be unforgivably cruel, as when a physician answers a young man asking if he has cancer with a curt Yes as he leaves the room. He may not have lied, but he has failed in every professional duty of respect and concern for his patient.

Once it has been established that lies should not be told, it still remains to be seen whether anything should be conveyed, and, if so, how this can best be done. The self-appointed removers of false beliefs from those for whom these beliefs may be all that sustains them can be as harmful as the most callous liars.

EXCUSES

If any lies, like other sins, steal upon us, they should seek not to be justified but to be pardoned.

—St. Augustine, "On Lying"

[Interview with Roc, age seven]: What happens when you tell lies?—*You get punished.* —And if you didn't get punished, would it be naughty to tell them?—*No.*—I'm going to tell you two stories. There were two kiddies and they broke a cup each. The first one says it wasn't him. His mother believes him and doesn't punish him. The second one also says it wasn't him. But his mother doesn't believe him and punishes him. Are both lies they told equally naughty? —*No.*— Which is the naughtiest? —*The one who was punished.*

—Jean Piaget, *The Moral Judgment of the Child*

The three exceptions to the rule of truthfulness [in the Talmud] are given as "tractate," "bed," and "hospitality." "Tractate" is explained by the commentaries to mean that if a scholar is asked if he is familiar with a certain portion of the Talmud he may, from modesty, untruthfully say that he is ignorant. An untruth is permitted if its aim is the avoidance of a parade of learning. "Bed" is understood by Rashi to mean that if a scholar is asked questions concerning his marital relations he may give an untruthful answer. [. . .] "Hospitality" is understood to mean that a scholar who had been generously treated by his host may decide not to tell the truth about his reception if he fears that as a result the host may be embarrassed by unwelcome guests. In addition there is a general principle of the Talmud that where peace demands it a lie may be told.

—Lewis Jacobs, "Truth," in *Jewish Values*

Types of Excuses

What is it, then, that can conflict with the requirement for truthfulness so as to make lies permissible at times? Say you are caught in a compromising lie. What excuses might you offer? What kinds of excuses?

An excuse seeks to extenuate, sometimes to remove the blame entirely from something which would otherwise be a fault. It can seek to extenuate in three ways. First, it can suggest that what is seen as a fault is not really one. Secondly, it can suggest that, though there has been a fault, the agent is not really blameworthy, because he is not responsible. And finally, it can suggest that, though there has been a fault, and though the agent is responsible, he is not really to blame because he has good reasons to do as he did.

A) Excuses of the first type may claim that the supposed lie is not really a lie, but a joke, perhaps, or an evasion, an exaggeration, a flight of fancy. Or else such an excuse may argue that since it is impossible to give objective distinctions between truth and falsehood, the supposed lie cannot be proved to be one.

B) The second type of excuse holds that, though there may have been deception, the agent is not really or not completely responsible. The liar may claim he never meant to mislead, or was incompetent, perhaps drunk, or talking in his sleep, or coerced into deceiving.* Or else he

---

*It is primarily this second type of excuse that J. L. Austin discusses in his well-known paper "A Plea for Excuses." Austin rightly stresses the difference between this type of excuse and the third type, which

may take refuge in arguing that no one can ever be held responsible for lies, that free choice in that respect is a myth.

Both these types of excuses obviously cover a vast territory and are in constant use by liars. But it is the third type which will be the focus of attention in this chapter and in Chapter VII—the type of excuse which is most fundamental for the process of evaluating deliberate lies. In this third type of excuse, the liar admits the lie, accepts responsibility for it, but offers reasons to show that he should be partially or even wholly cleared of blame. All three kinds of excuses are often present in the same effort to extenuate any one lie.

(There are, of course, reasons for lying which are never offered as excuses at all and which cannot function as such. "I lied to make you suffer" may be a true explanation; it is not an excuse, for it is not offered to extenuate. "I lie all the time and see nothing wrong in doing so" is not an excuse either, for it sees nothing to excuse.)

C) The third type of excuse, then, offers moral reasons for a lie, reasons to show that a lie ought, under the circumstances, to be allowed. People look for moral reasons when they are troubled or caught short; and generally when they need to persuade themselves or others that the usual presumption against lying is outweighed in their particular case. All the many reasons given to excuse lies can be grouped in a number of ways. I shall look at them from the point of view of the moral principles to which

---

he labels "justification." I prefer to call all three kinds of attempts at extenuation "excuses," however partial, however lame; and to reserve the term "justification" for those excuses of the third kind (offering *reasons*) that make at least a stab at removing blame. Only the more persuasive excuses of the third type are, therefore, genuine efforts at justification; and only a few of those efforts at justifying lies will, in fact, succeed in persuading those to whom the justification is addressed (unless it is the liar himself, in which case, the "liar's perspective" sees many more lies as justified).

they appeal. These principles can be given many names, many forms. They must certainly never be thought of as having some abstract existence of their own. Rather, we use them to give support and structure to the moral reasons we give for our choices. I shall set forth the reasons most commonly used to defend lies as appealing to four principles: that of avoiding harm, that of producing benefits, that of fairness, and that of veracity.*

Take the denial by a prime minister of the charge that his government helped to overthrow a neighboring regime. If the lie is discovered and he is pressed for reasons, what might he say? His answer cannot rely on claims that he was not really lying, or had not meant to lie, or that he lied under some coercion rendering him incompetent. Should he be pressed to give extenuating reasons, they might well appeal to one of these four principles.

The prime minister might give as a reason his desire to avoid through his lie some form of retaliation or international censure—some *harm*, in other words. Or he might argue that he had lied in order to give the new regime the legitimacy which might come from seeming to have overthrown the former government democratically. He would then claim that the lie was told in an attempt to achieve an overriding *benefit*. Alternatively, he might appeal to *fairness*—perhaps by claiming that, since everyone else lies under such circumstances, it would only be fair to excuse him for following standard procedure. Finally, he might argue that his lie served the cause of *veracity* and trustworthiness, or at least a semblance thereof: that he lied to uphold the confidence in his own government—confidence in the eyes of the world that his coun-

---

*In so doing, I follow the scheme of G. J. Warnock, who, in his book *The Object of Morality*, stresses the need, in human society, for these four "good dispositions whose tendency is directly to countervail the limitation of human sympathies." (p. 79).

try abides by international rules prohibiting such interference with other nations.

Of the four principles, the first two, which concern harm and benefit, are the most frequently invoked. They represent the most immediate approach to choice. But as soon as there is a question how to allocate harm and benefit, then the right to accept, reject, or request these is at issue, and appeals to the principle of fairness or justice enter in.

Veracity, finally, is indispensable to the proper functioning of the first three principles, to their having any force. It is, as I have pointed out earlier, the cornerstone of relationships among human beings; to the degree that it erodes, to that degree is the confidence in the benefits, protection from harm, and fairness one has come to count upon made haphazard, undermined.

These four principles are often invoked in a confused way. One may be invoked where a completely different one, or none at all, can serve. And they frequently intertwine and overlap. It may help, therefore, to try to set them forth explicitly in looking at the profusion of excuses given for different lies. When we do, we find that conflicts arise among the four principles only in the context of concrete choices. To say that veracity and fairness may conflict is obscure; but to say that a lawyer is troubled about how to satisfy both when only a lie can protect an innocent client from jail is not.*

*Similarly, while it is obscure to claim that weight and length conflict in the abstract, there are concrete cases where both cannot be satisfied, where you cannot get a thing the length you want and the weight you want, as where you need fifteen yards of heavy chain but only have the strength to carry home five pounds of it. In the same way, you cannot always make a choice, or expect others to make it, which achieves both the fairness and the beneficence you desire. Moral principles, just like length and weight, represent different dimensions by which we structure experience and can therefore present conflicts in concrete cases but never in the abstract. It is for this reason that the search for priority

Avoiding harm and producing benefit go together, yet it will be helpful to consider them separately. We can sense the difference in urgency between them. Law and morality surround the two with separate kinds of rules. And in medicine, the most frequently cited injunction to physicians is to help, but *above all* not to harm, their patients.

Just as lies intended to avoid serious harm have often been thought more clearly excusable than others, so lies meant to *do* harm are often thought least excusable. And lies which neither avoid nor cause harm occupy the middle ground. Throughout the centuries, beginning with Augustine, such distinctions have been debated, refined, altered. An Irish Penitential from around 800 A.D., for instance, requires different penances for lies differing in the harm occasioned:

> If anyone utters [such] a falsehood deliberately, without doing harm, he spends three days in silence except for the appointed prayers or readings; or else he receives 700 blows of a lash on his hands and keeps a half-fast or recites the 150 psalms.
>
> Anyone who utters a falsehood in words whereof good results, by giving a false description to a man's enemies, or by carrying pacific messages between disputants, or by anything that rescues a man from death, there is no heavy penance, provided it is done for God's sake.[1]

We have seen how Aquinas described all well-meant lies, whether to avoid harm or produce benefit, as "officious lies," and contrasted them with "malicious lies," intended to harm. A lie, for instance, told to a patient to

---

rules among moral principles in the abstract is doomed to fail; one might as well search for such priority rules among pounds, yards, and hours in the abstract.

prevent heart collapse, would be such an "officious lie." It would give time to forestall the danger which the bare truth could have brought at a moment of crisis and make possible a more humane and understanding approach.

Among lies which do harm, those which do the greatest harm are judged the worst. Lies which are planned are judged more harshly than those told without forethought; single lies less severely than repeated ones. Planned *practices* of deception are therefore especially suspect, no matter how repentant the liar claims to be between lies.

Many lies invoke self-defense—the avoidance of harm to oneself—as an excuse. Lies told in court by those dreading a sentence, or lies by those caught stealing or cheating; lies by those threatened by violence; lies to get out of trouble of all kinds, to save face, to avoid losing work— all employ in some form excuses claiming the overriding importance of avoiding harm to oneself. Self-defense is also invoked as an excuse for lies on behalf of entire groups or nations, as in national defense; at times the concept is even stretched to account for lies promoting aggressive schemes of "national defense" as well.

Self-defensive lies can permeate all one does, so that life turns into "living a lie." Professionals involved in collective practices of deceit give up all ordinary assumptions about their own honesty and that of others. And individuals who feel obliged to "pass" as a member of a dominant religious or racial group in order to avoid persecution deny what may be most precious to them. Political beliefs or sexual preferences unacceptable to a community compel many to a similar life-long duplicity, denying a central part of their own identity.

Producing Benefits

Lies to bring about some benefit are often harder to excuse than those which prevent harm. To say that one lied in self-defense is one thing; to admit that one lied in order to get more rent from a tenant is quite another, and, by itself, no excuse at all. In these two instances either the avoidance of harm or the production of benefits come first to mind; but there are, of course, innumerable instances where a lie can be seen equally well from both perspectives.

Because the prevention of harm seems more persuasive, those who formulate excuses for lies to benefit others or themselves very often place great stress on the harm those lies will prevent. But in their own eyes they tend to justify themselves by referring to the benefits they are bringing about. Thus social scientists who do deceptive experiments may stress publicly the suffering which the new knowledge will prevent, while having in mind also the benefits to be derived from the acquisition of knowledge and the advancement of science.

Sometimes an added excuse—that of altruism—enters the harm-benefit calculation. Lies are then believed better if they help—or avoid harm to—others rather than oneself. Yet the claim that altruism adds excusability has to be looked at with great care. In the two large categories of white lies and lies in life-threatening situations, for example, such a claim is not warranted. A lie to save one's own life from a murderer does not seem better or worse than the same lie to save the life of another. A white lie, if truly trivial, is equally so no matter who is thereby helped.

There seems, nevertheless, to be a difference, however elusive, in our attitude toward altruistic lies. Are we not quicker to accept—or at least sympathize with—the lie for the sake of another? Are we not more wary where the lie obviously benefits the liar? Perhaps we are, at least when sharing the perspective of the liar. But from every other point of view, altruism claimed by liars makes much less of a difference; first, because even the most self-serving liars use the shield of altruism whenever they can; and second, because even genuinely well-meant lies so often fail to achieve the intended benefits. It will be important, therefore, to look carefully in the chapters to come at the claim of altruism in the lies told for social benefit and for the supposed benefit of the deceived persons themselves —so-called "paternalistic lies."

The excuse of altruism is often grounded in the liar's general belief in his own good will. "I mean well; therefore my lies will help" is as frequent a leap of the mind as: "I mean no harm; therefore my lies can't hurt." The possibilities of error about one's good intentions are immense. But even if these intentions *are* good, they are obviously no guarantee of a good outcome.

Fairness

Appeals to fairness have a long history of special status in philosophy. Excuses which make such appeals claim to correct or forestall an injustice, or to help provide a fair distribution. The purpose is to give people their due treatment, reward, punishment, or share.* Giving people "their due" can be based on views about what they deserve, but also on a promise or a contract, as when a lawyer protects the confidentiality of a client.

Consider how Iago, in his unconvincing search for excuses for betraying Othello's trust appeals to his sense of unfairness or injustice in two ways:[2] He argues, first, that Othello has unfairly preferred Cassio to himself in

---

*I shall be using "justice" and "fairness" as synonymous. In doing so, I am not intending the larger sense of "justice" (all that is right or lawful), but the narrower sense distinguished by Aristotle in his *Nicomachean Ethics* (1130) of the just as rectifying what is disproportionate or wrong, distributing fairly. It concerns, then, both autonomy, or liberty, and equality. When lies are told to protect or further these, what is fundamentally at stake is an *equilibrium* to be prolonged, restored, or set up.

choosing one of them to be a lieutenant, in spite of Iago's seniority and better qualifications. Second, Iago mentions the rumor that Othello has been intimate with his wife. He acknowledges that he does not know this to be true, but that he "for mere suspicion in that kind will do as if for surety."[3]

Iago uses both claims as reasons for wanting to have his revenge upon Othello. We find these excuses feeble by comparison to the cruelty visited upon Othello and assume, rather, that the real motive for Iago's villainy was sheer malice, which explains rather than excuses what he did. But whether mere bows to convention or genuinely felt, the two excuses do make appeal to fairness of a kind.

Other deceptive schemes are held excusable by liars not so much because they punish those guilty of injustice as because they retrieve or protect what the liars think rightfully their own—their property, their liberty, or even their children, as in lies told to kidnappers. Still other lies appeal to fairness in a tit-for-tat way: "He lied to me, now it is all right for me to lie to him." Another way of appealing to fairness in an excuse for deception is to use a pseudonym when one is afraid that the use of one's real name might confer unfair advantages. Conversely, pseudonyms or disguises can be thought excusable also when they avoid unfair disadvantages for their bearers.[4]

Still another large category of excuses appealing in part to fairness are those which rely on confidentiality.[5] One may feel forced to lie to some persons in order to protect the privacy or the confidences of others. A priest bound by oath to conceal the fact that one of his parishioners is pregnant may feel excused, not only in avoiding questions about her state, but even in actually lying if need be so as to protect her secret. He acts so as to accord her what he believes is her due, on grounds of professional obligation. In such cases, those whose confidence is protected may well think that they have a *right* to such protection, a right based on some existing contract or promise.[6]

A final category where fairness is invoked is that where the dupes have agreed in advance to a practice involving deception. They have set rules for what is fair, for what can be expected. Anyone who agrees to the rules cannot complain of unfairness when deception is used, so long as the rules permitted it. In a game of poker, for instance, players accept the degree of deception allowed by the rules, just as in football they accept a degree of violence. And in medical experimentation, subjects who are competent[7] and who have agreed to participate in an experiment knowing it will use deception, are not being treated unfairly.

It is more often the case, however, that persons or groups or nations participate involuntarily in practices involving intentional deception. They are then forced to plan their strategy knowing that deception is possible or even likely. Should they be the only ones foregoing the bribe or the lie or the black-market operation, they might not survive in a corrupt community. While they may *expect* lies, then, they cannot be said to have *accepted* the practices as have those who play poker, since there may be no way for them to "leave the game." Nor can they therefore be said to be treated fairly in the same way as the card players.

Because claims to fairness involve deeply personal views about what one deserves or what is one's right, they are extraordinarily prone to misinterpretation and bias. Injustice, exploitation, the disparity of power—these are held to excuse innumerable lies. Those who believe they are exploited hold that this fact by itself justifies dishonesty in *rectifying* the equilibrium; those who have the upper hand often feel justified in using deceit so as to *maintain* that equilibrium.

Veracity

Veracity is not only in conflict with the other principles when lies are told. Some claim they lie so as to *protect* the truth. To lie for the sake of the truth—this is surely the most paradoxical of excuses.

Lies that make such an appeal to truth are more numerous than a first glance might reveal. The lie to undo the effect of another lie; the lie to further some larger or more important truth; the lie to preserve confidence in one's own truthfulness—all make appeal to truth in some sense. Each time such an excuse is given, it is crucial to separate the different meanings of "truth" and "truthfulness."

You make a small mistake, conceal it, and lie when asked about it. In part you want to avoid trouble. But in part you may also want to keep up my confidence that you are truthful in *other* matters. So the lie is told, and may have to be repeated, explained, kept up. You lie, then, in part to safeguard what you consider the justified belief in your truthfulness, your good word.

When do these lies begin to shade into the many forms of lying to keep up what you yourself know is a *false* front of apparent truthfulness and respectability? The difficulty in making such distinctions is almost as great for liars as for their dupes, because self-deception enters into such estimates to an extraordinary degree. Hypocrites half believe their own stories,* and sentimentality makes fraud take on the most innocuous tints. The lies to children to

---

* The word "hypocrisy" itself has revealing connotations. The Greek word originally meant "answer," including the kind of answers actors give each other on stage. By extension, it came to mean acting on a stage and then acting a part even offstage. Its present meaning is: the assumption of a false appearance of virtue or goodness, with dissimulation of real characters or inclinations.

preserve the appearance of adult rationality and blame-lessness; the lies to conceal a drinking habit or an addic-tion; the lies to retain confidence in a shaky business or a corrupt government—such lies become second nature. The greater the actual gap between role and reality, the more constant the need for concealment.

Once revealed, the gap is especially shocking in some-one whose profession ideally requires a concern for truth. When judges and scientists are caught in fraud, the sense of betrayal is great. A fraudulent scientist goes against the most fundamental standards of science. Yet he may, para-doxically, act fraudulently in part *on behalf* of what he takes to be science and truth.

A scientist, for example, may believe a new discovery or theory to be true, but find that the available data are as yet inconclusive. Confident that future experimentation will bear him out, he may then falsify the data in order to gain support for what he feels sure is true. He lies, in part, in the service of what he takes to be the truth. Sometimes these initial hunches turn out to be correct; often, they do not. In the latter case, he may be driven into ever more deceit.

Another motive for lying is to undo a false impression, thus once more promoting "truth." The ice cream adver-tised on television may in reality be mashed potatoes, which don't melt in the hot lights and therefore appear to the audience more like ice cream than the actual sub-stance. A city official may disguise a campaign contribu-tion that could, in his view, give the wrong impression about his allegiances. Such deception is often undertaken by those who know or assume that they have a more objective view of the situation than those to whom they speak. Lawyers in court, parents talking to children, bureaucrats to citizens—all can sincerely believe that they manipulate the facts in order to convey a "truer picture."

The extreme effort to provide a truer picture through deception is the lie to undo another lie's effect.[8] Say that an anxiety-ridden young man has been falsely told that rays are beamed at him that debilitate him and make him nervous. Someone who then, to calm him, invents a story about how the group aiming the rays has been arrested would be using one lie to undo the other—to revert, as it were, to the equilibrium before the first lie.

It is perhaps in this spirit that lies are told to convince people of some political or religious dogma. The belief that the dogma itself is true, and that it is, moreover, beneficial for the convert, will seem to excuse a lie told to speed conversion. In this way, the convert will gain a greater truth, as it were, and perhaps also be rescued from what is thought to be a false belief.[9] As so often, truth and truth-telling are here intertwined. The more dogmatic the belief that one possesses truth, the greater the liberties taken on its behalf with truth-telling!

The rescue from "false beliefs" finds contemporary illustration in the efforts at kidnapping and "deprogramming" engaged in by parents who believe that their son or daughter has been lured into a religious sect and duped into accepting false beliefs. To parental eyes, both deceit and violence may be excusable when undertaken to undo such damage.

How Persuasive?

There are, then, innumerable excuses for lying: not only those claiming that there was no lie, or disclaiming responsibility, but also those appealing to principles in extenuation for acknowledged lies. Inevitably, most of these excuses will fail to persuade. But what factors affect their persuasiveness, such as it is?

Perspective makes the biggest difference. Liars are persuaded by their own excuses to a degree that seems incredible to others. Those who are debating whether or not to lie do so from a liar's perspective. They tend to place a much more benevolent interpretation on their own excuses than when they are on the receiving end. They excuse themselves more easily by recourse to the two first types of excuses listed at the beginning of this chapter.

They are, first of all, much more likely to assume, in their own case, that "truth is unattainable" and to conclude that there is no clear distinction between truthfulness and falsehood; and much more likely to consider their message to be only marginally deceptive.

Second, they are much quicker to persuade themselves that no real deception was intended; much more likely to assume that they were "not themselves" when lying; and much more willing to claim that they were coerced, by persons or circumstances, into the lie.

The *reasons* for lying, finally, appeal to them much more when they share the perspective of liars than otherwise. Liars find the moral claims that their lies will be beneficial, perhaps prevent harm, or support fairness or prior obligations, much more persuasive than do those lied to or those not directly affected. Liars are quicker to argue that honesty will hurt them in practices where "everyone else cheats"; they are more easily convinced that a lie which benefits them will harm no one else; and their concern for the effect of deceit on their own character and practices is minimal.

Yet those who are lied to—and liars whenever they consider themselves lied to—are much less sanguine about these "good reasons." They have, in fact, few if any ways of distinguishing between lies told to them which are for good purposes and all the others. In part, this is so because they often have no way to tell a truthful statement made to them from a false one; in part also because they know from their experience *as* liars how easy it is to lie and how persuasive one's reasons then appear.

All these different excuses will be differently evaluated, also, depending on the expectations of the deceived. How much truthfulness were they expecting? By what rules did they communicate with the liars? Was there perhaps an explicit allowance for deception? Or was it, on the contrary, clearly ruled out? In a game of poker, deception is expected; in *Othello*, on the contrary, part of the horror comes from the knowledge of the great trust Othello had for Iago and from the fact that Iago played upon this trust:

> he holds me well,
> The better shall my purpose work on him.[10]

Most deception takes place in less well-defined circumstances. There is neither explicit trust nor an agreement to allow deception as part of the game. And even where liars claim that there *is* such an agreement, their bias operates to make them believe in one even when the dupe is not aware of it. Many lies to those who are very ill, for example, are taken by the liars themselves as understood and accepted by all involved, whereas those thus lied to have agreed to nothing of the sort.

A related factor which affects the excuses offered is that of the nature of the relationship between liar and deceived. Are the parties adversaries, neutral, or friends? Do contractual ties bind them, as professionals and clients, elected representatives and citizens, parents and children? And what is the power relationship between them? Can it *change* because of the lies, or are they so marginal as not to have that effect?

All excuses, finally, are affected by the alternatives to any one lie. There is no need even to begin to evaluate the reasons for a lie if the liar knew of a truthful alternative to secure the benefit, avoid the harm, or protect fairness. Even if a lie saves a life, it is unwarranted if the liar was aware that a truthful statement could have done the same. But here again, lines are hard to draw. How thoughtful or aware must the liar be? How much scope and ingenuity must he possess?

Because of the gradual nature of all these factors and

the difficulty of drawing lines, and because the reasons themselves are present to larger and smaller degrees, one cannot always say that a lie seems or does not seem excusable. Some lies will be excusable under all circumstances; others will vary greatly according to the context in which they are told. Some lies will be either ruled out or excused by most people; other lies will be more disputed.

The next task is to ask: Can we draw lines which demarcate *justifiable* lies? Are there criteria which help in drawing such lines? I hope to show how, just as the question of excusability exhibits the complexity of lying, so that of justification reduces the field once again. For while excuses abound, justification is hard to come by.

VII

JUSTIFICATION

Truthfulness is a condition of any collective undertaking. It is interesting to observe the growing recognition of the need of publicity wherever democratic institutions prevail. Secrecy is a sort of treason.

—Ralph B. Perry, *The Moral Economy*

[Justification] presumes a clash of views between persons or within one person, and seeks to convince others, or ourselves, of the principles upon which our claims and judgments are founded. Being designed to reconcile by reason, justification proceeds from what all parties to the discussion hold in common.

—John Rawls, *A Theory of Justice*

Justification and Publicity

How can we single out, then, justifiable lies from all those that their perpetrators regard as so highly excusable? Assume, as before, that we are dealing with clearcut lies, deliberate efforts to mislead. We can examine the alternatives confronting the liar, and the excuses he gives. Which excuses not only mitigate and extenuate, but remove moral blame? And if we accept the excuses for some lies, do we thereby merely remove blame from the liar retroactively? Or are we willing to allow those lies ahead of time under certain circumstances? Could we, finally, recommend a *practice* of telling such lies whenever those circumstances arise—whenever, for instance, an innocent life is otherwise threatened?

We have already seen how often the liar is caught in a distorting perspective; his efforts to answer questions of justification can then show a systematic bias. His appeals to principle may be hollow, his evaluation flimsy. The result is that he can arrive at diametrically opposed weighings of alternatives and reasons, depending upon what he puts into the weighing process in the first place.

Justification must involve more than such untested personal steps of reasoning. To justify is to defend as just, right, or proper, by providing adequate reasons. It means to hold up to some standard, such as a religious or legal or moral standard. Such justification requires an audience: it may be directed to God, or a court of law, or one's peers, or one's own conscience; but in ethics it is most appropriately aimed, not at any one individual or audience, but rather at "reasonable persons" in general.*

Someone seeking moral justification must, in Hume's words:

> depart from his private and particular situation and must choose a point of view common to him with others; he must move some universal principle of the human frame and touch a string to which all mankind have an accord and symphony.[1]

---

*See Virginia Held, "Justification, Legal and Political," *Ethics*, 1975, 1–16. It is interesting to compare justification in law, ethics, and religion, from the point of view of what one is attempting to justify: an action, a choice, or an entire life? One can then compare these different types of justification also from the point of view of how it is thought to take place, why it is needed, before whom it occurs, and what results are envisaged: vindication, forgiveness, permission to proceed, or a slate wiped clean. For a penetrating comment on justification by faith in Paul, see K. Stendahl, *Paul Among Jews and Gentiles* (Philadelphia: Fortress Press, 1976), pp. 23–40.

Moral justification, therefore, cannot be exclusive or hidden; it has to be capable of being made public. In going beyond the purely private, it attempts to transcend also what is merely subjective. Wittgenstein pointed to these elements of justification in observing that "justification consists in appealing to something independent."[2] Many moral philosophers have assumed that such an appeal is of the very essence in reasoning about moral choice. John Rawls has set it forth most explicitly, under the name of *publicity*, as a formal constraint on any moral principle worth considering. According to such a constraint, a moral principle must be capable of public statement and defense.[3] A secret moral principle, or one which could be disclosed only to a sect or a guild, could not satisfy such a condition.

Such publicity is, I believe, crucial to the justification of all moral choice. But it is, perhaps, particularly indispensable to the justification of lies and other deceptive practices. For publicity is connected more directly to veracity than to other moral principles. In ethics, publicity without truthfulness is misleading and thus worthless. In addition, lies, inherently secretive, may call for submission to public justification more than openly performed problematic acts. Such acts are more likely to arouse controversy eventually, whereas lies, if they succeed, may never do so.

I would like to combine this concept of *publicity* with the view of justification in ethics as being *directed to reasonable persons,* in order to formulate a workable test for looking at concrete moral choice. It will be a test to weigh the various excuses advanced for disputed choices, and therefore for lies. Such a test counters the self-deception and bias inherent in the liar's perspective. It challenges privately held assumptions and hasty calculations. It requires clear and understandable formulation of the arguments used to defend the lie—arguments which might otherwise have remained inchoate or seemed intuitively right without ever being questioned. Its advantages, moreover, are cumulative: the objectivity and ability to shift perspectives gained in each appeal to publicity carry over to subsequent ones. Basically, it is through the exercise of such appeals and the debates that they engender that a more finely tuned moral sense will develop.[4]

The test of publicity asks which lies, if any, would survive the appeal for justification to reasonable persons. It requires us to seek concrete and open performance of an exercise crucial to ethics: the Golden Rule, basic to so many religious and moral traditions.* We must share the perspective of those affected by our choices, and ask how we would react if the lies we are contemplating were told to us. We must, then, adopt the perspective not only of liars but of those lied to; and not only of particular persons but of all those affected by lies—the collective perspective of reasonable persons seen as potentially deceived. We must formulate the excuses and the moral arguments used to defend the lies and ask how they would stand up under the public scrutiny of these reasonable persons.

But exactly how is such a test best undertaken? Is the traditional appeal to conscience sufficient? Or, if there is to be more of a "public" involved, can it consist of just a few persons or need there be many? Need they be real or

---

*The Golden Rule has a very powerful negative form, as in the *Analects* of Confucius:

Tzu Kung asked: "Is there any one word that can serve as a principle for the conduct of life?" Confucius said: "Perhaps ... 'reciprocity': Do not do to others what you would not want others to do to you."

See also Rabbi Hillel's saying: "What is hateful to you do not do to your neighbour; that is the whole Torah, while the rest is commentary thereof;" (*Babylonian Talmud*, Order Mo'ed, Tractate Sabbath, Section 31a. Translated by Rabbi Isidore Epstein, London: Soncino Press, 1958, p. 140). See, also, the *Didache*, Vol. I, p. 309.

can they be merely imagined? And what are the limitations of such a test? I shall take up these questions in turn.

Levels of Justification

The initial and indispensable first effort at weighing moral choice from a reflective point of view that is already somewhat "public" is familiar: it is to have recourse to one's own conscience. Sometimes conscience is seen as another, and more exacting, self. But appealing to conscience often includes a confrontation with an inner judge as well. The judge may be an ideal one, perhaps even held divine; at other times, simply a commentator on one's acts to whom one tries to justify one's actions and beliefs. Seneca describes the appeal of such an onlooker in a letter to his friend Lucilius as follows:

> There is no real doubt that it is good for one to have appointed a guardian over oneself, and to have someone whom you may look up to, someone whom you may regard as a witness of your thoughts. It is, indeed, nobler by far to live as you would live under the eyes of some good person always at your side; but nevertheless I am content if you only act, in whatever you do, as you would act if anyone at all were looking on; because solitude prompts us to all kinds of evil.[5]

Some such method of personal soul-searching is undoubtedly necessary for even the most rudimentary moral choices. It is often all one can do. But it cannot be a *sufficient* guarantee that the conditions of publicity have been met. For while consciences can ravage, they can also be very accommodating and malleable. Most often, those who lie have a much easier time in justifying their behavior so long as their only audience is their own conscience or their self-appointed imaginary onlooker. And even for the well-intentioned, a conscience is unreliable as soon as matters of complexity and intensity must be weighed. Arguments may not be well formulated; implicit assumptions may go unchallenged; blurred analogies or faulty reasoning may continue unchecked. While the appeal to one's conscience is certainly indispensable, therefore, it does not provide for sufficient publicity. It can be quite unable to counter bias, and never more so than for those locked into the biased perspective of the liar.

For all the same reasons, appealing in one's mind to what others might say can come similarly to grief, no matter how numerous or how judicious one takes these others to be. It is doubtless helpful to imagine that one is justifying one's lie before a public assembly or a jury or even a television audience. And it certainly helps to try to formulate the maxim on which one is acting in order to see if it can serve as a maxim others could accept and live by. But so long as this process is purely an imagined one, so long as one is both actor and audience, both defender and jury, both law-giver and citizen, the risk of bias remains very high.*

In concrete problems of any gravity, then, publicity requires us to go beyond merely turning to our conscience or to imagined others for the justification of our lies. This is especially true for deceptive *practices*, as in government, where those who deceive occupy positions of trust. The

---

*An interesting example of how such a process incorporates bias is to be found in Kant's *The Groundwork of the Metaphysic of Morals*. Kant formulates the thought-experiment whereby one is to judge of particular duties: "Act as if the maxim of your action were to become through your will a universal law of nature." He then proceeds to give four applications of this method that are not equally persuasive—to suicide, to borrowing money with a false promise of repayment, to neglecting one's natural gifts, and to failing to help others.

following example may illustrate the need to reach out for advice:

> A newly elected high official was employing a "head-hunter" to find talented individuals to work for him. This "head-hunter," after locating good candidates for a position, had worked out a method for testing the strength of the recommendations provided. She wanted to make sure that these recommendations were not merely casually supportive. She therefore asked the colleagues of the candidates to respond to false statements about them and measured the strength of their protests. She might comment to them: "I hear X doesn't get along with his co-workers very well" or "People tell me X doesn't manage his affairs too competently" or "I understand X is not very innovative."

This "head-hunter" had no compunctions about her technique; on the contrary, she was proud of her new way to elicit accurate information. No inner guidelines troubled her; she felt no need to ask for justification. Yet had she asked others, it would not have taken long for someone to raise the very obvious moral problems implicit in such a technique.

The next "level" of public justification, then, goes beyond one's internal thought-experiment. Asking friends, elders, or colleagues for advice, looking up precedents, consulting with those who have a special knowledge in questions of religion or ethics—these are well-trodden paths which can bring objectivity, sometimes wisdom, to moral choices and lead to the demise of many an ill-conceived scheme.

Unfortunately, in the more difficult cases, where the stakes are high, such consultation is still insufficiently "public." It does not eliminate bias; nor does it question shared assumptions and fallacious reasoning. This is especially often the case, once more, in professional and powerful circles, where those who might object are not given a voice, and where those considered "wise" can be those most likely to agree with the questionable scheme. There *was* collegial consultation, for example, in the decision to deny falsely that the United States of America was bombing Cambodia. And there *was* consultation before the adoption of a deceptive cover story for the Bay of Pigs invasion. Irving Janis has described the failures of such systems of consultation among the like-minded in foreign policy decisions:

> The members' firm belief in the inherent morality of their group and their use of undifferentiated negative stereotypes of opponents enable them to minimize decision conflicts between ethical values and expediency, especially when they are inclined to resort to violence. The shared belief that "we are a wise and good group" inclines them to use group concurrence as a major criterion to judge the morality as well as the efficacy of any policy under discussion. "Since our group's objectives are good," the members feel, "any means we decide to use must be good." This shared assumption helps the members avoid feelings of shame or guilt about decisions that may violate their personal code of ethical behavior. Negative stereotypes of the enemy enhance their sense of moral righteousness as well as their pride in the lofty mission of the ingroup.[6]

More than consultation with chosen peers is needed whenever crucial interests are thus at stake. Those who are in positions of trust should be accountable for lies affecting the welfare of others. The same is true for deceptive practices, even those, like placebos or lying to the dying, which seem harmless enough in each instance, yet are cumulatively damaging. How can "publicity" enter sufficiently into efforts to justify such choices and practices?

A third "level" of public justification is required here. At this level, persons of all allegiances must be consulted, or at least not excluded or bypassed. "Publicity" in this sense rules out the hand-picking of those who should be consulted. It is not so much a matter of whether many or a few have access to the public justification, as that no one should be denied access. Naturally, the more complex and momentous the decision, the more consultation will be judged necessary.

We now have little public discourse about moral choice. It is needed in classes, in professional organizations, in government. It should be *open*, not closed to all but special interest groups. A good example of how it can operate at its best is to be found in the National Commission for the Protection of Human Subjects, established by Congress in 1974. It has examined very difficult, searing moral issues—of fetal research, psychosurgery, and the ethics of experimenting on prisoners, for example. Not only has it done so in complete openness, giving a chance for all views to be heard, but has arrived at conclusions in these difficult choices and, in so doing, has helped to shed light on much broader practices.[7]

There is great need for similar attention to issues of deception. If possible, such open discussion should take place before the initiation of the deceptive scheme, giving those to be deceived an opportunity to be heard. To do so is the only sure way of having the perspective of the deceived represented.

But is it not illogical to expect that those very persons lied to might be thus forewarned? Would this not eliminate any chance of the lie succeeding and thus rule out whatever benefit was hoped for? What is the use of prefacing a lie by consulting with those one plans to deceive?

Here we must distinguish, once again, between cases and practices. It would certainly be self-defeating to preface any one lie by consultation with the dupe. But it is not at all self-defeating to discuss deceptive policies beforehand, nor to warn the deceived themselves. For instance, in deceptive games, players obviously choose whether or not to participate. The same is true, as earlier mentioned, in those deceptive medical experiments where consent is required as a preliminary. Similarly, in the conduct of foreign policy, a national discussion of the purposes and limits of deception could set standards for allowable deception in times of emergency. Examples of past deceptions held necessary for national defense could be debated and procedures set up for coping with similar choices in the future.

What kind of consultation should be required beforehand? If consultation merely within an administration is inadequate, could federal judges or others be asked to give approval? And what degree of disclosure should be asked afterwards? How *soon* afterwards? The discussion of such questions publicly—in the press, in educational institutions, at public meetings—could use as examples different kinds of lies told as a matter of course by professionals.

Take the use of unmarked police cars. If a society has openly debated their use and chosen to allow it in order to lull speeders and others into false confidence, then those who still choose to break the speed laws will be aware of the deceptive practice and can decide whether to take their chances or not. Once again, while each deceptive *act* does not lend itself easily to public justification, nothing stands in the way of a public scrutiny of the *practice*.

Does the same hold true for more unsavory police practices, such as entrapment, where the police encourage a crime, often using decoys—in order to arrest and convict the criminal? Here, again, it is important not to bypass the requirement for publicity. So long as the deceptive element in entrapment is not recognized and balanced against possible alternatives and the reasons why its proponents think it necessary, we shall continue to have the present uneasy proliferation of troublesome practices haphazardly restrained by differing customs and regulations. What kind of society do we want to have?[8] What deviations threaten communities so much that entrapment might be the only way out? Once such issues have been decided, however, there is nothing illogical or self-defeating in the notion that publicity be given to deceptive practices and that dupes be forewarned.

The questions asked on page 93 about the nature of the publicity required for justifying lies can now be answered as follows. First, the "public" required for the justification of deceptive practices should ideally be wider than our conscience and more critical than the imagined audience, important though these are in their own right. If the choice is one of importance for others, or if, even though it seems trivial in itself, it forms part of a practice of deceit, then greater accountability should be required. Can the lie or the entire practice be defended in the press or on television? Can they be justified in advance in classrooms, workshops, or public meetings?

Second, there can be many or few in the public so addressed; but no one should be excluded from it on principle, least of all those representing the deceived or others affected by the lie.

If such issues were publicly addressed, then those who plan to enter professions where deceptive practices are common would have the opportunity in professional schools to consider how to respond before becoming enmeshed in situations which seem to require lying. They could confront hypothetical cases similar to many they will later encounter; articulate and weigh the reasons supporting the conflicting choices; and debate their strengths and weaknesses. A public test of this kind would remove the self-righteous belief in the unquestionable necessity for their lies on the part of those who operate with secret principles, fully trusting the blamelessness of their motives. And it would severely limit lies by professionals who believe that, as a group, they share a concern for the well-being of mankind which puts them beyond scrutiny.

The last question on page 94 asks about the limitations on this test of publicity. They are substantial. While the test is a useful check on bias and rationalization, and thus helps us go beyond our immediate intuitive judgments, it is no more than a check. It is obviously of no avail in situations where the opportunity to reflect and to discuss is absent, as where immediate action is required. Nor does the test work well in moral quandaries which have no good answer, given our limited information, powers of reasoning, and foreknowledge.

These two limitations can be reduced in scope: the test can be used in advance to consider what to do in situations where there will be no opportunity to reflect or to discuss; and it can help us to work out modes of response even to those circumstances where uncertainty prevents a clear choice to emerge as the best one—who is to decide at such times, for instance, and how. In this way, the process of consultation and discussion can push back the frontiers of the moral problems now thought too urgent or too difficult for reasoned consideration: limit them, and show that they are fewer in number than we think.

The test, finally, does not work well when there is a question about just how "reasonable" the available public actually is. One may even ask whether any public *can* be reasonable enough. This question is a crucial one for my scheme of applied publicity.

It is obviously impossible to be sure that the audience by which the choices of deception and truth-telling are discussed will be unbiased, let alone "reasonable" in any higher sense. Much has been written about the "tyranny of the majority." A shadowy gathering of imagined reasonable persons is one thing; the public in flesh and blood quite another. I have shown how an appeal to the former can be biased and incomplete; must I not recognize similar or worse defects in the latter? Surely such a public can persecute and oppress in a way the shadowy ones cannot.

This objection is extremely important, but it matters only for certain kinds of deception, for no public can discriminate against dupes in general without also discriminating against itself. When asked, therefore, whether lies to save a life or lies to repay a lie should be undertaken, members of any public can readily be made to share the perspectives of both liar and dupe. Because lying and being lied to are such universal experiences, mere publicity, without too much concern over the composition of the public, often suffices.

But as soon as the question becomes one of deceiving, not just any random person, but members of identifiable groups—then the composition of the public becomes crucial. Whether to lie to the incompetent, to children, to persons considered religiously, politically, or sexually deviant by the majority—such questions invite biased responses. An inflamed and threatened public can be unreasonable in the extreme. The more unlikely it is that the public will ever share the predicament of the deceived, the more difficult the shift of perspectives becomes, and the more bias can creep into the evaluation.

The composition of the public, under such circumstances, must be looked at with care. In the chapters dealing with lies to such definable groups, as, for example, lies to the sick and the dying, I make suggestions to meet this problem. In all group conflicts, a shift in perspectives which might permit identifying with the predicament of the opponent is difficult for many. It takes a conscious effort of the imagination and strong institutional incentives.

Apart from lies to members of these groups, the shift is easier to make. We are all too easily aware of having been both liar and dupe, agent and person affected. In spite of the fact that this shift of perspectives is so rarely performed when moral choice to lie or to tell the truth is at stake, the publicity given to such a choice would require its performance.

The test of publicity is not always needed; where needed it cannot always be implemented; if implemented it does not always bring forth solutions to moral quandaries. Given these limitations, it can nevertheless reduce the discrepancy of perspectives, shed light on moral reasoning, and facilitate moral choice.

Caution and Risk-taking

What steps does public justification require? What might reasonable persons do, when presented with someone's excuses for a particular lie? If they were asked to judge the degree of justification for, say, a practice of entrapment, how would they go about seeking an answer?

They would, first of all, look carefully for any alternatives of a non-deceptive nature available to the liar, for reasons explained in Chapter II. Assuming that lies always carry a negative value, they would only begin to consider possible excuses after ascertaining that no statement devoid of that negative value would do.

In the second place, they would proceed to the weighing of the moral reasons for and against the lie. In so doing, they would share the perspective of the deceived and those affected by lies. They would, therefore, tend to be much more cautious than those with the optimistic perspective of the liar. They would value veracity and accountability more highly than would individual liars or their apologists.

In weighing the moral reasons, the excuses advanced, and the principles invoked, these persons would keep in mind the analogy between the use of force and the use of deception. Both, in their view, would be acceptable when *consented* to, given certain restrictions. The consent would have to be based on adequate information and ability to make a choice; and there would have to be freedom to opt out of the violent or deceptive situation. Where such informed and voluntary consent obtains, there is no longer a discrepancy of perspectives between liar and dupe, agent and victim. Deceptive bargaining in a bazaar, for instance, where buyer and seller try to outwit one another, would present few problems to these reasonable persons. The same is true of professional boxing matches. But deception can be justified in such situations only if they are knowingly and freely entered into, with complete freedom to leave. The naïve newcomer may not be informed; many others have little genuine free choice; and if the practice is known to be deceptive yet entered into for survival, as in the case of a widespread black market, there is no longer freedom to leave.

Both violence and deception, moreover, would be more acceptable to these reasonable persons when used for the purposes of self-defense or life-saving. Finally, both would be more excusable the more trivial their effect on others.

But under all circumstances, these reasonable persons would need to be very wary because of the great susceptibility of deception to spread, to be abused, and to give rise to even more undesirable practices. The third step in their debate, therefore, would have to look beyond the individual excuses brought forth by liars and the individual counter-arguments on behalf of dupes. Here, the importance of practices would be stressed, and the harm to persons quite outside the deceptive situation considered. Spread multiplies the harm resulting from lies; abuse increases the damage for each and every instance. Both spread and abuse result in part from the lack of clear-cut standards as to what is acceptable. In the absence of such standards, instances of deception can and will increase, bringing distrust and thus more deception, loss of personal standards on the part of liars and so yet more deception, imitation by those who witness deception and the rewards it can bring, and once again more deception. Augustine described the process thus:

> [. . .] little by little and bit by bit this will grow and by gradual accessions will slowly increase until it becomes

such a mass of wicked lies that it will be utterly impossible to find any means of resisting such a plague grown to huge proportions through small additions.[9]

Reasonable persons might be especially eager to circumscribe the lies told by all those whose power renders their impact on human lives greater than usual. And they would wish to set up the clearest possible standards and safeguards in order to prevent these and other liars from drifting into more and more damaging practices—through misunderstanding, carelessness, or abuse.

The concern to counteract spreading practices of deception would lead these reasonable persons to opt for accountability wherever individuals now exert influence over others in ways for which they cannot be held to task. Their marked caution would be reinforced by attention to the practices of deception rather than to the individual instances alone.

Emphasis on either case or practice at the expense of the other deprives one of insight. It leaves human choice without texture or depth. Thus the reasonable persons should maintain to the best of their ability a dual perspective on both cases and practices, in addition to the dual perspective of liars and deceived. At times they might take precautions against a practice by refusing to justify it, while considering some individual instances as excusable. And at all times they have to look at the individual lie from the point of view of the likelihood that it might give rise to others.

Such, then, are the general principles which I believe govern the justification of lies. As we consider different kinds of lies, we must ask, first, whether there are alternative forms of action which will resolve the difficulty without the use of a lie; second, what might be the moral reasons brought forward to excuse the lie, and what reasons can be raised as counter-arguments. Third, as a test of these two steps, we must ask what a public of reasonable persons might say about such lies.

Most lies will clearly fail to satisfy these questions of justification. But what lies might actually satisfy them? The chapters which follow will take up some kinds of lies often regarded as justified by the liars themselves. I shall do no more than begin to explore them.

LIES IN A CRISIS

May not a singular necessity supercede the common rule of veracity, too? Suppose a Genghis Khan, or any such Eastern monster, resolved on the massacre of a whole city if he finds they have given any protection to his enemy, and asking a citizen in whom he confides about this fact, whether his enemy had ever been sheltered by the citizens; and that by deceiving the monster, he can preserve the lives of hundreds of thousands, and of their innocent babes; whereas telling him the truth shall occasion the most horrible slaughter: could a wise man's heart reproach him justly for breaking through the common law of veracity, and conquering the natural impulse toward it, upon such strong motives of humanity?

—Francis Hutcheson,
A System of Moral Philosophy

Though it wasn't true, Woodward told Deep Throat that he and Bernstein had a story for the following week saying that Haldeman was the fifth person in control of disbursements from the secret fund.

"You'll have to do it on your own," Deep Throat said. [. . .] Since he had not cautioned them on Haldeman, he was effectively confirming the story.

—Carl Bernstein and Bob Woodward, *All the President's Men*

The Acute Crisis

How might the test of publicity discriminate among the many crisis* situations where lies are told? Let us look back first at the case discussed by Kant and so many others —the murderer who asks where his victim has gone. This is a crisis in the most common sense of the word, a turning point at which a decisive change for better or worse may take place. It is a crisis, also, in the moral sense of that word: the turning point presents an opportunity to choose whether to intervene, and by what means. Not all crises afford such choice. The familiar scene from the past, where parents sat helpless by the bedside of a sick child whose illness had reached a critical point, is one of agonizing powerlessness. But here, the choice is clear, the stakes are high, and the likely damage without the lie irreversible. There seems no way to prevent the misdeed without the lie, and time is running out.

For those confronted with such a crisis, there is little time to reflect. But could they do so beforehand, they would, I believe, be able to justify such lies. First of all, they could argue, the limited time in which to make the decision rules out the chance to work out alternatives, such as appeals for assistance or rescue. (If, on the other hand, one could know a day ahead of time, there would, of course, be many alternative ways of protecting the victim.)

*The Greek word *"krisis"* means "discrimination," "judgment," "decision," "crisis," or "trial." It always involves human perception of an unfolding event—a war, an illness, a trial; but it can also sometimes stress the moral element of personal choice which goes along with perception when there is something at stake and opportunity to intervene. This double meaning is important for understanding the limitations a crisis may impose and the very different degrees to which personal choice can affect its course.

Second, if the claim that an innocent life can be saved is justified, it will offset in most minds the negative value ordinarily placed on lies. Non-maleficence, or the avoidance of harm, would be the principle invoked, and most would hold that it overrides the principle of veracity in these cases. Just as force would be justifiable as a means to prevent the murder, so it would be right to achieve the same objective through a lie.

Third, the life threatened is itself an innocent one. If, on the other hand, the pursued were a kidnapper, the lie to cover up for him would be very differently judged. One can conceive of innumerable variations in the degree of innocence of the pursued; of violence or coercion should the pursuer find him; and of loyalty to the pursued on the part of the person asked to reveal his whereabouts. All these variations could affect our judgment of how excusable the protective lie would be.

Finally, a lie to protect a murderer's intended victim is a very isolated instance. It would neither be likely to encourage others to lie nor make it much more likely that the person who lied to save a life might come to lie more easily or more often. In many lives, such emergencies arise rarely, if ever; should one arise, it is not likely to be repeated. And the situation is so extraordinary as to provide no reason to generalize the need for lying. There would be very little risk, therefore, of such a lie contributing in any way to a spreading deceptive practice.

For these reasons, the test of public justification could be satisfied. There would be no difficulty in defending openly the policy that persecutors searching for their innocent victims can be answered dishonestly. In fact, not only can it be defended; it could be advocated in advance as preferable to a policy of honesty at all times. Someone who advocated the opposite policy of total honesty to persecutors would be a dangerous individual in times where life-and-death crises arise more frequently; one who could be trusted with no confidential information at all.

Does such a justification apply only to those lying to save other people from extreme threats, or does it apply equally to those who might lie to save themselves? That is, is there some greater justification for altruistic lies here than for self-serving ones? I cannot see that one is more justifiable than the other in such a crisis. Both can be equally advocated in advance and excused in retrospect. (Though if one person gives himself up to save another, the situation changes; such an act cannot be expected in advance,[1] yet it must be admired in retrospect.)

It has been argued that although lying might be justifiable on such rare occasions, most of us will, in fact, never encounter a situation where a lie might be excusable. We should proceed in life, therefore, as if no lies should ever be told. This is a comforting thought and makes everyday choices simple, but it holds little consolation for those many whose lives are touched more often and more crushingly by crisis than one might think. More individuals than not lead their lives under a continuous threat to survival or to their political or religious freedom. And even in societies where there are no such threats, there are professional groups—doctors or military personnel, for example—whose members can expect frequent crises in their work. For them, there can be no such easy certainty that a crisis where a lie will be necessary will probably never come into their lives.

Prolonged Threats to Survival

A crisis may be acute, as in the life-saving cases; but a state of crisis can also become chronic. The same elements are present—great danger and no escape—but the time frame is entirely different, and there is no one critical turning point. The threat may be continuous, so that one lie after another barely staves off disaster, or it may recur over and over again, each time posing the issue of deception.

In extreme and prolonged threats to survival, as in plagues, invasions, and religious or political persecution, human choice is intolerably restricted. Survival alone counts; moral considerations are nearly obliterated. People may still give each other help and protection in extremes of physical and mental stress; they may still forego lies and still share alike; but such choice goes far beyond duty. And for many, the moral personality is itself crushed; the ability to choose is destroyed.

Hume, describing such conditions, wrote that justice itself can be expected only in an intermediate range of scarcity and benevolence—when there is neither such abundance that all have what they need nor such scarcity that not all can survive; and where people are neither so completely good that they act justly and lovingly spontaneously, nor so incurably evil that nothing can make them do so.*

And George Steiner evokes the "survival value" of lying under extreme circumstances:

*See David Hume, *An Enquiry Concerning the Principles of Morals*, Section III, Part I. While I agree with Hume about some floor *beneath* which justice cannot be expected, I do not share his optimism about its superfluity at the highest levels of abundance and human benevolence. In the first place, we are coming to realize how limitless human needs can become. And second, we have the experience of situations where grave problems of justice and moral choice arise among well-meaning persons even where scarcity is not a problem. In hospitals, for example, there are times where resources are plentiful, and where everyone wants to do what is best for a patient, yet where searing moral differences arise. Finally, benevolence can surely bring its own tyranny.

For a comparison with Hume, see Rawls, *A Theory of Justice*, pp. 126–130, and H. L. A. Hart, *The Concept of Law* (Oxford: Clarendon Press, 1961), pp. 189–195.

Fiction was disguise: from those seeking out the same waterhole, the same sparse quarry, or meagre sexual chance. To misinform, to utter less than the truth was to gain a vital edge of space or subsistence. Natural selection would favor the contriver. Folk tales and mythology retain a blurred memory of the evolutionary advantage of mask and misdirection. Loki, Odysseus are very late, literary concentrates of the widely diffused motif of the liar, of the dissembler elusive as flame and water, who survives.[2]

Under such circumstances, the luxury of alternatives is out of the question. The overwhelming justification is, once again, survival. It appeals to the most powerful aspect of the principle of avoiding harm—the battle against personal extinction. At such times, the spread of deceptive practices cannot be a consideration insofar as it has already taken place. Society *is* in a state of collapse, and a lie won't add to the chaos or the degradation. For all these reasons, public debate of how justifiable such lies are would then be largely beside the point.

These long-term threats to survival strain morality most of all. In shorter and more limited crises, as in mining disasters or shipwrecks, where some may survive and return to society, the ordinary expectations have more force. Such emergencies create exceptional circumstances, not qualifications of moral rules. Survivors may be brought to trial and held to existing standards, as in Conrad's *Lord Jim* or the famous lawsuit of *U.S.* v. *Holmes.*[3] In this case, the crew in a lifeboat threw overboard fourteen men to keep the vessel from sinking in a turbulent sea. One of the surviving crew members was convicted for unlawful homicide.

But to say that the long-term threats to survival strain morality is not to say that hindsight cannot make out differences in adherence to principles of justice or veracity at such times. Nor, obviously, is it to say that those who *impose* or tolerate such burdens for their fellow human beings must not be judged. It is merely to say that there comes a point of human endurance and of long-term threat beyond which justice is inoperative for sufferers, and where their adherence to moral principles cannot be evaluated by outsiders.*

Line-drawing

Acute, life-threatening crises, then, can justify lies to save innocent lives; and prolonged threats to survival suspend the *efforts* to evaluate lies told in self-defense. But there are a great many less crushing predicaments which are still perceived as a crises by liars. They may want to be freed from a chronic unpleasant burden, even though it is in no way life-threatening. Their moral excuses—their claims to innocence, for example, or the threat they perceive— may be much less powerful. Even if the threat is severe, it may not be immediate. It may not even be certain that a lie will remove the threat. There are innumerable variations on these themes, in all of which the liar may claim an urgent reason to lie. How can they be evaluated?

The following story from Plutarch is a good example of such a complex situation where a lie was told and ultimately highly praised:

> [. . .] anarchy and confusion long prevailed in Sparta, causing the death of the father of Lycurgus. For as he was trying to quell a riot, he was stabbed with a butcher's knife, and left the title of king to his eldest son, Polydectes. He too

*See Hannah Arendt, *The Origins of Totalitarianism* (New York: Harcourt Brace, 1966) p. 452:

> Totalitarian terror achieved its most terrible triumph when it succeeded in cutting the moral person off from the individualist escape and in making the decisions of conscience absolutely questionable and equivocal. The alternative is no longer between good and evil, but between murder and murder. Who could solve the dilemma of the Greek mother who was asked by the Nazis to choose which of her children should be killed?

dying soon after, the right of succession (as everyone thought) rested in Lycurgus; and reign he did, until it was found that the queen, his sister-in-law, was with child; upon which he immediately declared that the kingdom belonged to her issue, provided it were male, and that he himself only exercised the legal jurisdiction as his guardian. [. . .]

Soon after, an overture was made to him by the queen, that she would herself in some way destroy the infant, upon condition that he would marry her when he came to the crown. Abhorring the woman's wickedness, he nevertheless did not reject her proposal, but making show of closing with her, despatched the messenger with thanks and expressions of joy, but dissuaded her earnestly from procuring herself to miscarry, which would impair her health, if not endanger her life; he himself would see to it, he said, that the child, as soon as born, should be taken out of the way.

By such artifices having drawn on the woman to the time of her lying-in, when the baby was born, and a boy presented to him, he said to those about him:

"Men of Sparta, here is a king born unto us." [. . .] All were transported with his just and noble spirit.[4]

It is possible that Lycurgus could have talked the queen out of her evil designs upon her unborn baby and future king. But had he failed, she might well have carried them out. It is possible, alternatively, that, instead of lying to her, Lycurgus could have revealed her plans publicly and tried to guard her from hurting the baby. But this would have been at the cost of her reputation, perhaps life, and if he failed, his own life, as well as that of the baby, might have been endangered. His lie was not certain to remove the entire threat to the baby's life nor to his own. And having once begun to lie in the matter, he found that more and more deception became necessary to uphold the original lie.

Sometimes the danger comes, not just from one individual, but from an entire institution which is felt to be unjust. How do we respond to a law, a procedure, a whole network of corruption, perhaps oppression? Consider someone having to deal with a dishonest City Hall, an oppressive mental hospital, or a criminal syndicate. Should he adopt its standards merely to subsist and get his job done? Or should he resist? Openly or secretly? And at what risk?

In some such situations, lies are clearly justified, once again on the basis of self-defense. A person unjustly detained in a mental hospital, for instance, may have very few, if any, means of attaining freedom. If a lie brings him into contact with a lawyer who can take up his cause or make the authorities believe that someone on the outside is going to publicize his plight, it might well stand up to the test of publicity. The victim is powerless; his alternatives few and unsatisfactory. The danger is great and could be lifelong.[5] The risk that deception will spread is slight. While it is true that life itself is not threatened, the unjust deprivation of liberty would, I believe, be as powerful an excuse.

A more acute crisis, though less threatening to life or liberty, occurs when someone is forced to undergo sterilization, or is threatened with some unwarranted inroad on bodily integrity. In these circumstances, once again, I believe that self-defense through deception should be allowed where alternative forms of resistance are not available.

In a lighter vein, a crisis of sorts arose for a young woman I know who was making a university-sponsored visit to a village of former head-hunters. She was well received and presented with the special delicacy of the tribe: baby mice, taken by the tail, dipped in melted butter, and swallowed alive. After a moment's thought, she announced regretfully that she wished she could taste the mice, but that to do so would be against her religion.

But there are a number of common situations where the degree of danger, and the obligation to submit to it, are in dispute. Consider the young men who feel justified in falsely claiming physical or mental disabilities to avoid military service. And compare such lies when used, say, in peacetime, in World War II, and in the war in Vietnam. Or consider the following:

A pediatrician was approached by the mother of a child whom he had known for a long time. The child was a seven-year-old white boy living in Hyde Park, Massachusetts. Recently, the physician had been treating this child for bed-wetting and occasionally counseling the parents and the child because of mild emotional problems that had included aggressive behavior, trouble sleeping, and emotional lability. During the summer of 1975, the parents received a letter saying that he was to be bused to a school in Roxbury in September 1975. The parents, who were against forced busing, were very upset by this. Allegedly, the boy became particularly distraught. He began to wet his bed more often; he was quite anxious; and his parents reported that he was having frequent nightmares.

Late in August, the parents approached their pediatrician with a form requesting that the child be allowed to remain at his neighborhood school for "medical reasons." The pediatrician thought about this request. He felt that the boy might be having a stress reaction to the prospect of changing schools. In itself, this did not seem so abnormal. The physician was not convinced that the stress reaction was a "medical reason" to excuse the boy from forced busing. On the other hand, he had very good rapport with his family, and they desperately wanted him to fill out the form. He felt that the maintenance of this relationship was very important, and that they were really depending upon him at this time for help with what they perceived as a major crisis in their lives. This pediatrician himself was against forced busing in general.

The pediatrician decided to fill out the form, stating that he thought it was important, for this child's continuing emotional stability, that he not be bused. In the form, he described the alleged deterioration of the boy's behavior during the summer.[6]

Both for the parents of this boy and for potential draftees, there *are* honest alternatives to going along with the request they regard as unjust: they can refuse to submit, and accept the consequences. Many have had to weigh the choice between acceding to a demand they regard as threatening and unjust, or lying to evade it, or else resisting it overtly. In evaluating such choices one has to take into account the degree to which the request is indeed unjust, the available alternatives, the severity of the consequences of overt resistance, and the effects of lying, not least on the liars themselves.

Consider a couple driven to seek divorce in a society where it can be granted only for adultery. They may see two alternative ways to be allowed to divorce: committing adultery or lying to say that there has been adultery. A variant of the second way is to enact a charade wherein one spouse is caught in an incriminating situation. How should such a couple proceed, if both adultery and lies are distasteful to them and the marriage itself one they feel unable to continue? Some have chosen legal separation, in societies where divorce has been thus restricted; but for many, this alternative has represented such a sacrifice that a lie has seemed a small price to pay in order to achieve release from their marriage and the freedom to marry again.

Were such a case put to public debate, lying would seem excusable to some, who would argue that it is the system which, in presenting the choice in the first place, is degrading and in need of change. For the legislators or those who design the system are not caught in a crisis as are the divorcing spouses. There are many more alternatives open to those devising divorce legislation than to those caught in a system which punishes the honest. And the system obviously encourages the spread of dishonesty in a way that the individual crisis response does not. The system is, therefore, much less excusable than the individual deceit which forms a part of it. Others would argue, on the contrary, that the way to deal with laws one finds unjust is through lawful change, not through breaking the law surreptitiously.

These are but a few of a great many instances of human predicaments where what is perceived as a crisis makes lying one of the only ways out, but where unanimous resolutions may not be found. The factors that influence choice differ greatly. In some of these predicaments, only one lie or a few may be necessary. In others, and especially where survival within the institution is the only alternative, continuous lying may be at stake. People then have to choose between "living a lie" and breaking away in some way—through taking the risks of overt disregard for the prevailing norms, or of actual escape.

These situations also differ with respect to the proportion of persons who actually participate in the deceptive practices. They differ with respect to the degree of voluntariness of participation, depending upon the consequences of noncompliance. They differ, finally, in that some of the lies can be more openly acknowledged than others after the crisis is over.

In all these cases, the claims to justification vary. In all of them, liars will tend to overestimate the forces pushing them to lie. And in all, there comes a turning point where participants either comply, manage to leave, or are crushed.

Where is that turning point? What is the limit of expectable heroism? Where do powerlessness, external threat, and prevailing practice so work together that corruption is the norm, honesty the exception?

The absolutist rejection of all lies cannot suffice in such predicaments. Nor can the simple belief that, since most of us won't encounter dire emergencies that only a lie can dispel, we can follow the absolutists in practice, even though in principle we might admit an exception or two to their prohibition of all lies. This belief may be a sound basis for behavior in normal times; but it seems less applicable to many who live in the shadow of crises where lying seems the only alternative.

Line-drawing is a hard task once one leaves the domain of the clear-cut life-threatening crisis. It becomes difficult, then, to answer the questions relevant to moral justification. The first question, asking whether there are truthful alternatives, is hard to answer wherever there is uncertainty about the various alternatives and the hardships they may impose or avert. The second, asking what moral arguments can be made for and against the lie, will encounter problems connected with the excuses claiming non-maleficence: There will be disagreement as to how intense, how immediate, how irreversible, and how enduring the risks really involved are. And this disagreement will at times stem from widely varying estimates of the need to continue the practice calling forth the lies—the divorce laws, the busing regulations, the draft laws, and so on.

The test of publicity with respect to such lies would therefore have to address the debate, not only to the lies in isolation, but to the social practices of which they form a part. It would have to press the search for alternatives, both social and individual. And it would focus attention on the debilitating nature of participating in the deceptive practices, as well as the likelihood that these might spread and thus further injure the community.

Danger of Expanding Deceptive Practices

When should such a spread be thought most harmful? Surely when the opportunities to deceive flourish, and when the knowledge of these practices gives rise to a loss of trust, to imitation, to deceptive countermeasures. It is the fear of such spread which underlies the reluctance to condone professional deception, no matter how indicated it may seem in the individual case. There are a number of professions where crisis situations are not isolated incidents but frequent occurrences. Doctors, lawyers, journalists, secret-service agents, and military personnel, for example, may find themselves repeatedly in straits where serious consequences seem avoidable only through deception. Their chosen work exposes them frequently to such crises; their professions, moreover, reward competition and unusual achievement. Cutting corners may be one way to such achievements; and if deception is pervasive and rarely punished, then it will be all the more likely to spread. The accepted practices may then grow increasingly insensitive, and abuses and mistakes more common, resulting in harm to self, profession, clients, and society.

There is always an interweaving of self-serving and altruistic motives in such practices. One benefits personally by cutting corners, no one person seems to be too much harmed thereby, and the benefits one can bring about often seem important. But the self-serving motives are not clearly addressed; there is, in fact, rarely a clear professional standard or open discussion of the unspoken standards in professional organizations.

The excerpt from *All the President's Men* at the beginning of this chapter is a good case in point. Certainly, the situation was one of mounting crisis for the nation and of potential danger for investigating journalists who came too close to revealing the facts about Watergate. It is certain, too, that there was great pressure to be first with the revelations; the desire to advance professionally and to gain fame formed no small part of the undertaking. In pursuing their investigation, the two journalists came to tell more than one lie; a whole fabric of deception arose. Persons being interviewed were falsely told that others had already given certain bits of information or had said something about them. One of the reporters tried to impersonate Donald Segretti on the telephone. The other lied to Deep Throat in order to extract corroboration of a fact which this witness would have feared to reveal in other ways. And the newspaper was used to print information for which there was not always adequate evidence.

It is not clear that, beyond the secrecy which had to surround the investigation, deception was actually needed. Yet it is certain that the reporters deserve great credit for exposing the misdeeds of the Watergate scandal. It can be argued that, in order for this exposure to be possible, deception was needed; but what is more troubling in the book than the lies themselves is the absence of any acknowledgment of a moral dilemma. No one seems to have stopped to think that there was a problem in using deceptive means. No one weighed the reasons for and against doing so. There was no reported effort to search for honest alternatives, or to distinguish among different forms and degrees of deception, or to consider whether some circumstances warranted it more than others.

The absence of such reflection may well result in countless young reporters unthinkingly adopting some of these methods. And those who used them successfully at a time of national crisis may do so again with lesser provocation. The impression gained by the reading public is that such standards are taken for granted among journalists. The results, therefore, are severe, both in terms of risks to the personal professional standards of those directly involved, the public view of the profession, and to many within it or about to enter it.

The same risks confront other professions. In the care of the sick and the dying, in courtroom practice, in every kind of selling and advocacy—wherever the opportunities for deception abound, rewards are high, and time for considering alternatives often short—the danger of the formation of deceptive habits is much greater than in other lines of work. The word "crisis" then becomes a sufficiently elastic term to suit every occasion for lies. We need to look more closely, therefore, at particular cases in these occupations.

Out of the vast number of possible cases, I shall take up only a few in the chapters to come. Others could serve as well; it is my hope that as soon as a few practices are questioned, many more will be the more easily examined.

IX

LYING TO LIARS

A man ought to be a friend to his friend, and repay gift with gift. People should meet smiles with smiles and lies with treachery.

—The *Poetic Edda*

When my love swears that she is made of truth,
I do believe her, though I know she lies,
That she might think me some untutored youth,
Unlearned in the world's false subtleties.
Thus vainly thinking that she thinks me young,
Although she knows my days are past the best,
Simply I credit her false-speaking tongue;
On both sides thus is simple truth suppress'd.
But wherefore says she not she is unjust?
And wherefore say not I that I am old?
O, love's best habit is in seeming trust,
And age in love loves not t'have years told.
　　　Therefore I lie with her, and she with me,
　　　And in our faults by lies we flattered be.

—Shakespeare, Sonnet 138

Lying to Unmask Liars

In 385 A.D., Christian authorities executed the first of many "heretics": Priscillian, Bishop of Avila, was put to death on charges of immorality and sorcery. He professed a severely ascetic doctrine and advocated the renunciation of marriage and most bodily pleasures as the way to salvation. He based these views on the belief that all matter, and in particular human bodies, including that of Jesus Christ, had been created by devils.

After his death, his followers, not unreasonably, went into hiding or disguised their beliefs. They falsely professed faith in the prevailing dogmas, while continuing their own practices in secret. Consentius wanted to infiltrate their community so as to expose them, but worried about the deception in doing so. He wrote to ask Augustine's advice. Could one not justifiably lie to this heretical sect, he argued, considering that they themselves were lying about their beliefs?

Truthfulness was here dramatically at stake on both sides. Each acknowledged the importance of truthfulness in religious matters—of bearing witness to one's faith. The very word "martyr," which means "witness" in Greek, was taken over by Christians to mean also those who persisted in bearing witness to their Christian faith even if they had to undergo the penalty of death. And throughout the long, bloody history of religious persecution, the very same debates have arisen: among persecutors, whether or not to use deception to infiltrate the sects they wish to subdue or convert; among their victims, whether or not to conceal their beliefs.[1] The same debates arise in political persecution as well; but they have a special edge in religious hostilities, where lying about one's faith in God is thought the gravest of sins, while the highest importance is placed on converting the faithless or those with unacceptable beliefs.

To Consentius' question, Augustine answered that, though he was delighted with the zeal exhibited in "raging against even latent heretics," he did not think it would be right to draw them out of hiding by lies. To proceed against lies by lying, he wrote, would be like countering robbery with robbery, sacrilege with sacrilege, and adultery with adultery. Above all, for Christians who prided themselves on their truthfulness to lie to heretics whom they believe mired in falsity and deception would be to wipe out one of the major differences between the two.[2]

To repay in kind, to emulate the wrongdoing, immaturity, or incompetence of those one has to contend with, is certainly at times to accept lower standards. Such behavior is pushed to its ludicrous extreme in the question posed by a distraught mother: "Shall I bite my baby back?"[3] And yet it has seemed to many that there is indeed some justification for repaying lies with lies—perhaps not to children, but to a great many others who know what they are doing.

An Eye for an Eye

Such views go back as far as the kind of justice which demands an eye for an eye and a tooth for a tooth. They appeal, in the first place, to the excuses having to do with fairness: to lie to a liar is to give him what he deserves, to play by his own rules, to restore an equilibrium he himself has upset. In the same way, gifts are repaid by gifts, hospitality by hospitality, blows by blows.[4]

This sense of reciprocity forms a partial background to the ease with which those judged to be enemies are lied to. When President Nixon authorized the deception and burglary to acquire Daniel Ellsberg's files from his psychiatrist, he believed he was repaying him for past treachery. Had not Ellsberg forfeited his right to be dealt with truthfully? Would he not merely be getting "his due" if deceived in return?

Many find it easier to lie to those they take to be untruthful themselves. It is as though a barrier had been let down. And to Augustine's argument that countering a lie with a lie is like countering sacrilege with sacrilege, they might answer: Such an analogy cannot be stretched to conclude that it is always wrong to repay lies in kind. They might advance another analogy—that between lying and the use of force—and ask: If at times force can be used to counter force, why should lies never be used to counter lies? And they might contend that just as someone forfeits his rights to noninterference by others when he threatens them forcibly, so a liar has forfeited the ordinary right to be dealt with honestly.

Two separate moral questions are confused in such debates. The first asks whether a liar has the same claim to be told the truth as an honest person. The second asks whether one is more justified in lying to a liar than to others.

The first is a question about the grounds for complaint which a liar might have for being paid back in his own coin. The answer to this question, assuredly, is that the liar can have no such cause for complaint under normal circumstances. It would be hypocritical for him to complain that others do not uphold the rules which he has broken. It has seemed to many, as a result, that liars are fair game for deception.

But this conclusion short-circuits the second question: Should others lie in turn to the liar? Is it right for them to do so? For their choice does not depend merely on the liar's claims or on his trustworthiness; it must be subjected to scrutiny as carefully as all other lies and take into account as many possible effects.

In order to see this distinction most clearly, consider a pathological liar, known to all, and quite harmless; someone, perhaps, who is falsely immodest about athletic feats in his youth. Surely, there would be no reason to lie to him more often because of his own tall tales. For the harm to self, others, and general trust which can come from practices of lying has to be taken into account in weighing how to deal with this man, not merely his personal characteristics. To think otherwise would be to make oneself entirely dependent on the character deficiencies in others and to stoop always to the lowest common denominator in reciprocating lies for lies.

In addition, even if it were right to reciprocate in this way, it is often hard to know when others are lying. Even those who want to return the deception they encounter are bound to make mistakes. If we feel free to deceive those we suspect of having lied, we are likely to invite vast increases in actual deception and to escalate the seriousness of lies told in retaliation. Such a notion would not stand up well under the test of publicity.

In summary, there is an undoubted psychological easing of standards of truthfulness toward those believed to be liars. It is simply a fact, for instance, that one behaves differently toward a trusted associate and toward a devious, aggressive salesman. But this easing of standards merely explains the difference in behavior; it does not by itself justify lies to those one takes to be less than honest. Some of the harm the liar may have done by lying may be repaid by the harm a lie can do to him in return. But the risks to others, to general trust, and to those who lie to liars in retaliation merely accumulate and spread thereby. Only if there are separate, and more compelling, excuses, can lying to liars be justified.

What might these more compelling excuses be? One would be the complete harmlessness of the intended lie. A genuinely white lie may be excusable on those grounds, but not especially so when told to a liar. A second excuse would arise if the liar one intends to deceive has precipitated a crisis of the kind discussed in the last chapter. Again, then, the lie would not be specifically justified by the fact that one is then lying to a liar.

A third excuse often used is closely connected to the sense of reciprocity which makes lying to liars seem more natural than lying to the honest. It is the desire to teach the liar a lesson, to dramatize to him how it feels to be lied to.* The excuse given here makes a claim to some kind of benefit to be achieved through such a repayment. The liar has not only forfeited the right to be trusted, it is argued; he has injured trust. He and others will benefit if he can see his behavior for what it is and feel its results acutely —if, in other words, he can be made to share the perspective of the deceived.

But such a claim is patently insufficient to give added justification to deceiving liars. For if one really wants to teach the liar a lesson, there are many honest ways of doing so. The lie to teach a lesson is, therefore, in no way a last resort. Nor will it necessarily achieve the objective claimed for it by such an excuse—the lesson may well not be understood or even perceived. Often, the liar thus treated will merely conclude that he had been right in assuming that everyone else lies and in setting his standards accordingly. For this reason it is not only wrong to lie so as to teach a lesson; it is actually counterproductive to do so to those one takes to have an incomplete grasp of honesty. The child, the unthinking, the confused, and the mythomaniac will develop such a grasp only by experiencing the honesty of others, not the reverse.

Consentius, however, was making yet a fourth claim in his request to use deception to unmask heretics. He did not intend mere reciprocity or lesson-teaching. His lies were meant also to serve the principle of veracity at what he took to be the highest level. This aim was to be achieved in two ways. He wanted primarily to unveil the mendacity of the Priscillianists—both the falseness of their views about religion and the lies they told in self-protection. In so doing, he also hoped to advance what he believed to be the true faith and to weaken or destroy its enemies.

*This excuse often blends the retaliatory and the educational senses of "teaching someone a lesson."

Against this plea, Augustine retorted most vehemently:

> Do you not see how much this argument supports the very ones whom we are trying to catch as great quarry by our lies? That, as you yourself have shown, is precisely the opinion of the Priscillianists. To establish this opinion they produce evidence from Scripture, urging their followers to lie as if in accordance with the example of the Patriarchs, Prophets, Apostles, and angels, not hesitating to add even Christ our Lord Himself, thinking that they cannot otherwise prove their falsehood to be true except by saying that the Truth is mendacious. They must be refuted, not imitated.[5]

The appeal to veracity in order to excuse lying to liars does not stand up well under scrutiny, as Augustine pointed out. It is no better than appeals to fairness—either retributive or reciprocal—or to beneficence. But there is one context which does make such lies more excusable. It is when liar and dupe consent to a *mutually* deceptive relationship.

Mutual Deceits

The Shakespeare sonnet quoted at the beginning of this chapter describes a quite common, often poignant human arrangement, where two persons deceive one another, each knowing of the deceit, each preferring to have it continue rather than to confront what it masks. Each feigns belief in the flattery and trust which the other conveys:

> Therefore I lie with her, and she with me,
> And in our faults by lies we flattered be.[6]

Most friendships and families rely on some such reciprocity to sustain illusions, suppress some memory too painful to confront, and give support where it is needed.

Sometimes these bonds are willingly maintained; most often they are painfully upheld, with little or no freedom to begin afresh.

Such deception can resemble a game where both partners know the rules and play by them. It represents, then, a pact of sorts, whereby what each can do, what each gains by the arrangement, is clearly understood. A game of poker is such a pact. It mingles trust and distrust, bargaining and gambling. Mutual deceits can be short-lived, like a poker game, or they can last indefinitely. The stakes can be insignificant or very high. At best, the practice is voluntarily and openly undertaken, and terminable at will. It can then overcome most of the objections that deceit would otherwise provoke.*

But few mutual deceits represent such ideal compacts. Some are not compacts at all, though the liars call them that, often believing them to be so. For instance, many rationalize their lies to persons who are dying or chronically ill with the thought that "he knows that I know that he is dying," thereby escaping the necessity to speak more honestly. This is a kind of imprisonment for both parties, but especially for the patient, often too vulnerable to be able to secure truthful information. If, on the other hand, a sick man *asks* not to be burdened with discouraging news, such a pact, where each respects the agreement made, can arise. And, as always, the most difficult situations are those where one thinks that truthfulness is not wanted by the patient, but dare not ask for fear of blundering into the forbidden region.

In certain bargaining situations, we also play such mu-

---

*Consider the analogy here between deception and violence: A boxing match is ordinarily freely entered into and ended according to precise conventions. A duel may be voluntarily entered into, but is often socially coerced for at least one party. Once entered, it is left only with the greatest difficulty. An assault, finally, is neither freely entered by the victim, nor left except through the use of coercion in return.

tually deceptive roles: as buyer and seller, defense and prosecution, sometimes husband and wife. In a bazaar, for instance, false claims are a convention; to proclaim from the outset one's honest intention would be madness. If buyers and sellers bargain knowingly and voluntarily, one would be hard put to regard as misleading their exaggerations, false claims to have given their last bid, or words of feigned loss of interest. Both parties have then consented to the rules of the game.

Much greater problems in bargaining arise when one or both parties do not participate voluntarily, or where both parties are not equally aware of the ground rules allowing deception. It is easy for liars to stretch the analogy of voluntary mutual bargaining to excuse much more questionable practices. A factory owner, for example, may falsely predict that the plant will have to close down if the union wins the upcoming representation election. Such deception cannot be condoned as an element of mutually agreed-to bargaining. For all employees clearly will not know the "rules of the game" by which the employer is playing. They are also at a great disadvantage, since there is little they can do to deceive the employer in return. And even if they know the deceptive nature of what is told them, there may be no way for them to leave the bargaining situation if they do not have an equivalent job opportunity elsewhere.

Once a union has been formed, the false statement by the factory owner that he will have to close down the plant—say, if the union insists on a 10 percent wage increase—is often made in a context of possible deception suspected by each side. The union may retaliate by offering deceptive threats at the bargaining table. But while both parties may *know* the rules of the game, neither may have consented to play by these rules. Nor are they free to abandon the bargaining or to change the unspoken rules.

As these examples suggest, deception in bargaining

and selling is rarely as mutually and freely accepted as in games. Even when it is, there may still be reason to ask whether it can overflow into other practices, so that persons *not* consenting to the deception are misled, and whether it can affect the liars themselves, even though they do not injure each other in the least. Once again the analogy with games that allow lying and bluffing is helpful. Many such games have clear lines of demarcation; players know when they are playing, with whom, and by what rules. Certain bargaining situations are equally clearly distinguished from other undertakings. But many are not. It may then be difficult to know when one should and should not deceive, who is and is not a voluntary participant, and how much deception "the rules" allow.

These difficulties are intensified for those who spend large portions of their time in deceptive bargaining. They may then lose some ability to discriminate among kinds and degrees of falsehood; and unless the lines between circumstances where the rules allowing deception do and do not apply are very clear, the deceptive tactics may spill over into other relationships. In the end, the participants in deception they take to be mutually understood may end up with coarsened judgment and diminished credibility, even though the original bargaining practice seemed harmless in its own right.

Bargaining and salesmanship have a thousand shadings, and innumerable lines at which to take a stand or go along with what seems to be the accepted practice. These are the everyday contexts where many test their personal standards. A recent study shows that businessmen are increasingly concerned that their work brings pressure upon these standards by rewarding deception.[7] They find that "number manipulation" is a particularly acute problem, as are questions of honesty in advertising and in giving information to top management, clients, and the government.

To sum up: The fact that someone is himself a liar does

not by itself add strength to excuses for deception, such as the harmlessness of the lie, the existence of a crisis, or voluntary mutual consent in clearly delineated circumstances. Alternatives still have to be weighed, moral arguments considered, the test of publicity taken into account. But if, finally, the liar to whom one wishes to lie is also in a position to do one harm, then the balance may shift; not because he is a liar, but because of the threat he poses. We have already seen how the attempt to avoid serious harm can justify a lie, just as it allows the recourse to force. I would like, therefore, to take up in some greater detail the question of lying to those from whom one fears harm—to adversaries and those thought to be threats. For it is because of the believed *threat* that Consentius and Nixon really thought that lying to their foes was right, and not just to reciprocate lies, improve liars, or buttress what they believed true.

X

LYING TO ENEMIES

When a man denominates another his *enemy*, his *rival*, his *antagonist*, his *adversary*, he is understood to speak the language of self-love, and to express sentiments peculiar to himself and arising from his particular circumstances and situation. But when he bestows on any man the epithets of *vicious* or *odious* or *depraved*, he then speaks another language, and expresses sentiments in which he expects all his audience are to concur with him. He must here, therefore, depart from his private and particular situation and must choose a point of view common to him with others; he must move some universal principle of the human frame and touch a string to which all mankind have an accord and symphony.
 —David Hume, *Enquiry Concerning the Principles of Morals*

The great masses of the people [. . .] will more easily fall victims to a big lie than to a small one.
 —Adolf Hitler, *Mein Kampf*

I discovered in the earliest stages that pursuit of truth did not permit violence being inflicted on one's opponent, but that he must be weaned from error by patience and sympathy.
 —Gandhi, *Defense Against Charge of Sedition*

Giving Enemies Their Due

To believe someone an enemy is to think him hostile and capable of coercion through force, threats of force, or deception. The tax evader, the hostage holder, the invading nation are enemies of a society; but private adversaries, such as competitors in cutthroat businesses, or rivals in love or politics, can be equally hostile. In all such relationships, there is more than a casual link between the concepts of "enemy" and "liar." An enemy will often, though not always, lie to defeat you; and someone who lies to you will often, though not always, constitute an enemy in your mind.

Lying to enemies serves two purposes. First, it can divert their maneuvers. If the lie succeeds in making them think one is too strong to be defeated, or so paltry and unattractive as not to be worth attacking, it may even keep them from attacking altogether. Second, lying can help in the strategy to *defeat* the enemy. In World War II, for instance, the Allies not only kept information concerning the planned invasion of Normandy a secret; they also engaged in an elaborate hoax to make the Germans believe it would come at a different time and place.

Lying to enemies is closely related to the lies for survival and in great crises discussed in earlier chapters. But very often there is no immediate crisis, nor a pressing question of survival; yet lies to enemies are traditionally accompanied by a special sense of self-evident justification. Such lies appeal, first, to a sense of *fairness* through retribution. Enemies are treated as they deserve to be treated; they receive their due. In addition, the *defense from harm* is invoked in all adversary relationships. Self-defense is the excuse strained for even by those launching aggressive warfare far beyond their borders. And where self-defense cannot serve, the defense of another nation is invoked. Given these two excuses of retribution and self-defense, further examination is thought unnecessary. Hostilities polarize allegiances even more and strengthen the belief in the righteousness of one's cause. Each side then tries to persuade itself, as yet another barricade against self-doubt, that God or destiny or right is on its side.

This righteousness is often forced. Yet there are times when it may be justified. In this chapter, I want to look more carefully at the two main principles appealed to in lying to enemies: fairness and the avoidance of harm.

The first claim advanced to justify lying to enemies is that they deserve such treatment. Fairness requires, for the earliest and by far the most common intuitive moral judgments, that one should treat friends well and enemies badly. People should receive the treatment that their behavior merits. Enemies, through their own unfairness, their aggressive acts or intentions, have forfeited the ordinary right of being dealt with fairly. The idea that one should turn the other cheek to an enemy is profoundly alien to such intuitive morality.

Few have put the claim to justification for lying to enemies so bluntly or spread the net of "enemyhood" so widely as Machiavelli. He was an exponent of the strategic use of a combination of deception and violence; of the imitation of both fox and lion. He admonished the Prince to break faith whenever necessary on the ground that men "are bad":

> You must know, then, that there are two methods of fighting, the one by law, the other by force: the first method is that of men, the second of beasts; but as the first method is often insufficient, one must have recourse to the second. [. . .]
> A prince being thus obliged to know well how to act as a beast must imitate the fox and the lion, for the lion cannot protect himself from traps, and the fox cannot defend himself from wolves. One must therefore be a fox to recognize

traps, and a lion to frighten wolves. Those that wish to be only lions do not understand this. Therefore, a prudent ruler ought not to keep faith when by so doing it would be against his interest, and when the reasons which made him bind himself no longer exist. If men were all good, this precept would not be a good one; but as they are bad, and would not observe their faith with you, so you are not bound to keep faith with them. [. . .]

But it is necessary to be able to disguise this character well, and to be a great feigner and dissembler; and men are so simple and so ready to obey present necessities, that one who deceives will always find those who allow themselves to be deceived.[1]

In the preceding chapter, we already weighed the claim that others are deceitful and found that this, by itself, does not justify lying in retaliation or in retribution.

The question now is: Would the fact that "men are bad" give added justification for such lies beyond what we have already allowed for self-defense in a crisis? And what might Machiavelli have meant by saying that "men are bad" in order that this claim count as a justification for lies to them?

First, such a statement conveys the belief that men are likely to *act* badly, to pose threats which make it all right to lie to them in return. For some, such a judgment results from experience with those thus feared; others conclude from what they take to be class, racial, or religious characteristics that members of certain groups are threatening and must be treated in an underhanded way. Second, because some are believed bad in this way, they are thought automatically less worthy of truthfulness; since they cannot themselves be trusted, why should they be treated with honesty? Conversely, those who plan to deceive and to harm gain from making their adversaries seem bad, perhaps even less than human, so that they forfeit any right to decent treatment. Warring nations often go to absurd lengths in their slogans and propaganda to make their adversaries seem less than human, even inhumane, and therefore unworthy of honesty and respect.

Third, and as a result of the first two, the adversary is often thought to be outside the "social contract" which otherwise obtains among human beings or at least within any one society. The outsiders, it is held, do not, or cannot, comply with existing rules. They do not uphold their end of any social arrangements from which they benefit, and can therefore not expect the ordinary protections. This claim was vividly expressed by James Martineau in 1875:

> On the area of every human society, and mixed with its throngs, there are always some who are thus *in* it but not *of* it, who are there, not to serve it, but to prey upon it, to use its order for the impunity of disorder, and wrest its rights into opportunities of wrong. Assassins, robbers, enemies with arms in their hands, madmen beyond the pale. [. . .] Without a certain *moral consensus* the commonwealth of truth cannot be constituted, and cannot be entered.[2]

To Martineau it was clear that those who threatened society were outside its moral bounds, and, as a result, need not be treated with the honesty due to others. Armed with such a conviction, those who contemplate action against enemies may then throw ordinary moral inquiry to the winds. They see no reason to seek alternatives to lying and rarely question either their own motives or the process whereby they came to see their enemies *as* enemies, as outside the social contract. Yet, when rulers or revolutionaries, or rivals in love or business try to justify their deceit toward those they take to be their enemies, their words ring hollow, especially to our by now increasingly suspicious reasonable persons. For all the dangers from indiscriminate lying and corruption of power are increased when one's low opinion of the dupes seems to justify one's lies.

Most important, those who lie to enemies out of a conviction that justice allows it fail to take into account the effects of the lies on themselves as agents, on others who may be affected, and on general trust. Retribution may be called for; it does not follow that there is justification for deceit. On the contrary, lies for this purpose ought to give rise to exceptional caution.

For the harm from lies to enemies is peculiarly likely to spread because of this very casual way in which enemyhood is so often bestowed. Public justification for the coercion of hostile and harmful individuals would call for very clear and public evidence for so classifying them. But many, on the contrary, forgo such efforts at public justification. Sometimes paranoia governs them to such an extent that they imagine that the public itself constitutes the conspiracy they combat. And Machiavelli allows lying not only on retributive but on *preemptive* grounds. Because men "would not observe their faith with you," you in turn are not bound to "keep faith with them." No evidence of present hostility is needed; predictions of future breaches of faith will serve as well.

Paranoia is not an unusual occurrence when it comes to setting up "enemies" and deciding how to treat them. Worse, the more paranoiac an agent or a group—the more convinced they are both that there is a conspiracy against them and that their cause overrides all others—the more self-righteously will they see their lies as merited by the iniquity of their enemies. And just as paranoia and megalomania are pathological distortions of the liar's perspective, so they can also distort the perspective of the deceived. Both can come to see an enemy in every bush and to expect deceit and duress from every quarter. This distortion of the two perspectives can blur them, and each suspected transgression then invites more retaliations, new precautions.

Most claims that lies to enemies are justified would not, then, stand up in the face of reasonable scrutiny. The risks of bias are very much greater here than in lies to neutrals or those one intends to help. The more unreflective these claims and the more stereotyped the group seen as the enemy, the less likely it is that impartial onlookers will accept the excuses for lying to such an enemy. The harm to all those deceived, to the liars themselves, and the threat to others from all the lies told will then become all too evident, just as the imputation of malevolence to the group believed hostile will be shown to be unconvincing.

But surely there are some who are so overtly hostile, so obviously threatening, that there is little danger of misjudging them. And while it is no excuse to lie to them out of a sense of retribution, might their being adversaries not provide the added justification for lying? The question that must be raised now is: Can we go beyond the justification for lying which has already been allowed in crises? Does the very fact that a crisis is *imposed by an enemy* add to the justification for lying in response? Need there then be less of a crisis, or a less immediate one, for lies to be justified where enemies are concerned? Can one begin to resort to lies to enemies in a less threatening, less immediate crisis than in those brought about by forces of nature or even unwittingly by friends?

Countering Harm

We have already discussed the occasions when deception in self-defense and in countering unfair coercion is justified. Enmity multiplies the occasions for such crises as well as their intensity. Sieges, invasions, espionage and torture[3]—all are layered with deceit and counter-deceit. Once they have begun and taken hold, it is difficult to say at any one point that an individual cannot have recourse to deception in response. Thus, to mislead one's torturers through every possible stratagem would clearly meet the test of public justification. The victim has no other alternatives to avoid breaking confidences protecting the lives of others. The torturer has no claim to normally honest answers, having stooped to such methods in the first place. It is unlikely that the practice of lying will spread because of the victim's lie under duress. And the victim, finally, is in no position to take into account harm to self or to trust.[4]

If lies under such conditions are justified, can the same not be true about lies to prevent those conditions from arising? What of a series of deceits to cut short an unjust war? Or underhanded methods for learning about an attack so as perhaps to forestall it? Are these lies not extensions of the concept of self-defense? Would anyone claim, for instance, that it was not right for the Allies to deceive the Germans during World War II about the time and place of the Normandy landings?

In principle, much argues in favor of such an extension of the justification of lies in self-defense. The threats are real and extensive; alternatives may not exist; and deceit is certainly *expected* on both sides as part of the ongoing hostilities—the more so whenever force is already in open use. Self-defense—and the use of every kind of duplicity—can then also outweigh the ordinary risks of harm incurred by the lies themselves. Even though appeals to retribution and fairness do not excuse lies to enemies, therefore, appeals to self-defense and to the prevention of harm may well do so. Honesty ought not to allow the creation of an emergency by the enemy, when deception can forestall or avert it.

In practice, however, lying to enemies has enormous drawbacks. First, as already indicated, the great likelihood of error and discrimination in the selection of who is to count as an enemy necessitates the greatest caution. Second, lies to enemies carry very special dangers of backfiring. All too often, the lie directed at adversaries is a lie to friends as well; and when it is discovered, as some always are, the costs are high. The U-2 incident, for example, was intended as a routine lie to cover up for the reconnaissance mission of the pilot. It was for enemy consumption. But this lie was one of the crucial turning points in the spiraling loss of confidence by U.S. citizens in the word of their leaders.

Even if lying may be justified in the face of force and in the name of self-defense, this very defense of self requires great caution, for deception cannot always be *aimed* only at others with the precision of many forms of violence. The larger the deceptive scheme, the more likely it is to backfire.

Governments build up enormous, self-perpetuating machineries of deception in adversary contexts. And when a government is known to practice deception, the results are self-defeating and erosive. They can come to resemble the effects of brainwashing, as described by Hannah Arendt:

> It has frequently been noted that the surest result of brainwashing in the long run is a peculiar kind of cynicism, the absolute refusal to believe in the truth of anything, no matter how well it may be established. In other words, the result of a consistent and total substitution of lies for factual truth is not that the lie will now be accepted as truth, and truth be defamed as lie, but that the sense by which we take our bearings in the real world—and the category of truth versus falsehood is among the mental means to this end—is being destroyed.[5]

Even when the substitution of falsehood for truth is not total, but seems random or partial to the deceived, or when it affects matters they consider crucial, such a state of cynicism may result. For this reason, the many forms of international deception which are assumed to be merely a "part of the game" by governments can have far-reaching effects on both internal and external trust.

There is growing evidence that the world audiences to which propaganda is directed *are* becoming more distrustful. The sense of being manipulated is stronger, and the trust in one's own government or that of others is shrinking. As a result, citizens the world over have less confidence that they can influence what governments do.[6]

The loss in confidence benefits individuals to an extent. Those in a position to resist oppression by bureaucracies will do so, and fewer can be talked into fighting senseless wars. But the major effects are surely negative. For insofar as problems have to be met jointly—problems, for example, of disarmament, energy, or population—the fact that government information cannot be trusted is crippling. Bona fide efforts in the joint interest are thus undercut by the cynicism and sense of powerlessness which result from the knowledge of large-scale deception.

Lies to enemies just because they are enemies, then, are sometimes especially excusable, but are weighted with very special dangers; dangers of bias, self-harm, proliferation, and severe injuries to trust. And the very claim that lies to enemies are especially excusable, by allowing so many lies to go unquestioned, ends up adding to much of the oppression and the crises which might otherwise be avoided. So many forces push in the direction of growing dishonesty in adversary relations. They can never be eliminated; but every effort must be made to hold them down.

Are there any special circumstances where lying to enemies becomes more excusable? Could the test of publicity help to weed out all the spurious or biased excuses, and all those where lies might backfire or cause harm to general trust, while preserving certain conditions where lies to enemies are justified? If so, what features of hostile relationships would mark these circumstances?

Rules of the Game

A public test would look, first of all, for alternatives. No matter how hostile or dangerous a person, dealing with him honestly will always be preferable to deceit. Secondly, encounters with enemies where there is a clear element of crisis must allow for deception, though with the same caution as in all other crises. Whenever it is right to resist an assault or a threat by force, it must then be allowable to do so by guile. But the criteria for who is to count as presenting such a threat must be publicly justifiable. In this way, deceiving a kidnapper can be distinguished from deceiving adversaries in business.[7]

Finally, even apart from such crises, a special case might be made for deception in lawful, *declared* hostilities, as against tax-evaders or counterfeiters, or between openly warring parties. Such open declarations lessen the probability of error and of purely personal spite, so long as they are open to questioning and requests for accountability. They do not, however, lessen the possibility of joint discrimination by members of a group or society, and ought therefore to function only in combination with a strong protection of civil rights. Given such protection, the more openly and clearly the adversaries, such as criminals, can be pinpointed, and the more justifiable, therefore, the criteria for regarding them as hostile, the more excusable will it be to lie to them if honesty is of no avail.

If the designation of a foe is open, as in a declaration of war, deception is likely to be expected on all sides. While it can hardly be said to be *consented* to, it is at least known and often acquiesced in. But the more secret the choice and pursuit of foes, the more corruptible the entire process, as all the secret police systems of the world testify. There is, then, no public control over who counts as an adversary nor over what can be done to him. The categories of enemies swell, and their treatment grows increasingly inhumane.

But even where the designation of the enemy is public, the nature of this publicity poses special problems. For who is to constitute the public? And how is its reasonableness and objectivity to be assured? With the growing mili-

tarization of the world have come increased po
brutal internal policing.[8] Obviously the fact that so
military junta or dictator publicly declares a group as
constituting enemies of the state does not satisfy the test
of publicity. And even if the majority of the people in a
society has been whipped into a frenzy of hostility, one
cannot speak of "publicity" in the sense in which it has
been used up to now in this book.

In principle, then, both deception and violence find a
narrow justification in self-defense against enemies. In
practice, however, neither can be contained within these
narrow boundaries; they end up growing, perpetuating
themselves, multiplying, and feeding on one another, to
produce the very opposite of increased safety. Constant
efforts must, therefore, be made to contain them and to
limit their scope.

The language of enmity and rivalry, as Hume indicated in the passage quoted at the beginning of this
chapter, is private language not suited to moral inquiry.
If we want to produce excuses for lying to someone, these
excuses should be capable of persuading reasonable persons, not merely some particular public locked in hostility
to a particular group. Entering into hostilities is, in a
sense, to give up the ability to shift perspectives. But even
those who give up the language of morality during a period of hostility and adopt that of strategy instead, may do
well to remember Mark Twain's words: "When in doubt,
tell the truth. It will confound your enemies and astound
your friends."

XI

LIES PROTECTING
PEERS AND CLIENTS

[. . .] it is obviously a most effective protection for legitimate secrets that it should be universally understood and expected that those who ask questions which they have no right to ask will have lies told to them;

—H. Sidgwick, *The Methods of Ethics*

It is only the cynic who claims "to speak the truth" at all times and in all places to all men in the same way but who, in fact, develops nothing but a lifeless image of the truth. He dons the halo of the fanatical devotee of truth who can make no allowance for human weaknesses; but, in fact, he is destroying the living truth between men. He wounds shame, desecrates mystery, breaks confidence, betrays the community in which he lives.

—Dietrich Bonhoeffer, "What is Meant by 'Telling the
Truth'?"

I don't see why we should not come out roundly and say that one of the functions of the lawyer is to lie for his client; and on rare occasions, as I think I have shown, I believe it is.

—Charles Curtis, "The Ethics of Advocacy"

> Here is a crime contemplated but not yet consummated, without malice, it is true, but nonetheless wilful, and from the basest and most sordid motives. The prospective victim is most often a pure young woman, confiding in the love and honor of the man who is about to do her this unspeakable wrong. [...] A single word [...] would save her from this terrible fate, yet the physician is fettered hand and foot by his cast-iron code, his tongue is silenced, he cannot lift a finger or utter a word to prevent this catastrophe.

So wrote a physician in 1904, to whom a syphilitic patient had announced his plan to marry without letting his fiancée know of his condition.[1] At a time when venereal disease could almost never be cured and was a subject so sensitive that prospective spouses could not discuss it, many a physician was confronted by an agonizing choice: whether to uphold his duty of honoring the confidences of patients, or to help an innocent future victim, whose health might otherwise be destroyed, and whose children could be born malformed or retarded. Physicians still face similar conflicts: should they reveal the recurring mental illness of patients soon to be married? Severe sexual problems? Progressively incapacitating genetic disease? One doctor recently wrote that he had seen many "impossible marriages" contracted because he could not violate his oath of professional secrecy.[2] To keep silent regarding a patient's confidences is to honor one of the oldest obligations in medicine. Lawyers do the same for their clients, as do priests in hearing confessions.

Silence is often sufficient to uphold this obligation. But sometimes the silence is so interpreted that the secret stands revealed thereby. What if the parents of the young girl became suspicious and asked the physician if there was anything to prevent their daughter's marriage to the young man? For the doctor merely to stammer that he cannot reveal confidences is to confirm their suspicions. A lie is the simplest way to protect the secret, though some have worked out subtle forms of evasion in answering unauthorized questions regarding a professional secret, such as: "I know nothing about it" (with the mental reservation "to communicate to others").[3]

Difficult choices arise for all those who have promised to keep secret what they have learned from a client, a patient, or a penitent.[4] How to deflect irate fathers asking whether their daughters are pregnant and by whom; how to answer an employer inquiring about the psychiatric record of someone on his staff; how to cope with questions from the press about the health of a congressional candidate: such predicaments grow more common than ever. The line between appropriate and inappropriate requests for information may shift from one society to another and be revised over time; but wherever the line is drawn, those charged with secrets have to decide how best to protect them.

A similar loyalty also shields colleagues. Politicians, for instance, or doctors or lawyers are reluctant to divulge the incompetence or dishonesty of their fellows. Once again, when silence would give the game away, lying is one alternative. Some choose it even when they know that innocent persons will thereby be injured—mutilated through a clumsy operation, or embroiled in a law suit that never should have begun.

Are there limits to this duty of secrecy? Was it ever meant to stretch so as to require lying? Where does it come from and why is it so binding that it can protect those who have no right to impose their incompetence, their disease, their malevolence on ignorant victims?

At stake is fidelity, keeping faith with those who have confided their secrets on condition that they not be revealed. Fidelity to clients and peers is rooted in the most primeval tribal emotions: the loyalty to self, kin, clansmen, guild members as against the more diffusely perceived rest of humanity—the unrelated, the outsiders, the barbarians. Defending one's own is the rule long before justice becomes an issue. It precedes law and morality itself. Allied to the drive for self-preservation, it helps assure collective survival in a hostile environment. To reveal the truth about a friend can then come to mean that one is a "false friend." And to be "true" to kin and clan can mean confronting the world on their behalf with every weapon at one's disposal, including every form of deceit.[5]

This drive to protect self and kin, friends and associates, persists even where moral rules and laws are recognized. Certain limits are then established: fraud and assault come to be circumscribed. But the limits are uncertain where these strong personal and professional bonds are present. And so lies to protect confidentiality come to be pitted against the restrictions on harming innocent persons. Practices, some legitimate, others shoddy, persist and grow behind the shield of confidentiality.

In order to distinguish between them, we have to ask: How is confidentiality itself defended? On what principles does it rest? And when, if ever, can those principles be stretched to justify lies in the protection of confidences?

Three separate claims are advanced in support of keeping secrets confidential. First, that we have a right to protect ourselves and those close to us from the harm that might flow from disclosure; second, that fairness requires respect for privacy; and third, that added respect is due for that which one has *promised* to keep secret.

The first claim appeals to the principle of avoiding harm. The lie to cover up for a friend, a client, a colleague may prevent injuries to their lives, even their liberty. The pilot whose heart condition is revealed may lose his job; the syphilitic fiancé may be jilted; the physician accused of malpractice may be convicted. Yet this appeal to principle obviously has its limits. To lie to avoid harm to the pilot or the fiancé can bring on greater harm, or more undeserved harm, to the passengers or the young woman about to marry. It is here that the perspective *within* a profession can be limiting; the bond of confidentiality can dim the perception of the suffering imposed on outsiders. This is especially true when it is not certain that any one person will be harmed—if a surgeon's addiction, say, means that one out of ten patients who would otherwise have lived die during operations.

The second claim invokes the right to privacy. Many requests for information are unwarranted and inherently unjust. To respond to them with silence or to turn them down is, then, to provide no more than what is due; but many are so perplexed or so frightened that they lie instead. Bonhoeffer relates such a case:

> [. . .] a teacher asks a child in front of the class whether it is true, that his father often comes home drunk. It is true, but the child denies it.[6]

In this category fall also all the illegitimate inquiries regarding political beliefs, sexual practices, or religious faith. In times of persecution, honest answers to such inquiries rob people of their freedom, their employment, respect in their communities. Refusing to give information that could blacklist a friend is then justified; and in cases where refusal is difficult or dangerous, lying may fall into the category of response to a crisis. One has a right to protect oneself and others from illegitimate inquiries, whether they come from intruders, from an oppressive government, or from an inquisitorial religious institution. A large area of each person's life is clearly his to keep as secret as he wishes. This is the region of *privacy*, of personal concerns and liberty not to be tampered with.

The delineation of this region of private concerns is today in considerable disarray. Should contraceptive choices, for example, or choices to abort, be protected? Should employers be able to give job seekers lie-detector tests? How can privacy be secured against unwarranted inroads? Each year, ever more records are kept by schools, psychiatrists, employers, probation officers, and by vast government and insurance computer systems. Investigators collect derogatory (or what happens to be thought derogatory at any one time) information, which is then sought by many more groups—prospective employers, the government, scholars doing research, and the press. Personal privacy is under constant pressure; and the lines between legitimate and illegitimate inquiries need continuous vigilance.

But is the young fiancé's syphilis properly in this region of his private concerns? Surely his future wife has a stake in learning about it. And surely a physician's drug addiction or alcoholism is more than his private affair, just as the guilt of the client on whose behalf the lawyer cooperates in perjury is not a matter of privacy alone.

The third claim in defense of confidentiality allows disclosure of secrets to prevent harm and to guard privacy, unless a promise has been made not to reveal the information in question. Even when confidentiality is not otherwise fair or beneficial, the argument runs, a promise can make it so. And even when ordinary promises might well be broken, professional ones to clients, to patients, or to those coming for confession, remain inviolate. When a confessor protects a secret, he may do what he would not do for those to whom he has made no promise of secrecy. This promise may exert such a strong pull as to override not only veracity alone and not only the desire to allow no harm to be done, but both together.

What is it, then, about promises, that endows them with such power? In the first place, in making a promise, I set up expectations, an equilibrium; should I break my promise, I upset that equilibrium and fail to live up to those expectations; I am unfair, given what I had promised and what I now owe to another. Second, in breaking faith, I am failing to make my promise *come true.** If I make a promise, knowing I shall break it, I am lying. Third, professional promises to clients are granted special inviolability so that those who most need help will feel free to seek it. Without a social policy allowing the protection of such secrets, people might not confide in lawyers or clergy. In this way, many would fail to benefit from legitimate means to help them.

But even this appeal to the sanctity of promises must surely have its limits. We can properly promise only what is ours to give or what it is right for us to do in the first place. Having made a promise adds no justification at all to an undertaking to do something that is in itself wrong. Here again, the question which must be asked of the deceptive practices shielded by confidentiality is what, exactly, *can* be thought of as rightly having been promised to clients and peers. The three claims made for confidentiality must be kept separate, then, as we look at practices of professional confidentiality to clients and to colleagues. When they are not seen clearly, their limits grow dim; the rhetoric of loyalty may then take over, expanding those limits to include what was never meant to be protected by confidentiality. Or else the reverse may happen, so that the region of privacy shrinks in the face of unwarranted inquiries.

*Many philosophers have regarded promise-keeping as revealing the truth about what one promised. This would make promises one part of veracity. Others, such as Ross, have looked at veracity as part of promise-keeping: as a "general undertaking to tell the truth"—a promise of a kind. But all see the two as closely connected.

Fidelity to Colleagues

Is it ever right to lie to cover up for colleagues who are exposing innocent persons to risk? colleagues who through addiction, accident, or illness, have been unable to do their work properly? Those who work with mine operators, pilots, surgeons, and military commanders may have to choose between lies and truth, between silence and speaking out.

To protect one's colleagues is natural; the relationship of those who work together can be very close, and the bonds that join them as close as brotherhood. Professional codes often enjoin colleagues to treat each other as brothers. (The Hippocratic Oath requires doctors to swear to "hold my teacher in this art as equal to my own parents [...] and to consider his family as my own brothers." And the World Health Organization [WHO] reformulation of the Oath in 1948 states simply that "my colleagues will be as my brothers.")

Such a sense of kinship imposes special bonds. The ideal of brotherhood extends and deepens that of equality among blood brothers.* Brothers ideally share and share alike, face hardships together, divide their gains, cover up for one another, look after each other's families. In medicine, where these bonds have the longest professional tradition, doctors treat family members of other doctors free of charge; they avoid overt competition for patients; and they protect each other when necessary against censure from the outside world. The relationship established in learning the art of medicine creates a debt to the entire profession. But how far should this debt be carried? At what cost to society should colleagues—usually the first to

*It sets limits to equal treatment, on the other hand, vis-à-vis non-brothers.

know when one of their own places innocent persons at risk—avoid the exposure of a sick or incompetent fellow professional? At what point does it become their responsibility to stop covering up, perhaps even to disclose the risk to those who most need to know them?

Current codes of ethics require, in principle, that physicians do just that. Thus, Section 4 of the American Medical Association's (A.M.A.) Principles of Medical Ethics holds:

> The medical profession should safeguard the public and itself against physicians deficient in moral character or professional competence. Physicians should observe all laws, uphold the dignity and honor of the profession, and accept its self-imposed disciplines. They should expose, without hesitation, illegal or unethical conduct of fellow members of the profession.[7]

Yet in practice such exposure is extremely rare. Between three percent and five percent of physicians in the United States are estimated to be incompetent, whether because of debilitating illness, addiction, or lack of proper training. There are, therefore, over 10,000 physicians in that category just in the United States.[8] Yet fewer than one hundred physicians are deprived of their licenses each year. And when patients bring suits for malpractice, a "conspiracy of silence" puts immense pressure on physicians not to testify against their peers. The pressure is increased by the substantial risk that by testifying on behalf of a plaintiff, physicians may have their malpractice insurance policies cancelled.[9] Not only are cases of exposure rare, but lies and coverups keep *others* from acquiring information which might lead to exposure.

Questions of deception must have posed painful conflicts for the colleagues of Cyril and Stewart Marcus, two well-known, talented gynecologists with brilliant academic careers and prospering practices in New York, who died of barbiturate abuse in 1975. Slowly they had deteriorated physically while keeping up respected and lucrative careers. They had grown irrational, unable to perform the operations which they scheduled for their patients. They looked emaciated; their behavior was erratic and bewildering. At one time, one of them took the place of the other at the operating table without first informing either the patient or those assisting. Only two weeks before their death were they relieved of their practice at the hospital where they worked. Until then, their colleagues had agonized over how to deal with the problem they presented for the hospital. And even thereafter they were free to continue to see their patients.

Or consider the choices which must have confronted colleagues in the following case:

> ———, a Sacramento, California orthopedist has millions of dollars in malpractice judgments against him, has admitted under oath that he performed complicated and dangerous spinal surgery when it was unnecessary, and still has numerous suits pending against him involving patients left crippled or paralyzed. Several news reports confirm that colleagues lied for him, intervened at the operating table to keep him from botching delicate procedures, and, on occasion, performed follow-up operations to repair damage he caused, all without taking any action to restrict his further practice. When at long last his colleagues voted to restrict his hospital privileges, they did it so quietly that he simply continued to work at another hospital in the same town.[10]

There can be no excuse for lying to protect anyone who places patients at such risk. And only an overwhelming blindness to the suffering of those beyond one's immediate sphere can lead colleagues simply to oust an incompetent and dangerous surgeon from their own hospital so quietly that he can continue his "work" at another.

No complicated moral dilemmas exist in such extreme cases. Professional loyalty is clearly outweighed by the duty to prevent grievous harm. The very idea of asking what a reasonable person might think about such lies suffices to demonstrate how unacceptable they are. The problem here is one of practical application: How can the cover-up in such cases be broken before great injury has been wrought? And what are the alternatives for colleagues who want to prevent injury to patients while trying to help their own? Can the sick colleague be assigned to no-risk work while he is given support and therapy?

Moral dilemmas arise more often in the much more numerous borderline cases. What about colleagues who are not brutally incompetent, but merely mediocre? What about those who have made serious mistakes that might not recur?[11] What about entire hospitals where lack of training or equipment subjects patients to substantially greater risk than others? Ought patients to learn that with some individuals or in some institutions, their chances of recovery are, say, cut in half? If they ask, should they receive an honest answer?

No one likes to be an informer and to destroy a reputation or a career, perhaps even mistakenly. One cannot always be certain of one's suspicions; and in order to support them with clear evidence, steps may be required that few are willing to take. If the hospital environment became one where health professionals watched one another, informed on one another, the long-range repercussions, even for patients, might be undesirable. It is easy to sympathize, too, even where evidence is at hand, with the hesitation to use it, the fear of seeming to expose a friend, the hope that he will perhaps improve or recover if only given time. All can imagine finding themselves in a similar predicament, and needing, then, the support and protection of colleagues. They may also fear, finally, severe retribution should they undertake to expose one of their own. They may well be engaged in a risky law suit; and all manner of things can begin to go wrong more generally for those who betray the collectivity.

The problems for patients are equally severe. For while alcoholism and related conditions afflict persons in every walk of life, they cause the disabled physician to be especially dangerous. People can deteriorate in many kinds of work; but the effects, while serious in the long run, will rarely be as catastrophic for innocent victims as when a false diagnosis is made, the wrong medication prescribed, or incompetent surgery performed.

It is time for health professionals and the public to look closely at the threat which incompetence poses in certain walks of life and at the conflicts between loyalty and responsibility which then arise. Without such cooperation, the fear of abuses will merely lead to more litigation and so in turn to more defensive measures taken by medical professionals. Trust will continue to dwindle as it has in the last few decades.

Measures will have to be worked out, instead, which merit trust, while neither needlessly destroying careers nor endangering the relationships among health professionals beyond the breaking point. First of all, existing licensing bodies must be given sufficient funds, personnel, and support to do their work of protecting the public adequately. Second, ways must be found to place those who are unable to do certain kinds of risky work in other positions where they do no harm while receiving all the support which professionals *ought* to give to one another. Third, the regular testing procedures which some professionals, such as airline pilots, undergo ought to be instituted for all those who, in their daily work, would place individuals at risk should they no longer be competent.

Such measures would take the pressure off those who are in daily contact with the persons who place others at risk. There would then be fewer times when they would be torn between loyalty to their colleague and concern for others. But when those occasions do arise, then lying to cover up must be seen for what it is: taking on a shared responsibility for the malfeasance. In the end, such lies do not even serve the long-range interests of the person for whom they are told. It is no real act of brotherhood or help to a colleague in need to allow him, through one's lies, to get more and more deeply into trouble and have ever greater suffering on his conscience.

Fidelity to Clients

The relationship between a lawyer and his client is one of the intimate relations. You would lie for your wife. You would lie for your child. There are others with whom you are intimate enough, close enough, to lie for them when you would not lie for yourself. At what point do you stop lying for them? I don't know and you are not sure.

This statement by Charles Curtis, a well-known Boston lawyer, has stirred up much discussion and some censure.[12] Are there persons for whom one would lie when one would not lie for oneself? And why should there be such a difference? The same questions have arisen for clergymen and physicians who protect the secrets of their parishioners or patients. At stake here is not the protection of colleagues; it is the defense, thought more legitimate, of information given by clients to professionals in strictest confidence.

Most would agree with Curtis that the relationship between professional and client, like that between husband and wife, requires that certain secrets be protected. But few have come out in public to stretch that privilege so far as to include lying. Curtis himself drew the line at lying in court. More recently, however, Monroe Freedman, Dean of Hofstra Law School and author of a well-known book on legal ethics, has advocated some forms of deception even in the courtroom:

. . . the criminal defense attorney, however unwillingly in terms of personal morality, has a professional responsibility as an advocate in an adversary system to examine the perjurious client in the ordinary way and to argue to the jury, as evidence in the case, the testimony presented by the defendant.[13]

If, that is, a lawyer has a client who lies to the court and thus commits perjury, Professor Freedman holds that this defense lawyer has the professional responsibility to ask questions which do not contest this testimony and even to use the false testimony in making the best case for the client to the court officers and the jury. That this can involve lying is beyond doubt. Nor is there serious doubt that such instances are not rare in actual practice. Yet lying in court has traditionally been more abhorred than other lying. How is it, then, that it has come to be thus defended, albeit by a minority of commentators? Defended, moreover, not just as a regrettable practice at times excusable, but actually as a *professional responsibility*?

One reason, once again, lies in the tribal ethic of avoiding harm to oneself and one's own. But it is often supported by an argument upholding the overriding strength of the privilege of confidentiality whenever a client gives information in confidence. Such a privilege is often thought to need no justification. Lawyers see it as so manifestly different from the shadier privileges claimed through the ages, ranging from the feudal sexual privilege to the excesses of "executive privilege," as to require no defense.

And yet, if we are to understand whether it *should* absolve lying in court, we must ask: What underlies the special claim of this privilege of confidentiality? Lawyers advance three arguments to support it. They argue, first, that even the most hardened criminal has a right to advice, help, and skilled advocacy; the right to a person loyal to him in particular. Fairness demands that his concerns be given a hearing; but he can convey his predicament honestly only if he is assured that his confidence will not be betrayed.

We can accept this argument and still not see why it should be stretched to justify lies. The assumption that the privilege can be thus stretched goes counter to the long tradition barring false witness, and the very special proscription of perjury. In the Jewish and Christian traditions, for example, false witness and perjury are the most serious forms of deception, inviting the most dire punishment. And a number of distinctions relevant to the dilemmas for contemporary lawyers have been worked out in some detail. Look, for example, at the ninth-century Penitential of Cummean:

> 8. He who makes a false oath shall do penance for four years.
> 9. But he who leads another in ignorance to commit perjury shall do penance for seven years.
> 10. He who is led in ignorance to commit perjury and afterward finds it out, one year.
> 11. He who suspects that he is being led into perjury and nevertheless swears, shall do penance for two years, on account of his consent.[14]

A second argument for confidentiality goes beyond the individual client's rights. It holds that not only should we all be able to expect discretion from our lawyers, but that the social system as a whole will benefit if confidences can be kept. Otherwise, clients may not dare to reveal their secrets to their lawyers, who, in turn, will not be able to present their cases adequately. Even though injustice may result in individual cases when a zealous lawyer succeeds in concealing a client's misdeeds in court, the general level of justice will be raised, it is claimed, if clients can trust their lawyers to keep their secrets. For some, this argument stretches, once again, all the way to lying in court. And, once more, they adduce no further argument for so enlarging the principle.[15]

Such arguments are often cemented, finally, by an appeal to the principle of veracity. Veracity itself will be advanced, many argue, if each side pushes as hard as it can to defeat the other. In the "adversary system of justice," truth is held to be more likely to emerge as a result of the contest between opposing forces if the accused is both defended and prosecuted "zealously within the bounds of the law."[16] The adversary system is often contrasted by its supporters to the "inquisitorial system of law," wherein the state itself inquires into all the facts before bringing a trial.[17] In a sense, those who advocate building on perjurious testimony in court then claim that lies can be a mechanism for producing truth. Yet this claim has never, to my knowledge, been empirically established. There is no reason why it could not be experimentally tested, in simulated court situations, for example. In the meantime, it seems self-contradictory to press it to the point of saying that truth will be advanced if we loosen the restrictions on perjury in court.

How, then, can these claims be evaluated? The strain on lawyers within the adversary system becomes evident precisely at this point—where the principle of confidentiality collides with the necessity to stay "within the bounds of the law."

The task of evaluating these claims is hampered by the fact that they have received little genuine inquiry recently within the legal profession, and even less outside it. Those who take up the question, in courses and textbooks on professional responsibility, of what lawyers in today's courts should do give no references to the debates on such issues in moral philosophy and in theology; nor do they refer students and practitioners to authors within the legal profession itself who have confronted these questions, such as Grotius and Pufendorf.[18] This, in turn, is perhaps not to be wondered at, since philosophers themselves have paid little attention to such issues in the last few centuries.

But historical and professional insularity has dangers. It impoverishes; it leads to a vacuum of genuine analysis. Thus, one recent textbook on the professional responsibility of lawyers holds merely:

> There is simply no consensus, for example, as to the lawyer's duty to the court if he knows his client is lying. In that and other situations a lawyer can only be sensitive to the issues involved and resolve these difficult cases as responsibly as he or she is able.[19]

Closer to throwing up one's hands one cannot get. To leave such choice open to the sensitive and the responsible without giving them criteria for choice is to leave it open as well to the insensitive and the corrupt.[20] References to responsibility and sensitivity are made to take the place of analysis and broader inquiry.

The problem here, as with many other deceptive professional practices, is that the questions are too often left up to the professionals themselves, whereas the issues obviously touch the *public* welfare intimately. There is, then, a great need for a wider debate and analysis of these issues. When does the privilege of confidentiality exceed the boundaries of the law? When does the promise on which confidentiality is based turn out to be itself illegitimate? Do we want a society where lawyers can implicitly promise to guard their clients' secrets through perjury and lies? Such a debate would have to go far beyond the confines of the American Bar Association and the teaching of professional responsibility in law schools.

If the public were to enter such a debate, it is much more likely that we should see the concerns central to this book come to the foreground: concerns for the consequences of a professional *practice* and on those engaging in it, their peers, the system of justice and society at large; concerns for the ways in which such practices spread, and for the added institutional damage which then results.

The slope here is very slippery indeed. For if some lies

in court to protect a client's confidences are all right, why not others? If the lawyer is sole judge of what is a tolerable lie, what criteria will he use? Will there not be pressure to include other lies, ostensibly also to protect the client's confidence? And if lawyers become *used* to accepting certain lies, how will this affect their integrity in other areas?

One effect of a public debate of these questions would inevitably be increased knowledge about deceptive professional practices in the law. And it can be argued that this knowledge ought then to be shared with all who participate in trials—most especially judges and juries. Should juries perhaps then be instructed to take into account the fact that a number of lawyers believe it their right to build upon perjured testimony?

It is clear that even those lawyers willing to support such a right for themselves would not wish juries to be thus instructed. But if they ask themselves why, they may come to see their own behavior in a different perspective. The most important reasons they might advance showing why juries should not have such knowledge are that it should remain easy to mislead them, that their trust in the legal profession and in courtroom procedures should remain whole. More than that, once forewarned, any juror with even minimal sense would then have to be quite suspicious about every *other* possible form of deception on the part of lawyers.

Imagining such instructions to the jury shows, I believe, that those who wish to tell lies in court, even for the best of motives, cannot expose these motives to the light of publicity. They want to participate in a practice but not have it generally known that they do.

Can it be argued that such lies are so common by now that they form an accepted practice that everyone knows about—much like a game or bargaining in a bazaar? But in that case, why should lawyers feel so uncomfortable at the prospect of instructing the jury about the practice? The fact is that, even though lawyers may know about such a practice, it is not publicly known, especially to jurors, much less consented to.

I believe, therefore, that a public inquiry into the appropriateness of lying in court on behalf of perjurious clients would lead to a perception that there are limits to acceptable advocacy in court. And these limits, moreover, are not different because of the lawyer-client relationship. That relationship, with its privilege of confidentiality, does not in itself justify lying for clients. At the very least, the limits set would have to exclude actual presentation of perjury by lawyers as well as the more circuitous ways of building upon a client's perjury. Lawyers themselves might well be grateful for the standards to be publicly discussed and openly established. They could then more easily resist pressure from clients and resolve to their own satisfaction what might otherwise seem to present them with a confusing conflict of personal and professional principle.

Once again, what is needed is the ability to shift perspectives and to see not only the needs that press for perjury and lying, but the effect that such practices have upon the deceived and social trust. Judge Marvin E. Frankel describes thus such a shift:

> [. . .] our adversary system rates truth too low among the values that institutions of justice are meant to serve. [. . .] [O]ur more or less typical lawyer selected as a trial judge experiences a dramatic change in perspective as he moves to the other side of the bench.[21]

XII

LIES FOR THE
PUBLIC GOOD

"How then," said I, "might we contrive one of those opportune falsehoods of which we were just now speaking, so as by one noble lie to persuade if possible the rulers themselves, but failing that the rest of the city?"

[. . .] "While all of you are brothers," we will say, "yet God in fashioning those of you who are fitted to hold rule mingled gold in their generation, for which reason they are most precious—but in their helpers silver and iron and brass in the farmers and other craftsmen."

[. . .] "Do you see any way of getting them to believe this tale?" "No, not these themselves," he said, "but I do, their sons and successors and the rest of mankind who come after." "Well," said I, "even that would have a good effect in making them more inclined to care for the state and one another."

—Plato, *The Republic*

HUGO   And do you think the living will agree to your schemes?

HOEDERER We'll get them to swallow them little by little.

HUGO   By lying to them?

HOEDERER By lying to them sometimes.

. . . .

HOEDERER I'll lie when I must, and I have contempt for no one. I wasn't the one who invented lying. It grew out of a society divided into classes, and each one of us has inherited it from birth. We shall not abolish lying by refusing to tell lies, but by using every means at hand to abolish classes.

—Jean-Paul Sartre, *Dirty Hands*

The Noble Lie

In earlier chapters three circumstances have seemed to liars to provide the strongest excuse for their behavior—a crisis where overwhelming harm can be averted only through deceit; complete harmlessness and triviality to the point where it seems absurd to quibble about whether a lie has been told; and the duty to particular individuals to protect their secrets. I have shown how lies in times of crisis can expand into vast practices where the harm to be averted is less obvious and the crisis less and less immediate; how white lies can shade into equally vast practices no longer so harmless, with immense cumulative costs; and how lies to protect individuals and to cover up their secrets can be told for increasingly dubious purposes to the detriment of all.

When these three expanding streams flow together and mingle with yet another—a desire to advance the public good—they form the most dangerous body of deceit of all. These lies may not be justified by an immediate crisis nor by complete triviality nor by duty to any one person; rather, liars tend to consider them as right and unavoidable because of the altruism that motivates them. I want, in this chapter and the next, to turn to this far-flung category.

Naturally, there will be large areas of overlap between these lies and those considered earlier. But the most characteristic defense for these lies is a separate one, based on the benefits they may confer and the long-range harm they can avoid. The intention may be broadly paternalistic, as when citizens are deceived "for their own good," or only a few may be lied to for the benefit of the community at large. Error and self-deception mingle with these altruistic purposes and blur them; the filters through which we must try to peer at lying are thicker and more distorting than ever in these practices. But I shall try to single out, among these lies, the elements that are consciously and purposely intended to benefit society.

A long tradition in political philosophy endorses some lies for the sake of the public. Plato, in the passage quoted at the head of this chapter first used the expression "noble lie" for the fanciful story that might be told to people in order to persuade them to accept class distinctions and thereby safeguard social harmony. According to this story, God Himself mingled gold, silver, iron, and brass in fashioning rulers, auxiliaries, farmers, and craftsmen, intending these groups for separate tasks in a harmonious hierarchy.

The Greek adjective which Plato used to characterize this falsehood expresses a most important fact about lies by those in power: this adjective is *"gennaion,"* which means "noble" in the sense of both "high-minded" and "well-bred."[1] The same assumption of nobility, good breeding, and superiority to those deceived is also present in Disraeli's statement that a gentleman is one who knows when to tell the truth and when not to. In other words, lying is excusable when undertaken for "noble" ends by those trained to discern these purposes.

Rulers, both temporal and spiritual, have seen their deceits in the benign light of such social purposes. They have propagated and maintained myths, played on the gullibility of the ignorant, and sought stability in shared beliefs. They have seen themselves as high-minded and well-bred—whether by birth or by training—and as superior to those they deceive. Some have gone so far as to claim that those who govern have a *right* to lie.[2] The powerful tell lies believing that they have greater than ordinary understanding of what is at stake; very often, they regard their dupes as having inadequate judgment, or as likely to respond in the wrong way to truthful information.

At times, those who govern also regard particular circumstances as too uncomfortable, too painful, for most people to be able to cope with rationally. They may believe, for instance, that their country must prepare for long-term challenges of great importance, such as a war, an epidemic, or a belt-tightening in the face of future shortages. Yet they may fear that citizens will be able to respond only to short-range dangers. Deception at such times may seem to the government leaders as the only means of attaining the necessary results.

The perspective of the liar is paramount in all such decisions to tell "noble" lies. If the liar considers the responses of the deceived at all, he assumes that they will, once the deceit comes to light and its benefits are understood, be uncomplaining if not positively grateful. The lies are often seen as necessary merely at one *stage* in the education of the public. Thus Erasmus, in commenting on Plato's views, wrote:

> [. . .][H]e sets forth deceitful fictions for the rabble, so that the people might not set fire to the magistracy, and similar falsifications by which the crass multitude is deceived in its own interest, in the same way that parents deceive children and doctors the sick.
> [. . .]Thus for the crass multitude there is need of temporary promises, figures, allegories, parables [. . .] so that little by little they might advance to loftier things.[3]

Some experienced public officials are impatient with any effort to question the ethics of such deceptive practices (except actions obviously taken for private ends). They argue that vital objectives in the national interest require a measure of deception to succeed in the face of powerful obstacles. Negotiations must be carried on that are best left hidden from public view; bargains must be struck that simply cannot be comprehended by a politically unsophisticated electorate. A certain amount of illusion is needed in order for public servants to be effective. Every government, therefore, has to deceive people to some extent in order to lead them.

These officials view the public's concern for ethics as understandable but hardly realistic. Such "moralistic" concerns, put forth without any understanding of practical exigencies, may lead to the setting of impossible standards; these could seriously hamper work without actually changing the underlying practices. Government officials could then feel so beleaguered that some of them might quit their jobs; inefficiency and incompetence would then increasingly afflict the work of the rest.

If we assume the perspective of the deceived—those who experience the consequences of government deception—such arguments are not persuasive. We cannot take for granted either the altruism or the good judgment of those who lie to us, no matter how much they intend to benefit us. We have learned that much deceit for private gain masquerades as being in the public interest. We know how deception, even for the most unselfish motive, corrupts and spreads. And we have lived through the consequences of lies told for what were believed to be noble purposes.

Equally unpersuasive is the argument that there always has been government deception, and always will be, and that efforts to draw lines and set standards are therefore useless annoyances. It is certainly true that deception can never be completely absent from most human practices. But there are great differences among societies in the kinds of deceit that exist and the extent to which they are practiced, differences also among individuals in the same government and among successive governments within the same society. This strongly suggests that it is worthwhile trying to discover why such differences exist and to seek ways of raising the standards of truthfulness.

The argument that those who raise moral concerns are ignorant of political realities, finally, ought to lead, not to a dismissal of such inquiries, but to a more articulate description of what these realities are, so that a more careful and informed debate could begin. We have every reason to regard government as more profoundly injured by a dismissal of criticism and a failure to consider standards than by efforts to discuss them openly. If duplicity is to be allowed in exceptional cases, the criteria for these exceptions should themselves be openly debated and publicly chosen. Otherwise government leaders will have free rein to manipulate and distort the facts and thus escape accountability to the public.

The effort to question political deception cannot be ruled out so summarily. The disparagement of inquiries into such practices has to be seen as the defense of unwarranted power—power bypassing the consent of the governed. In the pages to come I shall take up just a few cases to illustrate both the clear breaches of trust that no group of citizens could desire, and circumstances where it is more difficult to render a judgment.

Examples of Political Deception

In September 1964, a State Department official, reflecting a growing administration consensus, wrote a memorandum advocating a momentous deceit of the American public.[4] He outlined possible courses of action to cope with the deteriorating military situation in South Vietnam. These included a stepping up of American participation in the "pacification" in South Vietnam and a "crescendo" of military action against North Vietnam, involving heavy bombing by the United States. But an election campaign was going on; the President's Republican opponent, Senator Goldwater, was suspected by the electorate of favoring escalation of the war in Vietnam and of brandishing nuclear threats to the communist world. In keeping with President Johnson's efforts to portray Senator Goldwater as an irresponsible war hawk, the memorandum ended with a paragraph entitled "Special considerations during the next two months," holding that:

> During the next two months, because of the lack of "rebuttal time" before election to justify particular actions which may be distorted to the U.S. public, we must act with special care—signaling to . . . [the South Vietnamese] that we are behaving energetically despite the restraints of our political season, and to the U.S. public that we are behaving with good purpose and restraint.

As the campaign wore on, President Johnson increasingly professed to be the candidate of peace. He gave no indication of the growing pressure for escalation from high administrative officials who would remain in office should he win; no hint of the hard choice he knew he would face if reelected.[5] Rather he repeated over and over again that:

> [T]he first responsibility, the only real issue in this campaign, the only thing you ought to be concerned about at all, is: Who can best keep the peace?[6]

The stratagem succeeded; the election was won; the war escalated. Under the name of Operation Rolling Thunder, the United States launched massive bombing raids over North Vietnam early in 1965. In suppressing genuine debate about these plans during the election campaign and masquerading as the party of peace, government members privy to the maneuver believed that they knew what was best for the country and that history would vindicate them. They meant to benefit the nation and the world by keeping the danger of a communist victory at bay. If a sense of *crisis* was needed for added justification, the Domino Theory strained for it: one regime after another was seen as toppling should the first domino be pushed over.

But why the deceit, if the purposes were so altruistic? Why not espouse these purposes openly before the election? The reason must have been that the government could not count on popular support for the scheme. In the first place, the sense of crisis and threat from North Vietnam would have been far from universally shared. To be forthright about the likelihood of escalation might lose many votes; it certainly could not fit with the campaign to portray President Johnson as the candidate most likely to keep the peace. Second, the government feared that its explanations might be "distorted" in the election campaign, so that the voters would not have the correct information before them. Third, time was lacking for the government to make an effort at educating the people about all that was at issue. Finally, the plans were not definitive; changes were possible, and the Vietnamese situation itself very unstable. For all these reasons, it seemed best to campaign for negotiation and restraint and let the Republican opponent be the target for the fear of United States belligerence.

President Johnson thus denied the electorate any chance to give or to refuse consent to the escalation of the war in Vietnam. Believing they had voted for the candidate of peace, American citizens were, within months, deeply embroiled in one of the cruelest wars in their history. Deception of this kind strikes at the very essence of democratic government. It allows those in power to override or nullify the right vested in the people to cast an informed vote in critical elections. Deceiving the people for the sake of the people is a self-contradictory notion in a democracy, unless it can be shown that there has been genuine consent to deceit. The actions of President Johnson were therefore inconsistent with the most basic principle of our political system.

What if all governments felt similarly free to deceive provided they believed the deception genuinely necessary to achieve some important public end? The trouble is that those who make such calculations are always susceptible to bias. They overestimate the likelihood that the benefit will occur and that the harm will be averted; they underestimate the chances that the deceit will be discovered and ignore the effects of such a discovery on trust; they underrate the comprehension of the deceived citizens, as well as their ability and their right to make a reasoned choice. And, most important, such a benevolent self-righteousness disguises the many motives for political lying which could *not* serve as moral excuses: the need to cover up past mistakes; the vindictiveness; the desire to stay in power. These self-serving ends provide the impetus for countless lies that are rationalized as "necessary" for the public good.

As political leaders become accustomed to making such excuses, they grow insensitive to fairness and to veracity. Some come to believe that any lie can be told so long as they can convince themselves that people will be better off in the long run. From there, it is a short step to the conclusion that, even if people will not be better off from a particular lie, they will benefit by all maneuvers to keep the right people in office. Once public servants lose their bearings in this way, all the shabby deceits of Watergate—the fake telegrams, the erased tapes, the elaborate cover-ups, the bribing of witnesses to make them lie, the televised pleas for trust—become possible.

While Watergate may be unusual in its scope, most observers would agree that deception is part and parcel of many everyday decisions in government. Statistics may be presented in such a way as to diminish the gravity of embarrassing problems. Civil servants may lie to members of Congress in order to protect programs they judge important, or to guard secrets they have been ordered not to divulge. If asked, members of Congress who make deals with one another to vote for measures they would otherwise oppose deny having made such deals. False rumors may be leaked by subordinates who believe that unwise executive action is about to be taken. Or the leak may be correct, but falsely attributed in order to protect the source.

Consider the following situation and imagine all the variations on this theme being played in campaigns all over the United States, at the local, state, or federal level:

A big-city mayor is running for reelection. He has read a report recommending that he remove rent controls after his reelection. He intends to do so, but believes he will lose the election if his intention is known. When asked, at a news conference two days before his election, about the existence of such a report, he denies knowledge of it and reaffirms his strong support of rent control.

In the mayor's view, his reelection is very much in the public interest, and the lie concerns questions which he believes the voters are unable to evaluate properly, especially on such short notice. In all similar situations, the sizable bias resulting from the self-serving element (the desire to be elected, to stay in office, to exercise power) is often clearer to onlookers than to the liars themselves. This bias inflates the alleged justifications for the lie—the worthiness, superiority, altruism of the liar, the rightness of his cause, and the inability of those deceived to respond "appropriately" to hearing the truth.

These common lies are now so widely suspected that voters are at a loss to know when they can and cannot believe what a candidate says in campaigning. The damage to trust has been immense. I have already referred to the poll which found 69 percent of Americans agreeing, both in 1975 and 1976, that the country's leaders had consistently lied to the American people over the past ten years. Over 40 percent of the respondents also agreed that:

> Most politicians are so similar that it doesn't really make much difference who gets elected.[7]

Many refuse to vote under such circumstances. Others look to appearance or to personality factors for clues as to which candidate might be more honest than the others. Voters and candidates alike are the losers when a political system has reached such a low level of trust. Once elected, officials find that their warnings and their calls to common sacrifice meet with disbelief and apathy, even when cooperation is most urgently needed. Law suits and investigations multiply. And the fact that candidates, should they win, are not expected to have meant what they said while campaigning, nor held accountable for discrepancies, only reinforces the incentives for them to bend the truth the next time, thus adding further to the distrust of the voters.

Political lies, so often assumed to be trivial by those who tell them, rarely are. They cannot be trivial when they affect so many people and when they are so peculiarly likely to be imitated, used to retaliate, and spread from a few to many. When political representatives or entire governments arrogate to themselves the right to lie, they take power from the public that would not have been given up voluntarily.

Deception and Consent

Can there be exceptions to the well-founded distrust of deception in public life? Are there times when the public itself might truly not care about possible lies, or might even prefer to be deceived? Are some white lies so trivial or so transparent that they can be ignored? And can we envisage public discussion of more seriously misleading government statements such that reasonable persons could consent to them in advance?

White lies, first of all, are as common to political and diplomatic affairs as they are to the private lives of most people. Feigning enjoyment of an embassy gathering or a political rally, toasting the longevity of a dubious regime or an unimpressive candidate for office—these are forms of politeness that mislead few. It is difficult to regard them as threats to either individuals or communities. As with all white lies, however, the problem is that they spread so easily, and that lines are very hard to draw. Is it still a white lie for a secretary of state to announce that he is going to one country when in reality he travels to another? Or for a president to issue a "cover story" to the effect that a cold is forcing him to return to the White House, when in reality an international crisis made him cancel the rest of his campaign trip? Is it a white lie to issue a letter of praise for a public servant one has just fired? Given the vulnerability of public trust, it is never more important than in public life to keep the deceptive element of white lies to an absolute minimum, and to hold down the danger of their turning into more widespread deceitful practices.

A great deal of deception believed not only innocent but highly justified by public figures concerns their private lives. Information about their marriages, their children, their opinions about others—information about their personal plans and about their motives for personal decisions—all are theirs to keep private if they wish to do so. Refusing to give information under these circumstances is justifiable—but the right to withhold information is not the right to lie about it. Lying under such circumstances bodes ill for conduct in other matters.[*]

---

[*]A lie by an experienced adult in a position of authority about private matters that can be protected by a refusal to speak is therefore much

Certain additional forms of deception may be debated and authorized in advance by elected representatives of the public. The use of unmarked police cars to discourage speeding by drivers is an example of such a practice. Various forms of unannounced, sometimes covert, auditing of business and government operations are others. Whenever these practices are publicly regulated, they can be limited so that abuses are avoided. But they must be *openly* debated and agreed to in advance, with every precaution against abuses of privacy and the rights of individuals, and against the spread of such covert activities. It is not enough that a public official assumes that consent would be given to such practices.

Another type of deceit has no such consent in advance: the temporizing or the lie when truthful information at a particular *time* might do great damage. Say that a government is making careful plans for announcing the devaluation of its currency. If the news leaks out to some before it can be announced to all, unfair profits for speculators might result. Or take the decision to make sharp increases in taxes on imported goods in order to rescue a tottering economy. To announce the decision beforehand would lead to hoarding and to exactly the results that the taxes are meant to combat. Thus, government officials will typically seek to avoid any premature announcement and will refuse to comment if asked whether devaluation or higher taxes are imminent. At times, however, official spokesmen will go further and falsely deny that the actions in question will in fact take place.

Such lies may well be uttered in good faith in an effort to avoid harmful speculation and hoarding. Nevertheless, if false statements are made to the public only to be ex-

---

less excusable than a lie by the school child described by Bonhoeffer in Chapter XI: too frightened by the bullying teacher to be able to stand up to him or think of a non-deceptive "way out" on the spur of the moment.

posed as soon as the devaluation or the new tax is announced, great damage to trust will result. It is like telling a patient that an operation will be painless—the swifter the disproof, the more likely the loss of trust. In addition, these lies are subject to all the dangers of spread and mistake and deterioration of standards that accompany all deception.

For these reasons, it is far better to refuse comment than to lie in such situations. The objection may be made, however, that a refusal to comment will be interpreted by the press as tantamount to an admission that devaluation or higher taxes are very near. Such an objection has force only if a government has not already established credibility by letting it be known earlier that it would never comment on such matters, and by strictly adhering to this policy at all times. Since lies in these cases are so egregious, it is worth taking care to establish such credibility in advance, so that a refusal to comment is not taken as an invitation to monetary speculation.

Another form of deception takes place when the government regards the public as frightened, or hostile, and highly volatile. In order not to create a panic, information about early signs of an epidemic may be suppressed or distorted. And the lie to a mob seeking its victim is like lying to the murderer asking where the person he is pursuing has gone. It can be acknowledged and defended as soon as the threat is over. In such cases, one may at times be justified in withholding information; perhaps, on rare occasions, even in lying. But such cases are so rare that they hardly exist for practical purposes.

The fact that rare circumstances exist where the justification for government lying seems powerful creates a difficulty—these same excuses will often be made to serve a great many more purposes. For some governments or public officials, the information they wish to conceal is almost never of the requisite certainty, the time never the right one, and the public never sufficiently dispassionate.

For these reasons, it is hard to see how a practice of lying to the public about devaluation or changes in taxation or epidemics could be consented to in advance, and therefore justified.

Are there any exceptionally dangerous circumstances where the state of crisis is such as to justify lies to the public for its own protection? We have already discussed lying to enemies in an acute crisis. Sometimes the domestic public is then also deceived, at least temporarily, as in the case of the U-2 incident. Wherever there is a threat—from a future enemy, as before World War II, or from a shortage of energy—the temptation to draw upon the excuses for deceiving citizens is very strong. The government may sincerely doubt that the electorate is capable of making the immediate sacrifices needed to confront the growing danger. (Or one branch of the government may lack confidence in another, for similar reasons, as when the administration mistrusts Congress.) The public may seem too emotional, the time not yet ripe for disclosure. Are there crises so exceptional that deceptive strategies are justifiable?

Compare, for instance, what was said and left unsaid by two United States Presidents confronted by a popular unwillingness to enter a war: President Lyndon Johnson, in escalating the war in Vietnam, and President Franklin D. Roosevelt, in moving the country closer to participating in World War II, while making statements such as the following in his 1940 campaign to be reelected:

> I have said this before, but I shall say it again and again and again: Your boys are not going to be sent into any foreign wars.[8]

By the standards set forth in this chapter, President Johnson's covert escalation and his failure to consult the electorate concerning the undeclared war in Vietnam was clearly unjustifiable. Consent was bypassed; there was no immediate danger to the nation which could even begin to excuse deceiving the public in a national election on grounds of an acute crisis.

The crisis looming before World War II, on the other hand, was doubtless much greater. Certainly this case is a difficult one, and one on which reasonable persons might not be able to agree. The threat was unprecedented; the need for preparations and for support of allies great; yet the difficulties of alerting the American public seemed insuperable. Would this crisis, then, justify proceeding through deceit?

To consent even to such deception would, I believe, be to take a frightening step. Do we want to live in a society where public officials can resort to deceit and manipulation whenever they decide that an exceptional crisis has arisen? Would we not, on balance, prefer to run the risk of failing to rise to a crisis honestly explained to us, from which the government might have saved us through manipulation? And what protection from abuse do we foresee should we surrender this choice?

In considering answers to these questions, we must take into account more than the short-run effects of government manipulation. President Roosevelt's manner of bringing the American people to accept first the possibility, then the likelihood, of war was used as an example by those who wanted to justify President Johnson's acts of dissimulation. And these acts in turn were pointed to by those who resorted to so many forms of duplicity in the Nixon administration. Secrecy and deceit grew at least in part because of existing precedents.[9]

The consequences of spreading deception, alienation, and lack of trust could not have been documented for us more concretely than they have in the past decades. We have had a very vivid illustration of how lies undermine our political system. While deception under the circumstances confronting President Roosevelt may in hindsight be more excusable than much that followed, we could no more consent to it in advance than to all that came later.

Wherever lies to the public have become routine, then, very special safeguards should be required. The test of public justification of deceptive practices is more needed than ever. It will be a hard test to satisfy, the more so the more trust is invested in those who lie and the more power they wield. Those in government and other positions of trust should be held to the highest standards. Their lies are not ennobled by their positions; quite the contrary. Some lies—notably minor white lies and emergency lies rapidly acknowledged—may be more *excusable* than others, but only those deceptive practices which can be openly debated and consented to in advance are *justifiable* in a democracy.[10]

How rectify situation where public perception is that gov. leaders routinely lie?

XIII

DECEPTIVE
SOCIAL SCIENCE RESEARCH

The use of deception has become more and more extensive, and is now a commonplace and almost standard feature of social psychological experiments. Deception has been turned into a game, often played with great skill and virtuosity.

[. . .] I sometimes feel that we are training a generation of students who do not know that there is any other way of doing research in our field. [. . .] Our attitude seems to be that if you can deceive, why tell the truth?
—Herbert Kelman, "Human Use of Human Subjects: The Problem of Deception in Social Psychological Experiments"

Encouraging styles of research and intervention that involve lying to other human beings [. . .] tends to establish a corps of progressively calloused individuals, insulated from self-criticism and increasingly available for clients who can become outspokenly cynical in their manipulating of other human beings, individually and in the mass.
—Margaret Mead, "Research with Human Beings: A Model Derived from Anthropological Field Practice"

The behavioral researcher whose study might reduce violence or racism or sexism, but who refuses to do the study because it involves deception, has not solved an ethical problem but only traded it in for another.

—Robert Rosenthal, unpublished working paper for a conference on deception in research

Social Science Experimentation

In Stanley Milgram's obedience experiments, first performed at Yale in 1963, subjects were ostensibly recruited to take part in a study of memory. They were then duped into believing they were to be "teachers" in an experiment in which they would administer painful electric shocks of increasing strength to "learners" whenever the latter made mistakes. The so-called learners were actually actors who grunted, screamed, begged to be released from the experiment. As the subject-teachers administered what they thought was ever stronger punishment, they were observed to see whether they continued or protested, and what their reactions were. A large fraction of them were induced to give the highest range of shock, even when the pseudo-learners cried out that they feared a heart attack.

The responses of one subject are described as follows:

He began the experiment calmly, but became increasingly tense as the experiment proceeded. After administering the 150-volt shock, he began to address the experimenter in agitated tones:

(150 volts delivered.) "You want me to keep going?" (165 volts delivered.) "That guy is hollering in there. There's a lot of them here. He's liable to have a heart condition. You want me to go on?"

(180 volts delivered.) "He can't stand it! I'm not going to kill that man in there! You hear him hollering? He's hollering. He can't stand it. What if something happens to him?

I'm not going to get that man sick in there. He's hollering in there. You know what I mean? I mean I refuse to take responsibility. He's getting hurt in there. He's in there hollering. Too many left here. Geez, if he gets them wrong. There's too many of them left. I mean who is going to take responsibility if anything happens to that gentleman?"

(The experimenter accepts responsibility.) "All right." (195 volts delivered.) "You see he's hollering. Hear that? Gee, I don't know." (The experimenter says: "The experiment requires that you go on.") "I know it does, sir, but I mean—huh—he don't know what he's in for. He's up to 195 volts."

(210 volts delivered.)

(225 volts delivered.)

(240 volts delivered.) "Aw, no! You mean I've got to keep going up with the scale? No, sir. I'm not going to kill that man! I'm not going to give him 450 volts!" (The experimenter says: "The experiment requires that you go on.") "I know it does, but that man is hollering in there, sir."

Despite his numerous, agitated objections, which were constant accompaniments to his actions, the subject unfailingly obeyed the experimenter, proceeding to the highest shock level on the generator. He displayed a curious dissociation between word and action. Although at the verbal level he had resolved not to go on, his actions were fully in accord with the experimenter's commands. This subject did not want to shock the victim, and he found it an extremely disagreeable task, but he was unable to invent a response that would free him from E's authority.[1]

The results were quite unexpected. Even the investigators themselves had had no idea that such a high proportion of the subjects could be talked into causing what seemed to be great pain to their fellow human beings. Sixty-two percent of the subjects turned out to obey the experimenter's commands completely.

But along with the shock came a profound sense of unease. Human beings had been duped into revealing sides of themselves they would never voluntarily have exhibited. They had been used, manipulated, without consent. Was this a legitimate way to experiment? And could the worth of the results somehow be "balanced" against the discomfort they had felt, the knowledge about themselves they had gained?

At first, these questions were debated mostly among psychologists. But, in 1974, when Milgram's book on the subject reached the general public, the debate spread. Up to that time, deceptive research in the social sciences had not been urgently questioned. In medicine, on the other hand, such deception had been found to have a long and sometimes tragic history.[2] As a result, it is now carefully regulated in all biomedical research.[3] Subjects can take part in a study only after their consent has been obtained; and if the study employs deception, as when placebos are used, the subjects must have consented to it in advance. The question arose: Should such a rule not apply to *all* research with human beings?

In principle, the Federal regulations do apply to all research so long as there is risk for human subjects. In practice, however, behavioral research is treated very differently—witness the recently revised *Ethical Standards of Psychologists*, adopted in January 1977. These standards merely suggest that investigators obtain informed consent, but make explicit exceptions for those studies which "necessitate concealment or deception":

> d. Openness and honesty are essential characteristics of the relationship between investigator and research participant. When the methodological requirements of a study necessitate concealment or deception, the investigator is required to insure as soon as possible the participant's understanding of the reasons for this action and of a sufficient justification for the procedures employed.

> g. The ethical investigator protects participants from physical and mental discomfort, harm, and danger. If a risk of such consequences exists, the investigator is required to inform the participant of that fact, secure consent before

proceeding, and take all possible measures to minimize distress. A research procedure must not be used if it is likely to cause serious or lasting harm to a participant.[4]

The rudimentary nature of these requirements is striking. When investigators can persuade themselves that deception is for a good purpose and presents no harm, they can proceed with secrecy, disguises, and lies. The choice is up to them, not their dupes. So is the determination of what might harm or cause discomfort.

One reason why the Ethical Standards are so permissive is that genuine informed consent might interfere with many studies, for a great deal of research in the social sciences is, by its very nature, deceptive, especially in sociology and social psychology. A situation is in some way contrived; human responses are then observed and measured. If the subjects do not know what is being tested, or even, sometimes, that a test is going on, their responses will be more spontaneous.

Beginning with a few isolated deceptive studies early in this century, a veritable flood of such research is now pouring forth from universities, market research organizations, private scholarly groups, and governments. Its results are published in hundreds of journals around the world and taught to thousands of students. If sufficiently striking, these results are then publicized in the press and on television.

In one such inquiry, male undergraduates were falsely led to believe that they had been sexually aroused by photographs of men, and their responses to such information studied. In another, subjects were surreptitiously given LSD. In still others, persons who responded to questionnaires on sensitive issues, expressly stated to be anonymous, were traced through invisible codes on the envelopes. In many studies, the subjects are never approached for even a spurious consent to a deceptive study;

social scientists may infiltrate groups such as Alcoholics Anonymous or religious or political organizations; they may train children to accost passers-by and make believe they are lost; or they may stage some accident or assault complete with victim, fake blood, and debris, to measure "helping" behavior among bystanders.

What excuses are offered for this interference with the subjects' freedom of informed choice? Investigators appeal to two principles: producing benefits and avoiding harm. First, they hope that the research will produce important benefits: not only the general benefit of advancing human knowledge, but more specific social advantages, such as improved teaching techniques or the reduction of violence. The knowledge leading to their goals can often, they argue, be most conclusively demonstrated by means of deceptive experimentation. Thus one investigator explains that:

> A plausible cover story not only masks the experimenter's intention, it can also provide a setting which has great impact on the subject.[5]

According to the second claim, since many experiments are utterly harmless, it is a waste of time and energy to impose upon them the kind of requirements which biomedical experiments might well require. This harmlessness is attested in two ways. First, the review committee to which experiments are often submitted does have the right to reject harmful experiments. If an experiment is not rejected, it cannot carry much of a risk for subjects. And second, investigators often accept the burden of explaining the deception to subjects after the experiment is over and justifying their questionable actions. This explanation, often referred to as "debriefing," is believed to prevent abuse and to wipe out any lingering discomforts and anxieties. Why then, ask investigators, in the light of such guarantees, should people want the right to refuse an experiment certain to do them no lasting harm? And is it not unethical *not* to do such harmless experiments which might uncover knowledge we urgently need to have?

A. ALTERNATIVES

If the public could debate these issues, the very first question would be: Given the fact that any deceptive practice harms not only those lied to, but also liars and trust more generally, what alternatives to deceptive studies are there in the first place? This question is a troublesome one for social science investigators. Unlike the case of a crisis where a lie may be the last resort, experimentation itself can hardly be called a last resort, and deceptive experimentation even less. One alternative to seeking knowledge through lies to subjects is to forego the knowledge sought altogether; another is to seek it nonexperimentally, through studying records and other data; a third alternative is to pursue the knowledge experimentally, but through an honest research design.[6]

If these alternatives were publicly discussed, I doubt that the debate would result in a blanket approval of all deceptive studies thought harmless by investigators. Each study would have to be separately evaluated from the point of view of available alternatives. Such a process, if seriously undertaken, would eliminate a great many of these studies. First to go would be those which seek no new knowledge in the first place, but merely train students in repeating the deceptive models of the past. For training is clearly as effective through honest as through dishonest research designs.

Second, those studies which could achieve the desired knowledge by honest means should be required to do so. This might require a greater expenditure of ingenuity and perhaps greater facility in working with records and with statistics. The search for alternatives may well require more training and more imagination than the leap to deceptive techniques.

Finally, those studies which can go ahead, even though subjects are asked in advance for their consent to the deceptive experiment, could be given priority over those where no such consent could be sought without invalidating the study.

To make such distinctions would require a real change of direction among investigators and experimentation committees. For manipulation has by now become a way of life, to the point where alternatives are not often considered. Every textbook recounts the well-known successes of past deceptive studies. They are repeated and emulated by each incoming generation of social scientists the world over. And committees set up to oversee experimentation often do not (unlike their counterparts overseeing biomedical research) require informed consent by subjects before deceptive studies can be undertaken.

But such changes raise a difficult problem. What about research of very likely benefit to society, where alternative models cannot possibly achieve the information a deceptive study might bring—a study, perhaps, designed to learn more about what makes adults abuse children? How might it stand up to the test of public justification? It is hard to imagine that persons might voluntarily reveal the character traits that they can be tricked into revealing in such studies. And it can at least be argued that we still have insufficient experimental documentation of these characteristics.

B. HARM AND BENEFIT

In order to answer this question, we have to consider carefully the harmlessness claimed for such studies. Most are now agreed, as the Ethical Standards make clear, that studies producing lasting damage to subjects ought not to be undertaken for the purposes of gaining knowledge in the social sciences: that studies such as the experiments where military personnel were unknowingly given LSD should never have gone forward. Studies such as Milgram's experiment on obedience, therefore, must claim to produce no such lasting harm. And any momentary stress or discomfort must be believed either to vanish by itself or to be removable by the "debriefing" process after the study is over. How would these two claims stand up in the light of public discussion by groups which include potential subjects of these deceptive experiments?

The response of potential subjects would doubtless be that they might well be willing to participate in some such experiments but not in others, and that, moreover, some of them might not want to participate in any. They would probably agree, therefore, that each should judge personally the harmlessness of what is planned for him. What seems painless to one may deeply injure another. What leaves unbearable marks of intrusion on personal privacy in one life will not affect another. To be made to act cruelly, or to be misinformed as to personal sexual responses, will hurt the vulnerable while others escape unharmed.

C. DEBRIEFING

But is there not added safety in the "debriefing" process? Can any residual stress or anxiety or sense of invaded privacy not be removed once the study is over? There are two parts to the claims of efficacy for debriefing: an honest description of the study once it is over, and psychological support given by the investigator to allow the subject to cope with the stress or the knowledge gained. Both require scrutiny from the perspective of those who are to receive the benefits of the "debriefing"—the experimental dupes.

The first claim for the process of "debriefing" is a very interesting one from the point of view of veracity. Where there has been an experimental inroad on veracity, the claim seems to be that the harm brought by a lie is "erased" by truthful information, much as an antidote for poison wipes out its effects. So long as the harm from the lie does not remain long with the dupe, it will then have had no effect. As Bacon said:

> [. . .] it is not the lie that passeth through the mind but the lie that sinketh in and settleth in it, that doth the hurt. . . .[7]

Truthfulness after the fact, then, is held to remove any residual harm the lie may have done, especially if it is conveyed without delay. Some investigators hold that this aspect of debriefing works especially well if they disclose their own discomfort at having lied, and explain why they feel, nevertheless, that the lies are justified. Subjects may respond with disappointment at being so easily duped and at having placed trust in a "cover story." But if the debriefing succeeds, investigators hope to have counteracted the disappointment and enlisted the subject as an ally in the experiment, to the point of promising not to tell *other* subjects about the deception they will encounter.

Unfortunately, debriefing does not always succeed.[8] The disappointment may remain; the anxiety or loss of privacy may not be overcome. The experiment may reveal something to subjects about themselves that no debriefing will erase. Subjects may become even more suspicious after the explanation, and thus less useful for further studies. And they may suffer from the discovery that someone in a position of a model and authority figure resorted to such devious tactics.

Some investigators argue that this is reason enough *not* to debrief subjects, except where the harm done can truly be alleviated. For others, the second claim connected with debriefing assumes even greater importance: that even if the antidote of truthfulness does not in itself work, even if it does not wipe out anxiety and guilt and a sense of having been exposed, the psychologist-investigator can. The Ethical Standards state that it is the responsibility of the investigator to "assure that there are no damaging consequences for the participant."[9]

Can the subjects be sure that their reactions to stress, anxiety, unpleasant and perhaps degrading discoveries about themselves will be so easy to erase or learn to live with? Do they have the requisite confidence in the ability of psychologists to restore the human spirit after injuries? And even if some are gifted with such an ability, are all? Each of us has a very different sense of privacy lost, of personal space invaded,[10] of knowledge gained that is hard to cope with. These are not always easy to erase or to overcome. To assume the contrary belies the complexity of human responses; it demands greater faith in the restorative skills of investigators than experience warrants.[11]

Subjects need, then, to be able to judge for themselves whether an experiment is risky for them and whether they have confidence in debriefing. The judgment of the investigator does not suffice. Such caution on the part of the public would stem neither from a hostility to research nor from a desire to limit academic freedom—two concerns often suspected by scientists to underlie the new turn toward protecting the rights of human subjects of experimentation. Rather, the caution is directed solely to the question of risks from the experiment; for academic freedom has never been construed to be freedom to place others at risk without their consent.

But this caution has limits. It cannot be stretched to mean that each and every study should have to go through the same consent procedures. For many studies in the social sciences are totally harmless even by the most exacting standards. Measurements, observations, and non-intrusive experiments can surely often proceed without the slightest risk. Take observations of what pedestrians do when an investigator's stooge jaywalks or talks to himself on street corners; or notes taken on how a crowd welcomes a returning war hero. It would be cumbersome for all and a bit mad to require strict consent to these. How, then, are they best separated out?

Review Committees

There is no need for new federal regulations, already proliferated beyond all reason. Rather, the standards already in use for biomedical research should govern behavioral research as well. These standards require informed consent from subjects in any research that adds "physical, psychological, sociological, or other" risk to their lives.[12] The professions themselves and the many institutional review committees already in existence are, in principle, best qualified to weigh such risks to human subjects. Their mandate is, after all, precisely to set standards and to screen projects: to screen away both those studies too dangerous to carry out, even if subjects could be found to consent to them, and those studies so trivial that no consent is needed.

In practice, however, committees do not always serve this function well for social science research. Many studies, and often the shoddiest in design, least competent in execution, never even come before these committees. Those that do are not now screened to require consent by subjects whenever there is a question of risk to subjects— witness the many controversial studies that *have* been passed by committees. This failure to see the risks for subjects is made more inevitable by the fact that so few committees have representation by laymen and potential subjects in the first place.

Committee structure and procedure must be reformed, therefore, before the public interest can be said to be safeguarded. Laymen and potential subjects must be represented. Most important, committees must use adequate criteria of what constitutes risk to the subjects of experimentation. They must make it clear that consent requires informing subjects of all that is relevant to their decision, including the purpose of the study and the fact that deception may enter into it. The committees should look sharply, too, whenever risk is possible, for even marginal efforts at coercing the consent of subjects. This may happen when students are required to participate in studies in order to take courses or receive degrees. Among the risks taken seriously must be psychological ones: the damage which some may experience from having revealed themselves unknowingly, from having their privacy invaded, or from discovering something about themselves that will be painful to live with.

Learning about people's private, even intimate, behavior and emotions without their consent is very much like surreptitiously listening in on their telephone conversations or looking through their keyholes. Such acts are no less intrusive for being done in the interests of research. The same barriers ought to protect us from these forms of invasion of privacy.[13]

If psychological risks are taken into account, deceptive studies such as the obedience research by Milgram could go forward only with subject consent. If consent is refused, this should be taken as an indication that the study ought not to have been done without consent in the first place. (In fact, it would be useful to list a number of deceptive studies merely as examples in a questionnaire, to see which would be more, and which less, acceptable to potential subjects.) If the study cannot be performed after informed consent because the surprise element is gone, two alternatives remain: to devise a marginally deceptive study so *harmless* to subjects that no consent is needed; or to ask a group of subjects for consent to a number of studies, detailing the risks, but asking consent to secrecy as to when any one would be likely to be in question. The review committee would then have to deliberate to see whether such a procedure provides sufficient protection.

Questions of Professional Responsibility

The greatest harm from deceptive experimentation may be that to the investigators themselves, to the students trained in their professions, and to the professions as such. Subjects, after all, may come into contact with deceptive experiments only briefly; but investigators plan the studies, execute them, explain them over and over again to subjects being debriefed, and teach students how to carry them out. The danger of spreading deceptive practices here is twofold. Individually, lies can become a way of life, manipulation habitual. And professionally, deceit can become more commonplace, with growing ranks of participants having fewer and fewer compunctions.

For the investigators themselves, the practices may be disagreeable at first; if forced to participate they may become inured to doing what they ordinarily would resist and thus lose a degree of moral sensitivity. Many begin as students and find it difficult to refuse to participate in giving a "cover story" or in the infiltration of a group, especially when they see their professors playing such roles. Neither in classrooms nor in textbooks are they encouraged to make distinctions of an ethical nature. The textbooks occasionally point to the presence of a problem with deception, only to add that research nevertheless requires it. But important distinctions of a moral nature are not made: distinctions between harm to dupes and harm to liars, between an accidental lie and a planned, repeated one, between lies and other deceptions, between routine practices and emergencies, between different excuses or different degrees of justification.

This absence of ethical analysis of a questionable research technique in common use leads to a larger question. Is there a place, in universities, for the teaching of deceptive research? Ought academic disciplines to include such techniques? Do other disciplines not exclude them? While every field has its share of duplicity, most do not *teach* it. The teaching function itself, then, has to be questioned where these techniques are concerned. We have to ask: What does it do to students to be placed in situations where professors teach them to deceive, where their grades and professional advancement may depend on their adaptability and ingenuity in working with deceptive techniques?

The accumulated effects on individual students must affect the professions themselves. And where the professions become known for such research, yet another problem arises—each deceptive study comes to contribute to a breakdown in trust. Few activities show such a spread as those of deceptive research. Academic uses have given rise to innumerable commercial uses. Psychologists know that public resistance to participating in research is growing. Pollsters are received with suspicion, often hostility; questionnaires remain unanswered; students—up to now the most easily available group of subjects—are increasingly sophisticated about research processes, to the point where there is real doubt about the validity of the research where their naïveté is assumed. One commentator on the vast deceptive practices in the name of social science holds that:

> These tricks simply strengthen the growing conviction that you can't trust people you don't know. If a mugger doesn't hit you, a credit checker doesn't spy on you, or a salesman doesn't take you to the cleaners, a social scientist will dupe you.[14]

It is in the interest of social scientists themselves, then, to protect their standing and the accuracy of their results by taking a stand against the resort to deception without consent and to other underhanded methods, even when no direct harm to subjects can be discerned; to refrain from teaching such methods; and to probe, with students and colleagues, the moral aspects of research.

I want to turn now to a group of experiments which do use deception and which do invade what some would like to keep private, but where the public interest in uncovering abuse and error is great. They serve to protect the public; this purpose gives them greater urgency. Does it suffice to justify the deception?

Pseudo-patient Studies

In fairy tales, princes dressed as shepherds go out among their people to learn what they won't be told at court—how the sick and the poor live; how the courtiers and the councilors do their work; how power is wielded. A curious analogue to these quests has sprung up in the last fifteen years with the help of social scientists: the pseudo-patient study. Investigators pretending to suffer from depression, delusions, aches and pains, go into clinics and hospitals to seek "help." They want to learn for themselves about the care of the sick and the needy, the use of public funds, and the day-to-day routines in mental hospitals and health clinics. These studies have now become so common that doctors have been advised to learn how to cope with a new kind of patient—the pseudo-patient.[15] And the response by health professionals has often been one of shock and hostility at the deviousness of the research techniques.

One of the most controversial of these studies was conducted by D. L. Rosenhan and his associates. Their article, entitled "On Being Sane in Insane Places"[16] has become widely known, both because of its striking and frightening results, and because it ignited a debate about the ethical aspects of such studies. The investigators wished to test the hypothesis that the distinction between sane and insane persons is difficult or impossible in psychiatric hospitals. Eight investigators sought to be admitted to twelve different hospitals. They used the following procedure:

> After calling the hospital for an appointment, the pseudo-patient arrived at the admissions office complaining that he had been hearing voices. Asked what the voices said, he replied that they were often unclear, but as far as he could tell, they said "empty," "hollow," and "thud."
> [. . .] Beyond alleging the symptoms and falsifying name, vocation, and employment, no further alterations of person, history, or circumstances were made.
> [. . .] Immediately upon admission to the psychiatric ward, the pseudo-patient ceased simulating *any* symptoms of abnormality.
> [. . .] Despite their public "show" of sanity, the pseudo-patients were never detected. Admitted, except in one case, with a diagnosis of schizophrenia, each was discharged with a diagnosis of schizophrenia "in remission."

In Australia, pseudo-patients were employed to find out the extent to which physicians prescribe drugs to patients claiming symptoms of depression, and to learn whether sex role stereotypes affect physicians in their efforts to help these patients.[17] Ten pseudo-patients, five male and five female, were trained to present themselves with typical symptoms of mild depression to preselected physicians. The authors recommend "pseudo-patient experience and feedback" as giving a perspective on health care that other methods may be incapable of achieving, and of "strengthening consumer perspectives on health care." They suggest the establishment of a permanent body to report regularly on health-care service by using pseudo-patient studies.

In the United States such studies are also gaining ground. In the fall of 1976, Senator Frank Moss made headlines when he published the results of investigations of the Medicaid system in New York in which he had personally participated.[18] As Chairman of the Senate Subcommittee on Long-Term Care, he acquired a Medicaid card and visited one medical center, sending Capitol Hill policemen and committee staff aides on 120 visits to other "Medicaid Mills" in New York City. They found widespread fraud. As patients, they were subjected to unnecessary tests, often given extensive referrals and a number of prescriptions.

Such, then, are the techniques now increasingly used to monitor professional practices in the health fields. Those who are subjected to them feel injured in two ways: They have been lied to, and the lies have caught them off guard, so that their private relationships with patients have been invaded. Why, they ask, should they be treated in this way? The deceits practiced upon them are not white lies nor lies in some emergency. And the entire health care system might be further debilitated by suspicion and law suits should the pseudo-patient research continue to proliferate.

How do the investigators respond? To what principles do they appeal? In the first place, some see no need to do so; for them, deception poses no problem. Schooled in the manipulative techniques of recent decades and passing them on to their own graduate students, they have overcome any hesitation about misleading experimental subjects. At times, they even refer to "equality" in the choice of subjects: If patients can be the subjects of deceptive research, why should doctors not be similarly used?[19] As a result of such insouciance about deceptive studies, they often do not see the need to seek honest alternatives to these studies.

Other investigators are more troubled. But there are times when they see no other way to expose the abuses and errors which they suspect. And these can be very serious indeed. The countless patients who have been wrongly treated in "Medicaid Mills" bear testimony to the injustice of the system and to the immense misuse of taxpayers' money. These investigators appeal, therefore, to the principles of avoiding harm and of producing benefits, and see them as overriding the concern for veracity in these cases.

As for the claim by spied-upon physicians that they have been assaulted in their private relationship with patients, the investigators might reply that these relationships *ought* to be open to public scrutiny. They are very different in this sense from private sexual or religious behavior. The law supports investigators in making this distinction, holding that publicity which would otherwise constitute an invasion of privacy is permitted for matters in which the public has a legitimate interest. The invasion of privacy at issue here is a very different matter from that in many other studies on such subjects as homosexuality or obedience to authorities requesting violent acts.

Investigators may also appeal to the principle of fairness. It is unfair for men and women to receive different treatment because of their sex, instead of receiving the treatment best suited to cope with the disease itself. It is unfair for the poor and those most easily exploited to receive such shoddy care as they are given in the "Medicare Mills," and for those most vulnerable to exploitation in mental hospitals to be subjected to the procedures documented by the pseudo-patient studies. Finally, investigators make claims that appeal to the principle of veracity itself: monitoring will lead to greater honesty in patient care in the future, they argue, greater respect for the patient who might be an investigator in disguise, and greater reluctance to go along with sex role biases.

In weighing these arguments, we need to distinguish two separate purposes of pseudo-patient studies—to gain scientific knowledge and to protect those at risk. If such studies are looked at, first, primarily as *research*, their claims are relatively weak. Even proponents of the studies admit that the *knowledge* thus acquired can be gained with non-deceptive methods as well, and that it is by now already well established. Deception is not, therefore, the only way to achieve the scientific purpose. Because of the harm from deception already described, honest studies must therefore be preferred. As for the causes of fairness to the underprivileged and greater honesty on the part of health professionals, they are but haphazardly served by these scattered studies.

If, on the other hand, the element of *monitoring* in these studies is separately evaluated, the arguments become stronger. After all, surreptitious monitoring is common in many lines of work, such as car repair, banking, restaurant service—there is no doubt that standards are thereby higher. But if the monitoring purpose of the pseudo-patient studies is to be predominant, then participants ought to know that they may be monitored, and they ought to have consented to such a practice. As with the use of unmarked police cars, it is not enough to assume that there is public or professional consent to the deceptive practice.

By providing pseudo-patient monitoring with the safeguards given to other forms of monitoring, it can be regarded as a way to oversee patient treatment. Pseudo-patient monitoring could then at the very least be seen as different from the run-of-the-mill deceptive research now so common in the social sciences. The purposes are important; the protection urgently needed. The surreptitious element in monitoring—so pervasive in deceptive research—would then be largely overcome through consent. There may, at times, be no alternative way of conducting the supervision. Such monitoring of professional relationships differs sharply from invading the privacy of unsuspecting subjects in ordinary deceptive research.

And yet, the deceit so practiced may levy its own toll. Our society already tolerates much surreptitious monitoring. We need to ask ourselves how much surveillance and infiltration we really want. Do we also want pseudo-students in the classrooms, pseudo-converts to religious creeds, pseudo-party members, clients, and patients? How far do we want to go to train some to spy on their fellows in order to find a few miscreants? And should there be any monitoring where no misdeed at all is suspected?

These are matters for public choice. The surreptitious practices have to be looked at together, and standards set for what communities regard as necessary and tolerable monitoring. Until such standards are set for pseudo-patient studies, health professionals should assume that they may become the subjects in surreptitious studies. To return to the fairy tale with which we began: the wisest course may yet turn out to be to treat all strangers well. Who knows—they may be princes in disguise.

XIV

PATERNALISTIC LIES

The first inference is that even if something which has a false significance is said to an infant or insane person no blame for falsehood attaches thereto. For it seems to be permitted by the common opinion of mankind that "The unsuspecting age of childhood may be mocked." Quintilian, speaking of boys, said: "For their profit we employ many fictions." The reason is by no means far to seek; since infants and insane persons do not have liberty of judgment, it is impossible for wrong to be done to them in respect to such liberty.

—Grotius, *The Law of War and Peace*

The abuse of truth ought to be as much punished as the introduction of falsehood.

As if there were two hells, one for sins against love, the other for those against justice!

—Blaise Pascal, *Pensées*

Tell all the Truth but tell it slant—
Success in Circuit lies
Too bright for our infirm Delight
The Truth's superb surprise
As Lightning to the Children eased
With explanation kind
The Truth must dazzle gradually
Or every man be blind—

Emily Dickinson, *Poems*

Paternalism

Conquest, birth, and voluntary offer: by these three methods, said Hobbes, can one person become subjected to another.[1] So long as questions are not asked—as when power is thought divinely granted or ordained by nature —the right to coerce and manipulate is taken for granted. Only when this right is challenged does the need for justification arise. It becomes necessary to ask: When *can* authority be justly exercised—over a child for instance? And the answer given by paternalism is that such authority is at the very least justified when it is exercised over persons for their own good.

To act paternalistically is to guide and even coerce people in order to protect them and serve their best interests, as a father might his children. He must keep them out of harm's way, by force if necessary. If a small child wants to play with matches or drink ammonia, parents must intervene. Similarly, those who want to ride motorcycles are forced in many states to wear helmets for their own protection. And Odysseus asked to be tied to the mast of his ship when approaching the Sirens, who were "weaving a haunting song across the sea,"[2] bidding his sailors to take more turns of the rope to muffle him should he cry or beg to be untied. Paternalistic restraints may be brief and self-imposed, as in the case of Odysseus, or of much longer duration, and much less voluntary.[3]

Among the most thoroughgoing paternalistic proposals ever made were those of Johann Peter Frank, often called the Father of Public Health,[4] in eighteenth-century Germany. In his six-volume *System for a Complete Medical Policing* he proposed ways to "prevent evils through wise ordinances." Laws should be passed, he argued, in every case where they might further the health of citizens. Sexual practices, marriage, and child rearing were to be regulated in the smallest detail; a law should be passed to prohibit the tight clothing women wore, if it interfered with their respiration; control of disease should be attempted in every village. Frank even suggested a law to require those who had been to a country dance to rest before leaving, lest the cool evening air give them a cold after their exertions.

The need for some paternalistic restraints is obvious. We survive only if protected from harm as children. Even as adults, we tolerate a number of regulations designed to reduce dangers such as those of infection or accidents. But it is equally obvious that the intention of guarding from harm has led, both through mistake and through abuse, to great suffering. The "protection" can suffocate; it can also exploit. Throughout history, men, women, and children have been compelled to accept degrading work, alien religious practices, institutionalization, and even wars alleged to "free" them, all in the name of what someone has declared to be their own best interest. And deception may well have outranked force as a means of subjection: duping people to conform, to embrace ideologies and cults—never more zealously perpetrated than by those who believe that the welfare of those deceived is at issue.

Paternalistic Deception

Apart from guidance and persuasion, the paternalist can manipulate in two ways: through force and through deception. I have already described large-scale manipulation by governments and its appeal to paternalism; in this chapter I shall focus on deception among family members and friends. It is here that most of us encounter the hardest choices between truthfulness and lying. We may never have to worry about whether to lie in court or as experimenters or journalists; but in our families, with our friends, with those whose well-being matters most to us, lies can sometimes seem the only way not to injure or disappoint. Far from the larger professional schemes of deceit for the public good or for the advancement of science, we are here concerned with the closest bonds human beings can share.

Lies to protect these bonds carry a special sense of immediacy and appropriateness. To keep from children the knowledge that their parents' marriage may be dissolving; to keep up a false pretense of good health; to reassure those struck by misfortune that all will be well again—in such situations, falsehoods may be told so as to shore up, comfort, protect.

Children are often deceived with the fewest qualms. They, more than all others, need care, support, protection. To shield them, not only from brutal speech and frightening news, but from apprehension and pain—to soften and embellish and disguise—is as natural as to shelter them from harsh weather. Because they are more vulnerable and more impressionable than adults, they cannot always cope with what they hear. Their efforts, however rudimentary, need encouragement and concern, rather than "objective" evaluation. Unvarnished facts, thoughtlessly or maliciously conveyed, can hurt them, even warp them, render them callous in self-defense.

But even apart from shielding and encouragement, strict accuracy is simply not very high on the list of essentials in speaking with children. With the youngest ones especially, the sharing of stories and fairy tales, of invention and play can suggest, in Erik Erikson's words,[5] at its best "some virgin chance conquered, some divine leeway shared"—leaving the conventionally "accurate" and "realistic" far behind.

A danger arises whenever those who deal with children fall into the familiar trap of confusing "truth" and "truthfulness." It may lead them to confuse fiction and jokes and all that departs from fact with lying.* And so they may lose track of what it means to respect children enough to be honest with them. To lie to children then comes to seem much like telling stories to them or like sharing their leaps between fact and fancy. Such confusion fails to recognize the fact that fiction does not *intend* to mislead, that it calls for what Coleridge called a "willing suspension of disbelief," which is precisely what is absent in ordinary deception.

Equally destructive are those dour adults who draw the opposite conclusion from their confusion of fiction and deception and who try to eradicate both from the lives of their children. They fear what they take to be the unreality and falsity of fairy tales. They see lies and perversion in the stories children tell. They stifle every expression of imagination at crushing costs to their families and to themselves. Edmund Gosse, in *Father and Son*, has described such an upbringing, uncommon only in its ex-

---

*The confusion of fiction and deception has long antecedents. Plato stated in the *Republic* (597E) that artists and playwrights are at "three removes" from nature. Augustine and others argued, on the contrary, that what they convey, and what is conveyed in the use of symbol and ritual, is not deceptive, because not intended to mislead. Samuel Coleridge, in *Biographia Literaria*, chap. 14, used the "willing suspension of disbelief" to stand for the poetic faith which fiction requires of its audience. Such a suspension of disbelief is a form of *consent*.

But even though fiction and lying are in themselves quite separate, there are, of course, a number of borderline regions and areas where one invades the other. If an author really means to manipulate through his writing, as in propaganda; if the author mingles fiction and purportedly factual statements without signaling where the "suspension of disbelief" is appropriate; if the conveyor of what the audience takes to be fiction or invention is presenting what to him is straightforward history, as when a schizophrenic recently published his daily journal; if the author of a play has no intention to deceive anyone but finds that a gullible enthusiast in the audience leaps to the rescue of a victim in distress on the stage; in all these cases, the elements of fiction and deception are interwoven.

Finally, there are times where deception is clearly present, as in plagiarism and forgery.

cess. Explaining that his parents had dedicated him at birth to the ministry, and that they wanted to make him "truthful," he wrote:

> I found my greatest pleasure in the pages of books. The range of these was limited, for story-books of every description were sternly excluded. No fiction of any kind, religious or secular, was admitted into the house. [. . .]
>
> [. . .] Never, in all my early childhood, did any one address to me the affecting preamble, "Once upon a time!" I was told about missionaries, but never about pirates; I was familiar with humming-birds, but I had never heard of fairies. Jack the Giant-Killer, Rumpelstiltskin and Robin Hood were not of my acquaintance, and though I understood about wolves, Little Red Ridinghood was a stranger even by name.[6]

Another reason for paternalistic deception stems from the very desire to *be* honest with children or those of limited understanding. In talking to them, one may hope to produce, for their own good, as adequate an idea of what is at stake as possible, so that they will be able to respond "appropriately"—neither too casually nor too intensely if it is a present danger, and without excessive worry if it is a future danger. The truth will then be bent precisely so as to convey what the speaker thinks is the right "picture"; it will compensate for the inexperience or the fears of the listener, much as raising one's voice helps in speaking to the hard of hearing and translation conveys one's meaning into another language.

Such "translation" into language the child can understand may seem very wide of the mark to bystanders, yet not be intended to deceive in the least, merely to evoke appropriate response. But it can, of course, be mixed with deception—to play down, for instance, dangers about which nothing can be done, or to create, conversely, some terror in the child to make sure he stays away from dangers he *can* do something to avoid. In this way, parents may tell a child that medicine won't taste bad, or that dressing a wound won't hurt. And they may exaggerate the troubles that befall those who don't eat the "right" foods. In each case, part of what the child learns is that grownups bend the truth when it suits them.

All these factors—the need for shielding and encouragement, the low priority on accuracy, and the desire to get meaningful information across in spite of difficulties of understanding or response—contribute to the ease with which children are deceived. Milton expressed the tolerance so commonly granted to misleading the young and the incapacitated:

> What man in his senses would deny that there are those whom we have the best grounds for considering that we ought to deceive—as boys, madmen, the sick, the intoxicated . . . ?[7]

Following Grotius, many have taken the step of arguing that children can be deceived because they have no right to truthful information in the first place. Since children have no "liberty of judgment" with respect to what is said to them, one cannot wrong them or infringe on their liberty by lying to them.

Whatever we may conclude about the rightness of paternalistic lying at exceptional times, the argument that it is all right to lie to children and to the incompetent simply *because* they belong to these groups is clearly untenable. Someone who lied to harm a child would surely be more to blame, not less, because the victim could not fully understand the danger. Children can be wronged by lies as much as, or more than, others. And liars themselves can be as injured by lying to children as to all others. Finally, the lie to a child often turns out to affect his family as well, either because family members participate in the deceit or because they are themselves deceived. The following is an example of how the deception of a child "for his own good" corroded the existence of an entire family:

An adolescent boy has only one kidney, as a result of having had cancer as a baby. The parents, wishing to avoid the worries that this knowledge might cause him and his siblings, told them instead the following story: that the boy, when very little, had been swinging, watched over by an eight year-old sister. He had fallen out and hurt himself so much that the kidney had been gravely injured and had been removed. The boy now has but one desire: to play contact sports. He knows he cannot do so with only one kidney. He is angry and resentful toward his older sister, who in turn feels deeply guilty.

But not only children and those in need of care are deceived on paternalistic grounds. We may weigh the same questions with respect to adults who are close to us or for whom we have some special responsibility—as teachers sometimes deceive their students in order not to hurt them, or as colleagues flatter failing judges that their acuteness is undiminished. We may express—falsely—assurance, approval, or love, to those who seek it so as not to let them down. This is especially likely in existing relationships, where a close bond is taken for granted—at work, for example, or between friends. To keep up appearances, to respect long-standing commitments, to refrain from wounding, lies are told which disguise and protect.

Even if an open rejection does take place—as when an applicant is denied work, a request for money is turned down, an offer of marriage refused—paternalistic lies may be told to conceal the real reasons for the rejection, to retain the civility of the interaction, and to soften the blow to the self-respect of the rejected. It is easier to say that one cannot do something, or that the rules do not allow it, than that one does not want to do it; easier to say that there is no market for a writer's proposed book than that it is unreadable; or that there is no opening for the job seeker than that he lacks the necessary skills.

An interesting contemporary development illustrating lies to conceal rejection is found in the choice not to allow one family member to donate a life-saving organ to another. It is known that a kidney given by a close family member is much more likely to be successfully transplanted than a kidney from an unrelated donor. Yet sometimes there is no one in the family who has a kidney suitable for donation; at other times, a family member may express a wish to give the kidney, yet at the same time be frightened, resentful, and unwilling to do so. Renée Fox and Judith Swazey describe one case as follows:

> Susan's mother expressed her willingness to be a donor, but the medical team had reason to believe she did not really want to give Susan a kidney. The team noted, for example, that while Mrs. Thompson was being worked up she developed gastro-intestinal problems and heart palpitations. As soon as she was told that she would not be the donor for her daughter, "she changed for the better." Mrs. Thompson does not know, nor does the daughter, that she was turned down for psychological reasons . . . Mrs. Thompson was told that she could not be a donor because she was "not a good tissue match."[8]

All such deceptive practices claim benevolence, concern for the deceived. Yet in looking at them, the discrepancy of perspectives stands out once again. We can share the desire to protect and to support that guides so many paternalistic lies; and recognize the importance of not using the truth as a weapon, even inadvertently. But from the perspective of the deceived, the power of paternalistic deception carries many dangers. Problems may go unexplored, as for the mother who was deceived about her suitability as a donor for the kidney her daughter so desperately needed. False hopes may be maintained, as for graduate students who have spent long years studying without ever being told that they could not hope to advance in their fields or even find employment. Unnecessary resentments may linger, as for the boy who was told that his sister was to blame for what an illness had caused. And eroded marriages and friendships may wear away further in the absence of an opportunity for the deceived to take stock of the situation.

One reason for the appeal of paternalistic lies is that they, unlike so much deception, are felt to be without bias and told in a disinterested wish to be helpful to fellow human beings in need. On closer examination, however, this objectivity and disinterest are often found to be spurious. The benevolent motives claimed by liars are then seen to be mixed with many others much less altruistic—the fear of confrontation which would accompany a more outspoken acknowledgement of the liar's feelings and intentions; the desire to avoid setting in motion great pressures to change, as where addiction or infidelity are no longer concealed; the urge to maintain the power that comes with duping others (never greater than when those lied to are defenseless or in need of care). These are motives of self-protection and of manipulation, of wanting to retain control over a situation and to remain a free agent. So long as the liar does not see them clearly, his judgment that his lies are altruistic and thus excused is itself biased and unreliable.

The perspective of the deceived, then, challenges the "helpfulness" of many paternalistic lies. It questions, moreover, even the benefits that are thought to accrue to the liar. The effects of deception on the liars themselves —the need to shore up lies, keep them in good repair, the anxieties relating to possible discovery, the entanglements and threats to integrity—are greatest in a close relationship where it is rare that one lie will suffice. It can be very hard to maintain the deceit when one is in close contact with those one lies to. The price of "living a lie" often turns out not even to have been worth the gains for the liars themselves.

Justification?

The two simplest approaches to paternalistic lying, then, have to be ruled out. It is not all right to lie to people just because they are children, or unable to judge what one says, or indeed because they belong to any category of persons at all. And the simple conviction voiced by Luther and so many others that the "helpful lie" is excused by its own altruism is much too uncritical.[9] It allows far too many lies to go unquestioned. Both of these views fail to take into consideration the harm that comes from lying, not only to the deceived but to the liars and to the bonds they share.

Are there other ways to sort out the few justifiable paternalistic lies, if they exist, from the many abuses of paternalism? A first possibility is to take into account the frequent parallels between force and deception noted throughout this book, and to ask: Is lying for paternalistic reasons justified whenever force is?

In a crisis, to be sure, where an innocent life is threatened, and other alternatives have been exhausted, deception would certainly seem to be warranted to the extent that force is. Both might, for example, be justified in rescuing a child too frightened to leave a burning building. Carrying him out by force, or falsely saying there is no risk in running out, might both be justified. But the parallel is not complete. The very fact that paternalism so often thrives in families and in other relationships of closeness and dependence has a special effect on the choice between manipulation by force and by deception. These relationships require more trust than most others, and over a longer period of time. As a result, whereas in many crises such as that of the murderer seeking his victim, it may be as good or better to lie than to attempt force, the opposite may well be the case in family crises and wherever trust obtains.

Consider, for example, two parents trying to keep a small child from falling into a pond. They may try distraction or persuasion and resort to force if these do not succeed. But what if they choose instead to tell the child there are monsters in the pond? While such a tale might effectively avoid the danger of drowning and save the parents a certain amount of physical exertion, the strategy does not bode well for the family in the long run. (If, on the other hand, the parents were too far away, or unable to move to lift the child away, deception might be acceptable as a last resort.)

Not only does paternalistic concern for those to whom we are close not *add* a new excuse to those few we have accepted earlier, such as lies in crises, truly white lies, or lies where the deceived have given their consent. On the contrary, the very closeness of the bonds turns out to *limit* the justifiability even of lies in those narrow categories. Crises, as we have just seen, should call forth paternalistic deception only if persuasion and force are useless.[10] And trivial lies mount up within families, among neighbors, close friends, and those who work together as they never can among more casual acquaintances. They can thus gather a momentum they would not otherwise have. For all such lies, there is the added harm to the relationship itself to be considered, and the fact that, as some of the lies come to be discovered, the liar will have to live with the resultant loss in trust at close hand.

Most problematic of all is the status of *consent* in paternalistic lying. It is rare that children, friends, or spouses will have consented in advance to being deceived for their own good. A variation of the requirement for consent is therefore sometimes brought forth: implied consent. Some day, this argument holds, those who are rightly deceived will be grateful for the restraints imposed upon them for their own good. And those who are wrongly deceived will not. This expectation of future gratitude is likened to the ordinary consent given in advance of an action in the following way: If those who are now being deceived for what is truly their own good were completely rational, sane, adult, or healthy, they would consent to what is being done for them.[11] If they were in the liar's position, they, too, would choose to lie out of this altruistic concern.

Can "implied consent" be used as a test of all the paternalistic lies told—in crises, under more trivial circumstances, to shelter or encourage or heal? It would then close the gap between the perspectives of liar and deceived; their aims—to benefit the deceived—would coincide. The way to tell rightful paternalistic lies from all the others would then be to ask whether the deceived, if completely able to judge his own best interests, would himself want to be duped. If he becomes rational enough to judge at a later time, one could then ask whether he gives his retroactive consent to the deceit—whether he is grateful he was lied to.

Sometimes the answer to such questions is clear. If someone asks in advance to be lied to or restrained, consent can often be assumed. Odysseus asked to be tied with ropes; some patients ask their doctors not to reveal an unhappy prognosis. At other times, there has been no prior consent, but every reasonable person would want to be thwarted, even lied to, for his own good. A temporarily deranged person who asks for a knife, or the child paralyzed with fear who has to be cajoled and lured out of a burning house, will not question the integrity of those who lied to them, once their good judgment has returned.

The questions work equally well to rule out cases where no one would give genuine consent to certain forms of coercion merely labeled paternalistic. To be incarcerated in mental hospitals in order to "help" one overcome political disagreement with a regime, for instance, is a fate for which there is no implied consent; and retroactive consent to such treatment is no longer free—it is the sign of a broken spirit.

Or take the example often cited in antiquity: that it is right to bring false reports of victory to soldiers wavering in battle, so that they will be encouraged and go on to defeat their enemy. Those who tell such falsehoods may have persuaded themselves that they are doing the soldiers a favor. And once victory is achieved, the deceived soldiers who happen to survive may think so, too. But before going into combat, they would not view matters so optimistically. They have reason to ask how such a course of action is justified if one does not know the outcome of the battle—how the liar can take it upon himself to consider future consent only after the outcome of victory, and only for the survivors. While the defense of such lies is phrased in paternalistic language, stressing the pride and future consent of the deceived soldiers once they have won, and their gratitude at having gained courage to fight on through a lie, there is little genuine concern for the soldier behind such words, nor is the view of the deceived soldiers as insufficiently rational to choose for themselves a tenable one. The lie is purely strategic, told entirely to advance the aims of those guiding the hostilities.

But many times it is not so clear whether or not a rational person might at some future time give consent to having been deceived. Paternalistic lies are so often told in very private circumstances, where intricate webs of long-standing dissimulation make it hard to sort out what is a realistic alternative, whether the deceived is in fact not able to cope with the truth, what will benefit or harm, even what is a lie in the first place.

Should parents, for example, who have adopted a child, pretend to him that they are his biological parents?* Should a critically ill wife, afraid of her husband's inabil-

---

*The current practice is to encourage parents to be open about this fact to an adopted child.

ity to cope, lie to him about her condition? If one looks at the many lies which have been told—and lived—to conceal these matters, the consequences of telling the truth are not at all uniform. Most, if told the truth, might well agree that they prefer to know; but some would grieve, and wish that they had never been told.

Except in very clear cases, where all would *agree* to consent or to refuse consent, relying on implied consent is very different from having actual consent. Actual consent makes false statements no longer deceptive, as in a game to which the players have consented; the same cannot be said of implied consent. Whether or not one believes that such consent will be given, one must therefore still ask whether the lie is otherwise justified. The bond between liar and deceived does not in itself justify paternalistic lies, nor does the liar's belief in his good intentions, in the inability of the deceived to act reasonably if told the truth, and in the implied consent of the deceived. In assuming such consent, all the biases afflicting the liar's perspective are present in force.

If we assume the point of view of potential dupes, it becomes important to try not to fall into any predicament where others might believe that we ought to be deceived. It is possible to discuss in advance the degree of veracity that one can tolerate in a marriage, or friendship, or working relationship and to work out the ground rules well before there is much to conceal. With paternalistic lies, just as with white lies (and these often overlap), it may be difficult to eliminate from one's life all instances of duplicity; but there is no reason not to make the effort to reduce them to the extent possible, to be on the lookout for alternatives, to let it be known that one prefers to be dealt with openly. (Needless to say, however, it is as important here as with white lies not to imagine that abandoning deception must also bring with it the giving up of discretion and sensitivity.)

Such a working out of standards can succeed among

spouses, friends, co-workers. But greater difficulties arise with respect to children and the retarded, who will not soon, perhaps never, reach the the point where they will be able to discuss with others how honestly they want to be treated. Present consent to deceiving them is therefore difficult to obtain; and retroactive consent in the future either impossible or so distant as to be more unreliable than ever.

The difficulty for these groups is made greater still by the fact that the recourse to public debate has often worked especially poorly in protecting their interests. Eminently "reasonable" thinkers have supported the most brutal practices of manipulation and deception of the immature, the incompetent, and the irrational. Even John Stuart Mill, who spoke so powerfully for liberty, agreed that exceptions had to be made for children, those taken care of, and those "backward states in which the race itself may be considered in its nonage." He held that:

> Despotism is a legitimate mode of government in deal-
> ing with barbarians, provided the end be their improve-
> ment, and the means justified by actually effecting that
> end.[12]

The appeal to "reasonable persons" never has protected the interests of those considered outsiders, inferiors, incompetent or immature. And they themselves have no way to distinguish between benevolent and malevolent motives for lying to them; nor would history give them many grounds for confidence that the benevolent motives predominate. Rather than accepting the common view, therefore, that it is somehow more justifiable to lie to children and to those the liars regard as being *like* children, special precautions are needed in order not to exploit them.

In summary, paternalistic lies, while they are easy to understand and to sympathize with at times, also carry very special risks: risks to the liar himself from having to lie more and more in order to keep up the appearance among people he lives with or sees often, and thus from the greater likelihood of discovery and loss of credibility; risks to the relationship in which the deception takes place; and risks of exploitation of every kind for the deceived.

It is nevertheless also the case that some would in fact prefer to be deceived for paternalistic reasons. The difficulty here is in knowing who they might be. If there is some reason why one cannot ask them, much rides on what in fact is likely to befall the deceived. It may not be fair or kind to a person to tell him certain falsehoods; but then, it may not be fair or kind to tell him the corresponding truths either. The very privacy of the communication in paternalistic deception only aggravates this difficulty, as does the failure to share the predicament of those who are less than ordinarily competent.

I propose to explore this question in greater detail in the next chapter, focusing on lies to those who are ill and those near death. There has long been a split of opinions about deception at such times. Empirical data are now beginning to be available about what information people actually want regarding their illness and the likelihood that death may be near—data which will have to be weighed in any choice of whether or not to be truthful with patients. In addition, the fact that such choices concern health professionals makes it more possible once again to bring public discussion to bear on these problems than on the many lies told in the penumbra of family life.

LIES TO THE
SICK AND DYING

The face of a physician, like that of a diplomatist, should be impenetrable. Nature is a benevolent old hypocrite; she cheats the sick and the dying with illusions better than any anodynes. [. . .]

Some shrewd old doctors have a few phrases always on hand for patients that will insist on knowing the pathology of their complaints without the slightest capacity of understanding the scientific explanation. I have known the term "spinal irritation" serve well on such occasions, but I think nothing on the whole has covered so much ground, and meant so little, and given such profound satisfaction to all parties, as the magnificent phrase "congestion of the portal system."

—Oliver Wendell Holmes, *Medical Essays*

This deception tortured him—their not wishing to admit what they all knew and what he knew, but wanting to lie to him concerning his terrible condition, and wishing and forcing him to participate in that lie. Those lies—lies enacted over him on the eve of his death and destined to degrade this awful, solemn act to the level of their visitings, their curtains, their sturgeon for dinner—were a terrible agony for Ivan Ilych.

—Leo Tolstoy, *The Death of Ivan Ilych*

When a man's life has become bound up with the ana-
lytic technique, he finds himself at a loss altogether for the
lies and the guile which are otherwise so indispensable to
a physician, and if for once with the best intentions he
attempts to use them he is likely to betray himself. Since
we demand strict truthfulness from our patients, we jeop-
ardize our whole authority if we let ourselves be caught by
them in a departure from the truth.

—Sigmund Freud, *Collected Papers,* II

Deception as Therapy

A forty-six-year-old man, coming to a clinic for a routine
physical check-up needed for insurance purposes, is diagnosed as having a form of cancer likely to cause him to die
within six months. No known cure exists for it. Chemotherapy may prolong life by a few extra months, but will
have side effects the physician does not think warranted
in this case. In addition, he believes that such therapy
should be reserved for patients with a chance for recovery
or remission. The patient has no symptoms giving him
any reason to believe that he is not perfectly healthy. He
expects to take a short vacation in a week.

For the physician, there are now several choices involving truthfulness. Ought he to tell the patient what he
has learned, or conceal it? If asked, should he deny it? If
he decides to reveal the diagnosis, should he delay doing
so until after the patient returns from his vacation? Finally, even if he does reveal the serious nature of the
diagnosis, should he mention the possibility of chemotherapy and his reasons for not recommending it in this
case? Or should he encourage every last effort to postpone
death?

In this particular case, the physician chose to inform
the patient of his diagnosis right away. He did not, how-

ever, mention the possibility of chemotherapy. A medical student working under him disagreed; several nurses also thought that the patient should have been informed of this possibility. They tried, unsuccessfully, to persuade the physician that this was the patient's right. When persuasion had failed, the student elected to disobey the doctor by informing the patient of the alternative of chemotherapy. After consultation with family members, the patient chose to ask for the treatment.

Doctors confront such choices often and urgently. What they reveal, hold back, or distort will matter profoundly to their patients. Doctors stress with corresponding vehemence their reasons for the distortion or concealment: not to confuse a sick person needlessly, or cause what may well be unnecessary pain or discomfort, as in the case of the cancer patient; not to leave a patient without hope, as in those many cases where the dying are not told the truth about their condition; or to improve the chances of cure, as where unwarranted optimism is expressed about some form of therapy. Doctors use information as part of the therapeutic regimen; it is given out in amounts, in admixtures, and according to timing believed best for patients. Accuracy, by comparison, matters far less.

Lying to patients has, therefore, seemed an especially excusable act. Some would argue that doctors, and *only* doctors, should be granted the right to manipulate the truth in ways so undesirable for politicians, lawyers, and others.[1] Doctors are trained to help patients; their relationship to patients carries special obligations, and they know much more than laymen about what helps and hinders recovery and survival.

Even the most conscientious doctors, then, who hold themselves at a distance from the quacks and the purveyors of false remedies, hesitate to forswear all lying. Lying is usually wrong, they argue, but less so than allowing the truth to harm patients. B. C. Meyer echoes this very common view:

> [O]urs is a profession which traditionally has been guided by a precept that transcends the virtue of uttering truth for truth's sake, and that is, "so far as possible, do no harm."[2]

Truth, for Meyer, may be important, but not when it endangers the health and well-being of patients. This has seemed self-evident to many physicians in the past—so much so that we find very few mentions of veracity in the codes and oaths and writings by physicians through the centuries. This absence is all the more striking as other principles of ethics have been consistently and movingly expressed in the same documents.

The two fundamental principles of doing good and not doing harm—of beneficence and nonmaleficence—are the most immediately relevant to medical practitioners, and the most frequently stressed. To preserve life and good health, to ward off illness, pain, and death—these are the perennial tasks of medicine and nursing. These principles have found powerful expression at all times in the history of medicine. In the Hippocratic Oath physicians promise to:

> use treatment to help the sick . . . but never with a view to injury and wrong-doing.[3]

And a Hindu oath of initiation says:

> Day and night, however thou mayest be engaged, thou shalt endeavor for the relief of patients with all thy heart and soul. Thou shalt not desert or injure the patient even for the sake of thy living.[4]

But there is no similar stress on veracity. It is absent from virtually all oaths, codes, and prayers. The Hippocratic Oath makes no mention of truthfulness to patients about their condition, prognosis, or treatment. Other early codes and prayers are equally silent on the subject. To be sure, they often refer to the confidentiality with which doctors should treat all that patients tell them; but there is no corresponding reference to honesty toward the patient. One of the few who appealed to such a principle was Amatus Lusitanus, a Jewish physician widely known for his skill, who, persecuted, died of the plague in 1568. He published an oath which reads in part:

> If I lie, may I incur the eternal wrath of God and of His angel Raphael, and may nothing in the medical art succeed for me according to my desires.[5]

Later codes continue to avoid the subject. Not even the Declaration of Geneva, adopted in 1948 by the World Medical Association, makes any reference to it. And the Principles of Medical Ethics of the American Medical Association[6] still leave the matter of informing patients up to the physician.

Given such freedom, a physician can decide to tell as much or as little as he wants the patient to know, so long as he breaks no law. In the case of the man mentioned at the beginning of this chapter, some physicians might feel justified in lying for the good of the patient, others might be truthful. Some may conceal alternatives to the treatment they recommend; others not. In each case, they could appeal to the A.M.A. Principles of Ethics. A great many would choose to be able to lie. They would claim that not only can a lie avoid harm for the patient, but that it is also hard to know whether they have been right in the first place in making their pessimistic diagnosis; a "truthful" statement could therefore turn out to hurt patients unnecessarily. The concern for curing and for supporting those who cannot be cured then runs counter to the desire to be completely open. This concern is especially strong where the prognosis is bleak; even more so when patients are so affected by their illness or their medication that they are more dependent than usual, perhaps more easily depressed or irrational.

Physicians know only too well how uncertain a diagnosis or prognosis can be. They know how hard it is to give meaningful and correct answers regarding health and illness. They also know that disclosing their own uncertainty or fears can reduce those benefits that depend upon faith in recovery. They fear, too, that revealing grave risks, no matter how unlikely it is that these will come about, may exercise the pull of the "self-fulfilling prophecy." They dislike being the bearers of uncertain or bad news as much as anyone else. And last, but not least, sitting down to discuss an illness truthfully and sensitively may take much-needed time away from other patients.

These reasons help explain why nurses and physicians and relatives of the sick and the dying prefer not to be bound by rules that might limit their ability to suppress, delay, or distort information. This is not to say that they necessarily plan to lie much of the time. They merely want to have the freedom to do so when they believe it wise. And the reluctance to see lying prohibited explains, in turn, the failure of the codes and oaths to come to grips with the problems of truth-telling and lying.

But sharp conflicts are now arising. Doctors no longer work alone with patients. They have to consult with others much more than before; if they choose to lie, the choice may not be met with approval by all who take part in the care of the patient. A nurse expresses the difficulty which results as follows:

> From personal experience I would say that the patients who aren't told about their terminal illness have so many verbal and mental questions unanswered that many will begin to realize that their illness is more serious than they're being told. [. . .]

Nurses care for these patients twenty-four hours a day compared to a doctor's daily brief visit, and it is the nurse many times that the patient will relate to, once his underlying fears become overwhelming. [. . .] This is difficult for us nurses because being in constant contact with patients we can see the events leading up to this. The patient continually asks you, "Why isn't my pain decreasing?" or "Why isn't the radiation treatment easing the pain?" [. . .] We cannot legally give these patients an honest answer as a nurse (and I'm sure I wouldn't want to) yet the problem is still not resolved and the circle grows larger and larger with the patient alone in the middle.[7]

The doctor's choice to lie increasingly involves co-workers in acting a part they find neither humane nor wise. The fact that these problems have not been carefully thought through within the medical profession, nor seriously addressed in medical education, merely serves to intensify the conflicts.[8] Different doctors then respond very differently to patients in exactly similar predicaments. The friction is increased by the fact that relatives often disagree even where those giving medical care to a patient are in accord on how to approach the patient. Here again, because physicians have not worked out to common satisfaction the question of whether relatives have the right to make such requests, the problems are allowed to be haphazardly resolved by each physician as he sees fit.

The Patient's Perspective

The turmoil in the medical profession regarding truth-telling is further augmented by the pressures that patients themselves now bring to bear and by empirical data coming to light. Challenges are growing to the three major arguments for lying to patients: that truthfulness is impossible; that patients do not want bad news; and that truthful information harms them.

The first of these arguments was already discussed in Chapter I. It confuses "truth" and "truthfulness" so as to clear the way for occasional lying on grounds supported by the second and third arguments. At this point, we can see more clearly that it is a strategic move intended to discourage the question of truthfulness from carrying much weight in the first place, and thus to leave the choice of what to say and how to say it up to the physician. To claim that "since telling the truth is impossible, there can be no sharp distinction between what is true and what is false"[9] is to try to defeat objections to lying before even discussing them. One need only imagine how such an argument would be received, were it made by a car salesman or a real estate dealer, to see how fallacious it is.

In medicine, however, the argument is supported by a subsidiary point: even if people might ordinarily understand what is spoken to them, patients are often not in a position to do so. This is where paternalism enters in. When we buy cars or houses, the paternalist will argue, we need to have all our wits about us; but when we are ill, we cannot always do so. We need help in making choices, even if help can be given only by keeping us in the dark. And the physician is trained and willing to provide such help.

It is certainly true that some patients cannot make the best choices for themselves when weakened by illness or drugs. But most still can. And even those who are incompetent have a right to have someone—their guardian or spouse perhaps—receive the correct information.

The paternalistic assumption of superiority to patients also carries great dangers for physicians themselves—it risks turning to contempt. The following view was recently expressed in a letter to a medical journal:

As a radiologist who has been sued, I have reflected earnestly on advice to obtain Informed Consent but have decided to "take the risks without informing the patient" and trust to "God, judge, and jury" rather than evade responsibility through a legal gimmick. [. . .]

[I]n a general radiologic practice many of our patients are uninformable and we would never get through the day if we had to obtain their consent to every potentially harmful study.

[. . .] We still have patients with language problems, the uneducated and the unintelligent, the stolid and the stunned who cannot form an Informed Opinion to give an Informed Consent; we have the belligerent and the panicky who do not listen or comprehend. And then there are the Medicare patients who comprise 35 percent of general hospital admissions. The bright ones wearily plead to be left alone. [. . .] As for the apathetic rest, many of them were kindly described by Richard Bright as not being able to comprehend because "their brains are so poorly oxygenated."[10]

The argument which rejects informing patients because adequate truthful information is impossible in itself or because patients are lacking in understanding, must itself be rejected when looked at from the point of view of patients. They know that liberties granted to the most conscientious and altruistic doctors will be exercised also in the "Medicaid Mills"; that the choices thus kept from patients will be exercised by not only competent but incompetent physicians; and that even the best doctors can make choices patients would want to make differently for themselves.

The second argument for deceiving patients refers specifically to giving them news of a frightening or depressing kind. It holds that patients do not, in fact, generally want such information, that they prefer not to have to face up to serious illness and death. On the basis of such a belief, most doctors in a number of surveys stated that they do not, as a rule, inform patients that they have an illness such as cancer.

When studies are made of what patients desire to know, on the other hand, a large majority say that they *would* like to be told of such a diagnosis.[11] All these studies need updating and should be done with larger numbers of patients and non-patients. But they do show that there is generally a dramatic divergence between physicians and patients on the factual question of whether patients want to know what ails them in cases of serious illness such as cancer. In most of the studies, over 80 percent of the persons asked indicated that they would want to be told.

Sometimes this discrepancy is set aside by doctors who want to retain the view that patients do not want unhappy news. In reality, they claim, the fact that patients say they want it has to be discounted. The more someone asks to know, the more he suffers from fear which will lead to the denial of the information even if it is given. Informing patients is, therefore, useless; they resist and deny having been told what they cannot assimilate. According to this view, empirical studies of what patients say they want are worthless since they do not probe deeply enough to uncover this universal resistance to the contemplation of one's own death.

This view is only partially correct. For some patients, denial is indeed well established in medical experience. A number of patients (estimated at between 15 percent and 25 percent) will give evidence of denial of having been told about their illness, even when they repeatedly ask and are repeatedly informed. And nearly everyone experiences a period of denial at some point in the course of approaching death.[12] Elisabeth Kübler-Ross sees denial as resulting often from premature and abrupt information by a stranger who goes through the process quickly to "get it over with." She holds that denial functions as a buffer after unexpected shocking news, permitting individuals to collect themselves and to mobilize other defenses. She describes prolonged denial in one patient as follows:

> She was convinced that the X-rays were "mixed up"; she asked for reassurance that her pathology report could not possibly be back so soon and that another patient's report must have been marked with her name. When none of this could be confirmed, she quickly asked to leave the hospital, looking for another physician in the vain hope "to get a better explanation for my troubles." This patient went "shopping around" for many doctors, some of whom gave her reassuring answers, others of whom confirmed the previous suspicion. Whether confirmed or not, she reacted in the same manner; she asked for examination and reexamination. . . . [13]

But to say that denial is universal flies in the face of all evidence. And to take any claim to the contrary as "symptomatic" of deeper denial leaves no room for reasoned discourse. There is no way that such universal denial can be proved true or false. To believe in it is a metaphysical belief about man's condition, not a statement about what patients do and do not want. It is true that we can never completely understand the possibility of our own death, any more than being alive in the first place. But people certainly differ in the degree to which they can approach such knowledge, take it into account in their plans, and make their peace with it.

Montaigne claimed that in order to learn both to live and to die, men have to think about death and be prepared to accept it.[14] To stick one's head in the sand, or to be prevented by lies from trying to discern what is to come, hampers freedom—freedom to consider one's life as a whole, with a beginning, a duration, an end. Some may request to be deceived rather than to see their lives as thus finite; others reject the information which would require them to do so; but most say that they want to know. Their concern for knowing about their condition goes far beyond mere curiosity or the wish to make isolated personal choices in the short time left to them; their stance toward the entire life they have lived, and their ability to give it meaning and completion, are at stake.[15] In lying or withholding the facts which permit such discernment, doctors may reflect their own fears (which, according to one study,[16] are much stronger than those of laymen) of facing questions about the meaning of one's life and the inevitability of death.

Beyond the fundamental deprivation that can result from deception, we are also becoming increasingly aware of all that can befall patients in the course of their illness when information is denied or distorted. Lies place them in a position where they no longer participate in choices concerning their own health, including the choice of whether to be a "patient" in the first place. A terminally ill person who is not informed that his illness is incurable and that he is near death cannot make decisions about the end of his life: about whether or not to enter a hospital, or to have surgery; where and with whom to spend his last days; how to put his affairs in order—these most personal choices cannot be made if he is kept in the dark, or given contradictory hints and clues.

It has always been especially easy to keep knowledge from terminally ill patients. They are most vulnerable, least able to take action to learn what they need to know, or to protect their autonomy. The very fact of being so ill greatly increases the likelihood of control by others. And the fear of being helpless in the face of such control is growing. At the same time, the period of dependency and slow deterioration of health and strength that people undergo has lengthened. There has been a dramatic shift toward institutionalization of the aged and those near death. (Over 80 percent of Americans now die in a hospital or other institution.)

Patients who are severely ill often suffer a further distancing and loss of control over their most basic functions.

Electrical wiring, machines, intravenous administration of liquids, all create new dependency and at the same time new distance between the patient and all who come near. Curable patients are often willing to undergo such procedures; but when no cure is possible, these procedures merely intensify the sense of distance and uncertainty and can even become a substitute for comforting human acts. Yet those who suffer in this way often fear to seem troublesome by complaining. Lying to them, perhaps for the most charitable of purposes, can then cause them to slip unwittingly into subjection to new procedures, perhaps new surgery, where death is held at bay through transfusions, respirators, even resuscitation far beyond what most would wish.

Seeing relatives in such predicaments has caused a great upsurge of worrying about death and dying. At the root of this fear is not a growing terror of the *moment* of death, or even the instants before it. Nor is there greater fear of *being* dead. In contrast to the centuries of lives lived in dread of the punishments to be inflicted after death, many would now accept the view expressed by Epicurus, who died in 270 B.C.:*

> Death, therefore, the most awful of evils, is nothing to us, seeing that, when we are, death is not come, and, when death is come, we are not.

The growing fear, if it is not of the moment of dying nor of being dead, is of all that which now precedes dying for so many: the possibility of prolonged pain, the increas-

*See Diogenes Laertius, *Lives of Eminent Philosophers*, p. 651. Epicurus willed his garden to his friends and descendants, and wrote on the eve of dying:

"On this blissful day, which is also the last of my life, I write to you. My continual sufferings from strangury and dysentery are so great that nothing could augment them; but over against them all I set gladness of mind at the remembrance of our past conversations." (Letter to Idomeneus, *Ibid*, p. 549.)

ing weakness, the uncertainty, the loss of powers and chance of senility, the sense of being a burden. This fear is further nourished by the loss of trust in health professionals. In part, the loss of trust results from the abuses which have been exposed—the Medicaid scandals, the old-age home profiteering, the commercial exploitation of those who seek remedies for their ailments;[17] in part also because of the deceptive practices patients suspect, having seen how friends and relatives were kept in the dark; in part, finally, because of the sheer numbers of persons, often strangers, participating in the care of any one patient. Trust which might have gone to a doctor long known to the patient goes less easily to a team of strangers, no matter how expert or well-meaning.

It is with the working out of all that *informed consent** implies and the information it presupposes that truthtelling is coming to be discussed in a serious way for the first time in the health professions. Informed consent is a farce if the information provided is distorted or withheld. And even complete information regarding surgical procedures or medication is obviously useless unless the patient also knows what the condition is that these are supposed to correct.

Bills of rights for patients, similarly stressing the right to be informed, are now gaining acceptance.[18] This right is not new, but the effort to implement it is. Nevertheless, even where patients are handed the most elegantly phrased Bill of Rights, their right to a truthful diagnosis

---

*The law requires that inroads made upon a person's body take place only with the informed voluntary consent of that person. The term "informed consent" came into common use only after 1960, when it was used by the Kansas Supreme Court in Nathanson vs. Kline, 186 Kan. 393,350, p. 2d, 1093 (1960). The patient is now entitled to full disclosure of risks, benefits, and alternative treatments to any proposed procedure, both in therapy and in medical experimentation, except in emergencies or when the patient is incompetent, in which case proxy consent is required.

and prognosis is by no means always respected.

The reason why even doctors who recognize a patient's right to have information might still not provide it brings us to the third argument against telling all patients the truth. It holds that the information given might hurt the patient and that the concern for the right to such information is therefore a threat to proper health care. A patient, these doctors argue, may wish to commit suicide after being given discouraging news, or suffer a cardiac arrest, or simply cease to struggle, and thus not grasp the small remaining chance for recovery. And even where the outlook for a patient is very good, the disclosure of a minute risk can shock some patients or cause them to reject needed protection such as a vaccination or antibiotics.

The factual basis for this argument has been challenged from two points of view. The damages associated with the disclosure of sad news or risks are rarer than physicians believe; and the *benefits* which result from being informed are more substantial, even measurably so. Pain is tolerated more easily, recovery from surgery is quicker, and cooperation with therapy is greatly improved. The attitude that "what you don't know won't hurt you" is proving unrealistic; it is what patients do not know but vaguely suspect that causes them corrosive worry.

It is certain that no answers to this question of harm from information are the same for all patients. If we look, first, at the fear expressed by physicians that informing patients of even remote or unlikely risks connected with a drug prescription or operation might shock some and make others refuse the treatment that would have been best for them, it appears to be unfounded for the great majority of patients. Studies show that very few patients respond to being told of such risks by withdrawing their consent to the procedure and that those who do withdraw are the very ones who might well have been upset enough to sue the physician had they not been asked to consent beforehand.[19] It is possible that on even rarer occasions especially susceptible persons might manifest physical deterioration from shock; some physicians have even asked whether patients who die after giving informed consent to an operation, but before it actually takes place, somehow expire because of the information given to them.[20] While such questions are unanswerable in any one case, they certainly argue in favor of caution, a real concern for the person to whom one is recounting the risks he or she will face, and sensitivity to all signs of distress.

The situation is quite different when persons who are already ill, perhaps already quite weak and discouraged, are told of a very serious prognosis. Physicians fear that such knowledge may cause the patients to commit suicide, or to be frightened or depressed to the point that their illness takes a downward turn. The fear that great numbers of patients will commit suicide appears to be unfounded.[21] And if some do, is that a response so unreasonable, so much against the patient's best interest that physicians ought to make it a reason for concealment or lies? Many societies have allowed suicide in the past; our own has decriminalized it; and some are coming to make distinctions among the many suicides which ought to be prevented if at all possible, and those which ought to be respected.[22]

Another possible response to very bleak news is the triggering of physiological mechanisms which allow death to come more quickly—a form of giving up or of preparing for the inevitable, depending on one's outlook. Lewis Thomas, studying responses in humans and animals, holds it not unlikely that:

> [. . .] there is a pivotal movement at some stage in the body's reaction to injury or disease, maybe in aging as well, when the organism concedes that it is finished and the time

for dying is at hand, and at this moment the events that lead to death are launched, as a coordinated mechanism. Functions are then shut off, in sequence, irreversibly, and, while this is going on, a neural mechanism, held ready for this occasion, is switched on. . . .[23]

Such a response may be appropriate, in which case it makes the moments of dying as peaceful as those who have died and been resuscitated so often testify. But it may also be brought on inappropriately, when the organism could have lived on, perhaps even induced malevolently, by external acts intended to kill. Thomas speculates that some of the deaths resulting from "hexing" are due to such responses. Lévi-Strauss describes deaths from exorcism and the casting of spells in ways which suggest that the same process may then be brought on by the community.[24]

It is not inconceivable that unhappy news abruptly conveyed, or a great shock given to someone unable to tolerate it, could also bring on such a "dying response," quite unintended by the speaker. There is every reason to be cautious and to try to know ahead of time how susceptible a patient might be to the accidental triggering—however rare—of such a response. One has to assume, however, that most of those who have survived long enough to be in a situation where their informed consent is asked have a very robust resistance to such accidental triggering of processes leading to death.

When, on the other hand, one considers those who are already near death, the "dying response" may be much less inappropriate, much less accidental, much less unreasonable. In most societies, long before the advent of modern medicine, human beings have made themselves ready for death once they felt its approach. Philippe Ariès describes how many in the Middle Ages prepared themselves for death when they "felt the end approach." They awaited death lying down, surrounded by friends and relatives. They recollected all they had lived through and done, pardoning all who stood near their deathbed, calling on God to bless them, and finally praying. "After the final prayer all that remained was to wait for death, and there was no reason for death to tarry."[25]

Modern medicine, in its valiant efforts to defeat disease and to save lives, may be dislocating the conscious as well as the purely organic responses allowing death to come when it is inevitable, thus denying those who are dying the benefits of the traditional approach to death. In lying to them, and in pressing medical efforts to cure them long past the point of possible recovery, physicians may thus rob individuals of an autonomy few would choose to give up.

Sometimes, then, the "dying response" is a natural organic reaction at the time when the body has no further defense. Sometimes it is inappropriately brought on by news too shocking or given in too abrupt a manner. We need to learn a great deal more about this last category, no matter how small. But there is no evidence that patients in general will be debilitated by truthful information about their condition.

Apart from the possible harm from information, we are coming to learn much more about the benefits it can bring patients. People follow instructions more carefully if they know what their disease is and why they are asked to take medication; any benefits from those procedures are therefore much more likely to come about.* Similarly, people recover faster from surgery and tolerate pain with

---

*Barbara S. Hulka, J. C. Cassel, et al. "Communication, Compliance, and Concordance between Physicians and Patients with Prescribed Medications," *American Journal of Public Health*, Sept. 1976, pp. 847–53. The study shows that of the nearly half of all patients who do not follow the prescriptions of the doctors (thus foregoing the intended effect of these prescriptions), many will follow them if adequately informed about the nature of their illness and what the proposed medication will do.

less medication if they understand what ails them and what can be done for them.*

Respect and Truthfulness

Taken all together, the three arguments defending lies to patients stand on much shakier ground as a counter-weight to the right to be informed than is often thought. The common view that many patients cannot understand, do not want, and may be harmed by, knowledge of their condition, and that lying to them is either morally neutral or even to be recommended, must be set aside. Instead, we have to make a more complex comparison. Over against the right of patients to knowledge concerning themselves, the medical and psychological benefits to them from this knowledge, the unnecessary and sometimes harmful treatment to which they can be subjected if ignorant, and the harm to physicians, their profession, and other patients from deceptive practices, we have to set a severely restricted and narrowed paternalistic view—that *some* patients cannot understand, *some* do not want, and *some* may be harmed by, knowledge of their condition, and that they ought not to have to be treated like everyone else if this is not in their best interest.

Such a view is persuasive. A few patients openly request not to be given bad news. Others give clear signals to that effect, or are demonstrably vulnerable to the shock or anguish such news might call forth. Can one not in such cases infer implied consent to being deceived?

Concealment, evasion, withholding of information

*See Lawrence D. Egbert, George E. Batitt, et al., "Reduction of Post-operative Pain by Encouragement and Instruction of Patients," *New England Journal of Medicine*, 270, pp. 825–827, 1964.

See also: Howard Waitzskin and John D. Stoeckle, "The Communication of Information about Illness," *Advances in Psychosomatic Medicine*, Vol. 8, 1972, pp. 185–215.

may at times be necessary. But if someone contemplates lying to a patient or concealing the truth, the burden of proof must shift. It must rest, here, as with all deception, on those who advocate it in any one instance. They must show why they fear a patient may be harmed or how they know that another cannot cope with the truthful knowledge. A decision to deceive must be seen as a very unusual step, to be talked over with colleagues and others who participate in the care of the patient. Reasons must be set forth and debated, alternatives weighed carefully. At all times, the correct information must go to *someone* closely related to the patient.

The law already permits doctors to withhold information from patients where it would clearly hurt their health. But this privilege has been sharply limited by the courts. Certainly it cannot be interpreted so broadly as to permit a general practice of deceiving patients "for their own good." Nor can it be made to include cases where patients might calmly decide, upon hearing their diagnosis, not to go ahead with the therapy their doctor recommends.[26] Least of all can it justify silence or lies to large numbers of patients merely on the grounds that it is not always easy to tell what a patient wants.

For the great majority of patients, on the contrary, the goal must be disclosure, and the atmosphere one of openness. But it would be wrong to assume that patients can therefore be told abruptly about a serious diagnosis—that, so long as openness exists, there are no further requirements of humane concern in such communication. Dr. Cicely Saunders, who runs the well-known St. Christopher's Hospice in England, describes the sensitivity and understanding which are needed:

> Every patient needs an explanation of his illness that will be understandable and convincing to him if he is to cooperate in his treatment or be relieved of the burden of unknown fears. This is true whether it is a question of

giving a diagnosis in a hopeful situation or of confirming a poor prognosis.

The fact that a patient does not ask does not mean that he has no questions. One visit or talk is rarely enough. It is only by waiting and listening that we can gain an idea of what we should be saying. Silences and gaps are often more revealing than words as we try to learn what a patient is facing as he travels along the constantly changing journey of his illness and his thoughts about it.

[. . .] So much of the communication will be without words or given indirectly. This is true of all real meeting with people but especially true with those who are facing, knowingly or not, difficult or threatening situations. It is also particularly true of the very ill.

The main argument against a policy of deliberate, in-variable denial of unpleasant facts is that it makes such communication extremely difficult, if not impossible. Once the possibility of talking frankly with a patient has been admitted, it does not mean that this will always take place, but the whole atmosphere is changed. We are then free to wait quietly for clues from each patient, seeing them as individuals from whom we can expect intelligence, cour-age, and individual decisions. They will feel secure enough to give us these clues when they wish.[27]

Above all, truthfulness with those who are suffering does not mean that they should be deprived of all hope: hope that there is a chance of recovery, however small; nor of reassurance that they will not be abandoned when they most need help.

Much needs to be done, however, if the deceptive prac-tices are to be eliminated, and if concealment is to be restricted to the few patients who ask for it or those who can be shown to be harmed by openness. The medical profession has to address this problem. Those who are in training to take care of the sick and the dying have to learn how to speak with them, even about dying. They will be helped to do so if they can be asked to consider alternative approaches to patients, put themselves in the situation of a patient, even confront the possibility of being themselves near death.

Until the day comes when patients can be assured that they can trust what doctors tell them, is there anything they can do to improve the chances for themselves? How can they try to avoid slipping into a dependent relationship, one in which they have no way of trusting what anyone tells them? Is there any way in which they can maintain a degree of autonomy, even at a time of great weakness?

Those who know who will take care of them when they become seriously ill or approach death can talk this matter over well ahead of time. If they do, it is very likely that their desires will be respected. Growing numbers are now signing statements known as *living wills,* in which they can, if they so wish, specify whether or not they want to be informed about their condition. They can also specify conditions under which they do not want to have their lives prolonged.[28] Still others, who may not have thought of these problems ahead of time, can insist on receiving adequate information once they are in need of care. It is the great majority—those who are afraid of asking, of seeming distrustful—who give rise to the view that patients do not really want to know since they never ask.

The perspective of needing care is very different from that of providing it. The first sees the most fundamental question for patients to be whether they can trust their care-takers. It requires a stringent adherence to honesty, in all but a few carefully delineated cases. The second sees the need to be free to deceive, sometimes for genuinely humane reasons. It is only by bringing these perspectives into the open and by considering the exceptional cases explicitly that the discrepancy can be reduced and trust restored.

CONCLUSION

Certainly, it is heaven upon earth to have a man's mind move in charity, rest in providence, and turn upon the poles of truth.

—Bacon, "Of Truth"

Nearly every kind of statement or action can be meant to deceive. Clearly intended lies—the most sharply etched forms of duplicity—have been in the foreground throughout this book. More marginal forms, such as evasion, euphemism, and exaggeration, have been close at hand, ready to prop up these lies or take their place. And all around have clustered the many kinds of deception intended to mislead without even marginally false statements: the changes of subject, the disguises, the gestures leading astray, all blending into the background of silence and inaction only sometimes intended to mislead.

We lead our lives amidst all these forms of duplicity. From childhood on, we develop ways of coping with them —of believing some, seeing through others, and consciously ignoring still others. We may end by tolerating even certain practices of outright lying without knowing how to distinguish them from those that we reject out of hand: tolerating, for instance, lies believed to serve the "best interests" of groups or individuals, those undertaken for purposes of advocacy, or those construed to serve the objectives of self-defense. I have wanted to convey the *levels* of deception that we must all live with as a result and to focus on the burden they impose.

Must we take these levels of deception to be our lot? Are they somehow immutable? There is no reason to think so. They vary from one family to another, from one profession or society to the next. As a result, there is ample room for change. But how can it be brought about? What steps can individuals take by themselves, and which measures require collective action?

Individuals, without a doubt, have the power to influence the amount of duplicity in their lives and to shape their speech and action. They can decide to rule out deception wherever honest alternatives exist, and become much more adept at thinking up honest ways to deal with problems. They can learn to look with much greater care at the remaining choices where deception seems the only way out. They can make use of the test of publicity to help them set standards to govern their participation in deceptive practices. Finally, they can learn to beware of efforts to dupe them, and make clear their preference for honesty even in small things.

But individuals differ greatly in their ability to carry through such changes. They differ in their knowledge of deception and its alternatives; in their desire to bring about changes; and in their understanding of what lying can do to them, either as deceiver or as deceived. Many who might be able to change the patterns of duplicity in their own lives lack any awareness of the presence of a moral problem in the first place, and thus feel no need to examine their behavior and explore the alternatives carefully. Others are beyond caring.

Still another difference among individuals cuts sharply into the capacity of many to make changes: the difference in the power to carry through a change and in the freedom and security from repercussions should they challenge deeply rooted habits of duplicity. The lack of power and freedom to cope with the consequences of battling deceptive practices reinforces the lack of awareness or concern wherever it exists; it puts great pressure even on those least comfortable with deceit.

Thus, the cub reporter who will lose his job if he is not aggressive in getting stories, or the young politician whose career depends on winning an election, may in principle be more sorely tempted to bend the truth than those whose work is secure; but this difference may be more than outweighed by the increased callousness of the latter to what they have come to regard as routine deception.

The very stress on individualism, on competition, on achieving material success which so marks our society also generates intense pressures to cut corners. To win an election, to increase one's income, to outsell competitors —such motives impel many to participate in forms of duplicity they might otherwise resist. The more widespread they judge these practices to be, the stronger will be the pressures to join, even compete, in deviousness.

The social incentives to deceit are at present very powerful; the controls, often weak. Many individuals feel caught up in practices they cannot change. It would be wishful thinking, therefore, to expect individuals to bring about major changes in the collective practices of deceit by themselves. Public and private institutions, with their enormous power to affect personal choice, must help alter the existing pressures and incentives.

What role can the government play in such efforts? First, it can look to its own practices, to the very "climate" of its dealings with the public. It will take time and great effort to try to reverse the injuries to trust and to public life of the last decades. Second, the government could move forcefully to carry out the existing laws prohibiting fraud and perjury. Here again, government members have to be the first to be held to such standards. Third, the laws and rules in our society must be examined from the point of view of whether they encourage deception needlessly. Some regulations put great pressures on individuals to deceive—in order to continue to receive welfare payments, for example, or to be allowed to have a divorce in societies with very strict rules against divorce. Some laws even *require* deception, as in those states where criminal records officials are compelled by law to deny that certain felons have a police record when asked by prospective employers.

Private institutions can play a parallel role in reducing the incentives to cut corners. Recent studies indicate that businessmen regard unethical practices as very widespread, and pressures to conform as strong.[1] These pressures can be communicated directly from top management, with an immediate effect on lower level managers. Three quarters of those surveyed agree that, like the junior members of Nixon's reelection committee, young executives automatically go along with superiors to show loyalty. Very often, however, there is no such communication from top management; the pressures are conveyed indirectly. For example, a company may set high goals for production or sales. When economic conditions become adverse, it may be next to impossible to meet these targets without moral compromises. If the incentives for achieving the goals—retaining one's job, most importantly, but also promotions, bonuses, or salary increases— are felt to be too compelling, the temptation to lie and to cheat can grow intolerable.

Such conditions came to light in the momentous price-fixing scandal in 1960 involving General Electric and the sale of heavy electrical machinery. For years, subordinate officials participated in illegal price-fixing activities involving sales valued at more than a billion dollars a year. They conspired to fix prices, rig bids, split markets. By means of secret meetings, misleading code-words, falsified expense accounts, these activities were covered up, and the responsibilities passed from one manager to the next. At the very same time as top management sent around stern prohibitions of price-fixing to all subordinates, it put greater and greater pressures on each to raise the percentage of available business.[2]

There is strong insistence now that business ought to have a code of ethics. But codes of ethics function all too often as shields; their abstraction allows many to adhere to them while continuing their ordinary practices. In business as well as in those professions that have already developed codes, much more is needed. The codes must be but the starting point for a broad inquiry into the ethical quandaries encountered at work. Lay persons, and especially those affected by the professional practices, such as customers or patients, must be included in these efforts, and must sit on regulatory commissions. Methods of disciplining those who infringe the guidelines must be given teeth and enforced.

Throughout society, then, all would benefit if the incentive structure associated with deceit were changed: if the gains from deception were lowered, and honesty made more worthwhile even in the short run. Sometimes it is easy to make such a change. Universities, for instance, have found in recent years that parents of incoming students all too often misrepresent their family incomes in order to gain scholarships for their children at the expense of those in greater need of assistance. If, on the other hand, parents are told in advance that they may have to produce their income tax statements on request, such misrepresentation is much less likely to take place.

Very often, however, there can be no such checks—as where people communicate estimates, or vote their preference, or make sealed bids in auctions. In large organizations, for instance, specialists often communicate skewed estimates and false prognostications in order to affect the final choices made in what they regard as the "right" direction.

It ought not to be beyond human ingenuity to increase the incentives for honesty even in such circumstances. Many are beginning to devote thought to possible changes of this kind. Economists, in particular, are seeking procedures that reward honesty in such activities as voting, giving expert advice, bargaining, and bidding at auctions.[3] Their efforts combine mathematical economics with policy-making in the public interest. They suggest that such changes be made in common social procedures that, when people choose strategically, it will also be in their best interest to be honest. In this way, social practices that have sprung up helter-skelter, and that at present appear to reward deception, may be altered in such a way that all benefit thereby.

Educational institutions have a very large role to play as well. First of all, they, too, have to look to their own practices. How scrupulously honest are they in setting an example? How do they cope with cheating, with plagiarism, and with fraudulent research? What pressures encourage such behavior? To what extent, and in what disciplines, are deceptive techniques actually *taught* to students? What lines do law school courses, for instance, draw with respect to courtroom tactics, or business school courses with respect to bargaining and negotiation? Second, what can education bring to the training of students, in order that they may be more discerning, better able to cope with the various forms of duplicity that they will encounter in working life? Colleges and universities, as well as nursing schools, police academies, military academies, accounting schools, and many others need to consider how moral choice can best be studied and what standards can be expected, as well as upheld.

Some professions, such as medicine and law, have longer traditions of ethical inquiry than others; courses are springing up in these fields, and materials for teaching have been assembled. Other professions are only at the beginning of such an endeavor.[4] But in all these fields, much too little effort is being devoted to train persons who are competent to teach such courses. As a result, existing courses are often inadequate, leaving students confirmed in their suspicion that moral choice is murky and best left to intuition.

In developing courses, and in training those who will teach them, there is no need to start from scratch. We are not the first to face moral problems such as those of deception. Others have experienced them, argued about them, arrived at conclusions. The structure of lies and the possible justifications have long been studied. We need to make use of the traditional approaches. We need to consider, for example, in the context of working life, why it has been thought worse to *plan* to lie than to do so on the spur of the moment; worse to induce others to lie (and thus to *teach* deception, whether in families, work places or schools) than to do so oneself; worse to lie to those with a *right* to truthful information than to others; worse to lie to those who have entrusted you with their confidence about matters important to them than to your enemies.

We now have resources that these earlier traditions lacked. We have access to information and to methods that can sharpen and refine the very notions of what is "helpful" and what is "harmful" among the consequences of lies. There is much room for study; but we are learning, for example, what proportion of those who are very ill *want* to be treated truthfully; what happens to adopted children who are deceived about the identity of their parents; how the public responds to government deceit. We are learning, also, much more about how the mechanisms of bias and rationalization work. Finally, we can go far beyond the anecdotes available to earlier thinkers in documenting the deceptive practices themselves.

These practices are not immutable. In an imperfect world, they cannot be wiped out altogether; but surely they can be reduced and counteracted. I hope to have shown how often the justifications they invoke are insubstantial, and how they can disguise and fuel all other wrongs. Trust and integrity are precious resources, easily squandered, hard to regain. They can thrive only on a foundation of respect for veracity.

APPENDIX

Excerpts from works by Augustine, Aquinas, Bacon, Grotius, Kant, Sidgwick, Harrod, Bonhoeffer, and Warnock

AUGUSTINE
ON LYING

(25) The first type of lie is a deadly one which should be avoided and shunned from afar, namely, that which is uttered in the teaching of religion, and to the telling of which no one should be led under any condition. The second is that which injures somebody unjustly: such a lie as helps no one and harms someone. The third is that which is beneficial to one person while it harms another, although the harm does not produce physical defilement. The fourth is the lie which is told solely for the pleasure of lying and deceiving, that is, the real lie. The fifth type is that which is told from a desire to please others in smooth discourse. When these have been avoided and rejected, a sixth kind of lie follows which harms no one and benefits some person, as, for instance, when a person, knowing that another's money is to be taken away unjustly, answers the questioner untruthfully and says that he does not know where the money is. The seventh type is that which is harmful to no one and beneficial to some person, with the exception of the case where

From Augustine, "Lying," in *Treatises on Various Subjects*, ed. R. J. Deferrari, Fathers of the Church (New York: Catholic University of America Press, 1952), vol. 14, chap. 14.

a judge is questioning, as happens when a person lies because he is unwilling to betray a man sought for capital punishment, that is, not only a just and innocent person but even a criminal, because it belongs to Christian discipline never to despair of the conversion of anybody and never to block the opportunity for repentance. Now, I have spoken at length concerning these last two types, which are wont to evoke considerable discussion, and I have presented my opinion, namely, that by the acceptance of sufferings which are borne honorably and courageously, these lies, too, may be avoided by strong, faithful, and truthful men and women. The eighth is that type of lie which is harmful to no one and beneficial to the extent that it protects someone from physical defilement, at least, from that defilement which we have mentioned above. Now, the Jews considered it defilement to eat with unwashed hands. If anyone considers that as defilement, then a lie must not be told in order to avoid it. However, we are confronted with a new problem if a lie is such that it brings injury to any person, even though it protects another person from that defilement which all men detest and abhor. Should such a lie be told if the injury resulting from it is not in the nature of the defilement of which we have been treating? The question here does not concern lying; rather, it is whether harm should be done to any person, not necessarily through a lie, so that such defilement may be warded off from another person. I am definitely inclined to oppose such license. Even though the most trivial injuries are proposed, such as that one which I mentioned above in regard to the one lost measure of grain, they disturb me greatly in this problem as to whether we ought to do injury to one person if, by that wrong, another person may be defended, or protected against defilement. But, as I have said, that is another question.

AUGUSTINE
AGAINST LYING

You have sent me much to read, dear brother Consentius, you have sent me much to read. [. . .] I am quite delighted with

From Augustine, "Against Lying," in *Treatises on Various Subjects*, ed. R.J. Deferrari, Fathers of the Church (New York: Catholic University of America Press, 1952), vol. 16, chaps. 1, 2, 18.

your eloquence, with your memory of sacred Scripture, with your adroitness of mind, with your distress in stinging indifferent Catholics, with your zeal in raging against even latent heretics. But I am not persuaded that they should be drawn out of hiding by our lies. For, why do we try with so much care to track them and hunt them down? Is it not so that, when they have been caught and brought into the open, we may either teach them the truth themselves or else, by convicting them of error, keep them from harming others? Is it not, in short, so that their falsehood may be blotted out or guarded against and God's truth be increased? Therefore, how can I suitably proceed against lies by lying? Or should robbery be proceeded against by means of robbery, sacrilege by sacrilege, and adultery by adultery? 'But if through my lie the truth of God has abounded,' are we, too, going to say, 'why should we not do evil that good may come from it?' You see how much the Apostle detests this. But what is it to say: 'Let us lie in order to bring lying heretics to the truth,' if not the same as saying, 'Why should we not do evil that good may come from it?' Or is lying sometimes a good, or sometimes not an evil? Why, then, has it been written: 'Thou hatest all the workers of iniquity: thou wilt destroy all that speak a lie'? He has not made exception of some or said indefinitely: 'Thou wilt destroy tellers of lies,' so as to allow that certain ones be understood, but not every one. But he has brought forth a universal proposition, saying: 'Thou wilt destroy all that speak a lie.' Or, because it has not been said: 'Thou wilt destroy all that speak any lie or that speak any lie whatsoever,' are we to think, therefore, that room has been made for a certain kind of lie and that God will not destroy those who tell a certain kind of lie, but only those who tell unjust lies, not any lie whatsoever, because there are found just lies, too, which ought actually to be matter for praise rather than reproach?

(2) Do you not see how much this argument supports the very ones whom we are trying to catch as great quarry by our lies? That, as you yourself have shown, is precisely the opinion of the Priscillianists. To establish this opinion they produce evidence from Scripture, urging their followers to lie as if in accordance with the example of the Patriarchs, Prophets, Apostles, and angels, not hesitating to add even Christ our Lord

Himself, thinking that they cannot otherwise prove their false-hood to be true except by saying that the Truth is mendacious. They must be refuted, not imitated. We must not participate with the Pricillianists in that evil in which they are proved to be worse that all other heretics, for they alone, or at least they especially, in order to hide what they think is their truth, are found to give dogmatic sanction to lying. And this great evil they deem just, for they say that what is true must be kept in the heart, but that it is no sin to utter what is false with the tongue to strangers. They say that it has been written: 'He that speaketh truth in his heart,' as if that were sufficient for justice, even if one tells a lie with his tongue when a stranger and not a neighbor is listening. On this account they even think that the Apostle Paul, when he had said: 'Put away lying and speak truth,' at once added: 'each one with his neighbor, because we are members of one another,' so that it plainly might be law-ful and dutiful to tell a lie to those who are not our neighbors in the community of truth and not, as it were, our comem-bers.[. . .]

(36) But, because we are men and live among men, I confess that I am not yet in the number of those who are not troubled by compensatory sins. Often, in human affairs, human sympa-thy overcomes me and I am unable to resist when someone says to me: 'Look, here is a patient whose life is endangered by a serious illness and whose strength will not hold out any longer if he is told of the death of his dearly beloved only son. He asks you whether the boy is still alive whose life you know is ended. What will you answer when, if you say anything except "He is dead" or "He is alive" or "I don't know," the patient will believe that he is dead, because he realizes that you are afraid to say and do not want to lie? It will be the same no matter how hard you try to say nothing. Of the three convincing answers, two are false: "He is alive" and "I don't know," and you cannot utter them without lying. But, if you make the one true answer, namely, that he is dead, and if the death of the anguished father follows hard upon it, people will cry that he was slain by you. And who can bear to hear them exaggerate the evil of avoiding a beneficial lie and of loving homicide as truth?' I am moved by these arguments—more powerfully than wisely! For, when I put before my mind's eye the intellectual beauty of Him from

whose mouth nothing false proceeded, then, although my weakness reverberates in palpitation before the radiance of the truth shining ever more brightly, I am so inflamed by love of such great beauty that I despise all human considerations that call me back from there. It is hard for this feeling to persist so far that its effect is not lost in time of temptation. Indeed, when I am contemplating the luminous good on which there is cast no shadow of a lie, I am not moved by the fact that, when we are unwilling to lie and men die upon hearing what is true, truth is called homicide. Why, if a shameless woman expects to be defiled and then dies of her fierce love because you do not consent, will chastity also be homicide? Or, indeed, because we read: 'We are the fragrance of Christ for God, alike as regards those who are saved and those who are lost; to these an odor that leads to death, but to those an odor that leads to life,' shall we also pronounce the fragrance of Christ to be homicide? But, because we are men and because human sympathy generally overcomes or harasses us amid such questions and objections, therefore, he, too, added, And for such offices; who is sufficient?

(37) Besides this there is the more distressing fact that, if we grant that we ought to lie about the son's life for the sake of that patient's health, little by little and bit by bit this evil will grow and by gradual accessions will slowly increase until it becomes such a mass of wicked lies that it will be utterly impossible to find any means of resisting such a plague grown to huge proportions through small additions. Hence, it has been most providentially written: 'He that contemneth small things, shall fall by little and little.' What of the fact that such lovers of this life as do not hesitate to prefer it to the truth want us not only to lie but also to perjure ourselves in order that a man may not die, nay, in order that a man who must sooner or later die may die a little later? They would have us take the name of the Lord our God in vain in order that the vain health of a man may not pass away a little sooner. And there are in these matters learned men who even make rules and set limits for when we ought and when we ought not to be perjured. O where are you, ye fountains of tears? And what shall we do? Where shall we go? Where shall we hide ourselves from the wrath of truth, if we not only disregard the avoidance of lies, but venture in addition to teach perjuries? Let the advocates and defenders of lies look to what

kind or kinds of lying it pleases them to justify! Only in the worship of God may they grant that we must not lie; only from perjuries and blasphemies may they restrain themselves; only where God's name, God's testimony, God's oath is introduced, only where talk of divine religion is brought forth, may no one lie, or praise or teach or enjoin lying or say that lying is just. About other kinds of lies, let him who believes that we ought to lie choose for himself what he thinks is the mildest and most innocent kind of lying. This much I know, that even he who teaches that we ought to lie wants to appear to be teaching the truth. For, if what he teaches is false, who would want to study the false doctrine where the teacher deceives and the learner is deceived? But if, in order that he may be able to find some pupil, he declares that he is teaching the truth when he teaches that we ought to lie, how will that lie be of the truth, since John the Apostle protests that no lie is of the truth?' Therefore, it is not true that sometimes we ought to lie. And what is not true we should never try to persuade anyone to believe.

THOMAS AQUINAS
WHETHER LIES ARE SUFFICIENTLY DIVIDED INTO OFFICIOUS, JOCOSE AND MISCHIEVOUS LIES?

We proceed thus to the Second Article:—

Objection 1. It seems that lies are not sufficiently divided into *officious, jocose* and *mischievous* lies. For a division should be made according to that which pertains to a thing by reason of its nature, as the Philosopher states (*Metaph.* vii, text. 43: *De Part. Animal.* i. 3). But seemingly the intention of the effect resulting from a moral act is something beside and accidental to the species of that act, so that an indefinite number of effects can result from one act. Now this division is made according to the intention of the effect: for a *jocose* lie is told in order to make fun, an *officious* lie for some useful purpose, and a mischievous lie in order to injure someone. Therefore lies are unfittingly divided in this way.

Obj. 2. Further, Augustine (*Contra Mendac.* xiv) gives eight

---

From Thomas Aquinas, *Summa Theologica* 2. 2. ques. 110, art. 2.

kinds of lies. The first is *in religious doctrine;* the second is *a lie that profits no one and injures someone;* the third *profits one party so as to injure another;* the fourth *is told out of mere lust of lying and deceiving;* the fifth *is told out of the desire to please;* the sixth *injures no one, and profits someone in saving his money;* the seventh *injures no one and profits someone in saving him from death;* the eighth *injures no one, and profits someone in saving him from defilement of the body.* Therefore it seems that the first division of lies is insufficient.

Obj. 3. Further, the Philosopher (*Ethic.* iv. 7) divides lying into *boasting,* which exceeds the truth in speech, and *irony,* which falls short of the truth by saying something less: and these two are not contained under any one of these kinds mentioned above. Therefore it seems that the aforesaid division of lies is inadequate.

On the contrary, A gloss on Ps. v. 7, *Thou wilt destroy all that speak a lie,* says *that there are three kinds of lies; for some are told for the wellbeing and convenience of someone; and there is another kind of lie that is told in fun; but the third kind of lie is told out of malice.* The first of these is called an officious lie, the second a jocose lie, the third a mischievous lie. Therefore, lies are divided into these three kinds.

I answer that, Lies may be divided in three ways. First, with respect to their nature as lies: and this is the proper and essential division of lying. In this way, according to the Philosopher (*Ethic.* iv. 7), lies are of two kinds, namely, the lie which goes beyond the truth, and this belongs to *boasting,* and the lie which stops short of the truth, and this belongs to *irony.* This division is an essential division of lying itself, because lying as such is opposed to truth, as stated in the preceding Article: and truth is a kind of equality, to which more and less are in essential opposition.

Secondly, lies may be divided with respect to their nature as sins, and with regard to those things that aggravate or diminish the sin of lying, on the part of the end intended. Now the sin of lying is aggravated, if by lying a person intends to injure another, and this is called a *mischievous* lie, while the sin of lying is diminished if it be directed to some good—either of pleasure and then it is a *jocose* lie, or of usefulness, and then we have the *officious* lie, whereby it is intended to help another person, or to save him from being injured. In this way lies are divided into the three kinds aforesaid.

Thirdly, lies are divided in a more general way, with respect to their relation to some end, whether or not this increase or diminish their gravity: and in this way the division comprises eight kinds, as stated in the *Second Objection*. Here the first three kinds are contained under *mischievous lies*, which are either against God, and then we have the lie *in religious doctrine*, or against man, and this either with the sole intention of injuring him, and then it is the second kind of lie, which *profits no one, and injures someone*; or with the intention of injuring one and at the same time profiting another, and this is the third kind of lie, *which profits one, and injures another*. Of these the first is the most grievous, because sins against God are always more grievous, as stated above (I–II, Q. 73, A. 3): and the second is more grievous than the third, since the latter's gravity is diminished by the intention of profiting another.

After these three, which aggravate the sin of lying, we have a fourth, which has its own measure of gravity without addition or diminution, and this is the lie which is told *out of mere lust of lying and deceiving*. This proceeds from a habit, wherefore the Philosopher says (*Ethic*. iv. 7) that *the liar, when he lies from habit, delights in lying*.

The four kinds that follow lessen the gravity of the sin of lying. For the fifth kind is the jocose lie, which is told *with a desire to please*: and the remaining three are comprised under the officious lie, wherein something useful to another person is intended. This usefulness regards either external things, and then we have the sixth kind of lie, which *profits someone in saving his money*; or his body, and this is the seventh kind, which *saves a man from death*; or the morality of his virtue, and this is the eighth kind, which *saves him from unlawful defilement of his body*.

Now it is evident that the greater the good intended, the more is the sin of lying diminished in gravity. Wherefore a careful consideration of the matter will show these various kinds of lies are enumerated in their order of gravity: since the useful good is better than the pleasurable good, and life of the body than money, and virtue than the life of the body.

This suffices for the *Replies* to the *Objections*.

THOMAS AQUINAS
WHETHER EVERY LIE IS A MORTAL SIN?

We proceed thus to the Fourth Article:—

Objection 1. It seems that every lie is a mortal sin. For it is written (Ps. vi. 7): *Thou wilt destroy all that speak a lie,* and (Wis. i. 11): *The mouth that belieth killeth the soul.* Now mortal sin alone causes destruction and death of the soul. Therefore every lie is a mortal sin.

Obj. 2. Further, whatever is against a precept of the decalogue is a mortal sin. Now lying is against this precept of the decalogue: *Thou shalt not bear false witness.* Therefore every lie is a mortal sin.

Obj. 3. Further, Augustine says (*De Doctr. Christ.* i. 36): *Every liar breaks his faith in lying, since forsooth he wishes the person to whom he lies to have faith in him, and yet he does not keep faith with him, when he lies to him: and whoever breaks his faith is guilty of iniquity.* Now no one is said to break his faith or *to be guilty of iniquity,* for a venial sin. Therefore no lie is a venial sin.

Obj. 4. Further, the eternal reward is not lost save for a mortal sin. Now, for a lie the eternal reward was lost, being exchanged for a temporal meed. For Gregory says (*Moral.* xviii) that *we learn from the reward of the midwives what the sin of lying deserves: since the reward which they deserved for their kindness, and which they might have received in eternal life, dwindled into a temporal meed on account of the lie of which they were guilty.* Therefore even an officious lie, such as was that of the midwives, which seemingly is the least of lies, is a mortal sin.

Obj. 5. Further, Augustine says (*Lib. De Mend.* xvii) that *it is a precept of perfection, not only not to lie at all, but not even to wish to lie.* Now it is a mortal sin to act against a precept. Therefore every lie of the perfect is a mortal sin: and consequently so also is a lie told by anyone else, otherwise the perfect would be worse off than others.

From Thomas Aquinas, *Summa Theologica* 2. 2. ques. 110, art. 4.

On the contrary, Augustine says on Ps. v. 7, *Thou wilt destroy, etc.: There are two kinds of lie, that are not grievously sinful yet are not devoid of sin, when we lie either in joking, or for the sake of our neighbor's good.* But every mortal sin is grievous. Therefore jocose and officious lies are not mortal sins.

I answer that, A mortal sin is, properly speaking, one that is contrary to charity whereby the soul lives in union with God, as stated above (Q. 24, A. 12; Q. 35, A. 3). Now a lie may be contrary to charity in three ways: first, in itself; secondly, in respect of the evil intended; thirdly, accidently.

A lie may be in itself contrary to charity by reason of its false signification. For if this be about divine things, it is contrary to the charity of God, whose truth one hides or corrupts by such a lie; so that a lie of this kind is opposed not only to the virtue of charity, but also to the virtues of faith and religion: wherefore it is a most grievous and a mortal sin. If, however, the false signification be about something the knowledge of which affects a man's good, for instance if it pertain to the perfection of science or to moral conduct, a lie of this description inflicts an injury on one's neighbor, since it causes him to have a false opinion, wherefore it is contrary to charity, as regards the love of our neighbor, and consequently is a mortal sin. On the other hand, if the false opinion engendered by the lie be about some matter the knowledge of which is of no consequence, then the lie in question does no harm to one's neighbor; for instance, if a person be deceived as to some contingent particulars that do not concern him. Wherefore a lie of this kind, considered in itself, is not a mortal sin.

As regards the end in view, a lie may be contrary to charity, through being told with the purpose of injuring God, and this is always a mortal sin, for it is opposed to religion; or in order to injure one's neighbor, in his person, his possessions or his good name, and this also is a mortal sin, since it is a mortal sin to injure one's neighbor, and one sins mortally if one has merely the intention of committing a mortal sin. But if the end intended be not contrary to charity, neither will the lie, considered under this aspect, be a mortal sin, as in the case of a jocose lie, where some little pleasure is intended, or in an officious lie, where the good also of one's neighbor is intended. Accidentally a lie may be contrary to charity by reason of scandal or any other injury resulting therefrom: and thus again it will be a mortal sin, for instance if a man were not deterred through scandal from lying publicly.

Reply Obj. 1. The passages quoted refer to the mischievous lie, as a gloss explains the words of Ps. v. 7, *Thou wilt destroy all that speak a lie.*

Reply Obj. 2. Since all the precepts of the decalogue are directed to the love of God and our neighbor, as stated above (Q. 44, A. 1, *ad* 3: I-II, Q. 100, A. 5 *ad* 1), a lie is contrary to a precept of the decalogue, in so far as it is contrary to the love of God and our neighbor. Hence it is expressly forbidden to bear false witness against our neighbor.

Reply Obj. 3. Even a venial sin can be called *iniquity* in a broad sense, in so far as it is beside the equity of justice; wherefore it is written (1 John iii. 4): *Every sin is iniquity.* It is in this sense that Augustine is speaking.

Reply Obj. 4. The lie of the midwives may be considered in two ways. First as regards their feeling of kindliness towards the Jews, and their reverence and fear of God, for which their virtuous disposition is commended. For this an eternal reward is due. Wherefore Jerome (in his exposition of Isa. ixv. 21, *And they shall build houses*) explains that God *built them spiritual houses.* Secondly, it may be considered with regard to the external act of lying. For thereby they could merit, not indeed eternal reward, but perhaps some temporal meed, the deserving of which was not inconsistent with the deformity of their lie, though this was inconsistent with their meriting an eternal reward. It is in this sense that we must understand the words of Gregory, and not that they merited by that lie to lose the eternal reward as though they had already merited it by their preceding kindliness, as the objection understands the words to mean.

Reply Obj. 5. Some say that for the perfect every lie is a mortal sin. But this assertion is unreasonable. For no circumstance causes a sin to be infinitely more grievous unless it transfers it to another species. Now a circumstance of person does not transfer a sin to another species, except perhaps by reason of something annexed to that person, for instance if it be against his vow: and this cannot apply to an officious or jocose lie. Wherefore an officious or a jocose lie is not a mortal sin in perfect men, except perhaps accidentally on account of scandal. We may take in this sense the saying of Augustine that *it is a precept of perfection not only not to lie at all, but not even to wish to lie:* although Augustine says this not positively but dubiously, for he begins by saying: *Unless perhaps it is a precept,* etc. Nor does it matter that they are placed in a position to safeguard the truth: because they are bound to safeguard the truth by virtue of their office in judging or teaching, and if they lie in these matters their lie will be a mortal sin: but it does not follow that they sin mortally when they lie in other matters.

FRANCIS BACON
OF TRUTH

What is truth? said jesting Pilate, and would not stay for an answer. Certainly there be that delight in giddiness, and count it a bondage to fix a belief; affecting free-will in thinking, as well as in acting. And though the sects of philosophers of that kind be gone, yet there remain certain discoursing wits which are of the same veins, though there be not so much blood in them as was in those of the ancients. But it is not only the difficulty and labour which men take in finding out of truth, nor again that when it is found it imposeth upon men's thoughts, that doth bring lies in favour; but a natural though corrupt love of the lie itself. One of the later school of the Grecians examineth the matter, and is at a stand to think what should be in it, that men should love lies; where neither they make for pleasure, as with poets; nor for advantage, as with the merchant; but for the lie's sake. But I cannot tell: this same truth is a naked and open day-light, that doth not shew the masques and mummeries and triumphs of the world, half so stately and daintily as candle-lights. Truth may perhaps come to the price of a pearl, that sheweth best by day; but it will not rise to the price of a diamond or carbuncle, that sheweth best in varied lights. A mixture of a lie doth ever add pleasure. Doth any man doubt, that

From Francis Bacon, "Of Truth," in *Essays Civil and Moral* (London: Ward, Lock & Co., 1910).

if there were taken out of men's minds vain opinions, flattering hopes, false valuations, imaginations as one would, and the like, but it would leave the minds of a number of men poor shrunken things, full of melancholy and indisposition, and unpleasing to themselves? One of the fathers, in great severity, called poesy *vinum daemonum*, because it filleth the imagination, and yet it is but with the shadow of a lie. But it is not the lie that passeth through the mind, but the lie that sinketh in and settleth in it, that doth the hurt, such as we spake of before. But howsoever these things are thus in men's depraved judgments and affections, yet truth, which only doth judge itself, teacheth that the inquiry of truth, which is the love-making or wooing of it, the knowledge of truth, which is the presence of it, and the belief of truth, which is the enjoying of it, is the sovereign good of human nature. The first creature of God, in the works of the days, was the light of the sense; the last was the light of reason; and his sabbath work, ever since, is the illumination of his Spirit. First he breathed light upon the face of the matter or chaos; then he breathed light into the face of man; and still he breatheth and inspireth light into the face of his chosen. The poet that beautified the sect that was otherwise inferior to the rest, saith yet excellently well: *It is a pleasure to stand upon the shore, and to see ships tost upon the sea: a pleasure to stand in the window of a castle, and to see a battle and the adventures thereof below: but no pleasure is comparable to the standing upon the vantage ground of truth* (a hill not to be commanded, and where the air is always clear and serene), *and to see the errors, and wanderings, and mists, and tempests, in the vale below:* so always that this prospect be with pity, and not with swelling or pride. Certainly, it is heaven upon earth, to have a man's mind move in charity, rest in providence, and turn upon the poles of truth.

To pass from theological and philosophical truth, to the truth of civil business: it will be acknowledged, even by those that practise it not, that clear and round dealing is the honour of man's nature; and that mixture of falsehood is like allay in coin of gold and silver; which may make the metal work the better, but it embaseth it. For these winding and crooked courses are the goings of the serpent; which goeth basely upon the belly, and not upon the feet. There is no vice that doth so cover a man with shame as to be found false and perfidious. And therefore Mountaigny saith prettily, when he inquired the reason, why the word of the lie should be such a disgrace and such an odious charge? saith he, *If it be well weighed, to say that a man lieth, is as much to say as that he is brave towards God and a coward towards men.* For a lie faces God, and shrinks from man. Surely the wickedness of falsehood and breach of faith cannot possibly be so highly expressed, as in that it shall be the last peal to call the judgements of God upon the generations of men; it being foretold, that when Christ cometh, *he shall not find faith upon the earth.*

HUGO GROTIUS
THE CHARACTER OF FALSEHOOD

XI.—*The character of falsehood, in so far as it is unpermissible, consists in its conflict with the right of another; this is explained*

1. In order to exemplify the general idea of falsehood, it is necessary that what is spoken, or written, or indicated by signs or gestures, cannot be understood otherwise than in a sense which differs from the thought of him who uses the means of expression.

Upon this broader signification, however, a stricter meaning of falsehood must be imposed, carrying some characteristic distinction. This distinction, if we regard the matter aright, at least according to the common view of nations, can be described, we think, as nothing else than a conflict with the existing and continuing right of him to whom the speech or sign is addressed; for it is sufficiently clear that no one lies to himself, however false his statement may be.

By right in this connexion I do not mean every right without relation to the matter in question, but that which is peculiar to it and connected with it. Now that right is nothing else than the liberty of judgement which, as if by some tacit agreement, men who speak are understood to owe to those with whom they converse. For this is merely that mutual obligation which men

From Hugo Grotius, *On the Law of War and Peace*, trans. Francis W. Kelsey (New York: Bobbs-Merrill Co., 1925), bk. 3, chap 1.

had willed to introduce at the time when they determined to make use of speech and similar signs; for without such an obligation the invention of speech would have been void of result.

2. We require, moreover, that this right be valid and continuing at the time the statement is made; for it may happen that the right has indeed existed, but has been taken away, or will be annulled by another right which supervenes, just as a debt is cancelled by an acceptance or by the cessation of the condition. Then, further, it is required that the right which is infringed belong to him with whom we converse, and not to another, just as in the case of contracts also injustice arises only from the infringement of a right of the contracting parties.

Perhaps you would do well to recall here that Plato, following Simonides, refers truth-speaking to justice; that falsehood, at least the type of falsehood which is forbidden, is often described in Holy Writ as bearing false witness or speaking against one's neighbour; and that Augustine himself in determining the nature of falsehood regards the will to deceive as essential. Cicero, too, wishes that inquiry in regard to speaking the truth be referred to the fundamental principles of justice.

3. Moreover, the right of which we have spoken may be abrogated by the express consent of him with whom we are dealing, as when one says that he will speak falsely and the other permits it. In like manner it may be cancelled by tacit consent, or consent assumed on reasonable grounds, or by the opposition of another right which, in the common judgement of all men, is much more cogent.

The right understanding of these points will supply to us many inferences, which will be of no small help in reconciling the differences in the views which have been cited above.

XII.—*The view is maintained that it is permissible to say what is false before infants and insane persons*

The first inference is that even if something which has a false significance is said to an infant or insane person no blame for falsehood attaches thereto. For it seems to be permitted by the common opinion of mankind that

The unsuspecting age of childhood may be mocked.

Quintilian, speaking of boys, said: 'For their profit we employ many fictions.' The reason is by no means far to seek; since infants and insane persons do not have liberty of judgement, it is impossible for wrong to be done them in respect to such liberty.

XIII.—*It is permissible to say what is false when he to whom the conversation is not addressed is deceived, and when it would be permissible to deceive him if not sharing in it*

1. The second inference is that, so long as the person to whom the talk is addressed is not deceived, if a third party draws a false impression therefrom there is no falsehood.

There is no falsehood in relation to him to whom the utterance is directed because his liberty remains unimpaired. His case is like that of persons to whom a fable is told when they are aware of its character, or those to whom figurative language is used in 'irony', or in 'hyperbole', a figure which, as Seneca says, reaches the truth by means of falsehood, while Quintilian calls it a lying exaggeration. There is no falsehood, again, in respect to him who chances to hear what is said; the conversation is not being held with him, consequently there is no obligation toward him. Indeed if he forms for himself an opinion from what is said not to him, but to another, he has something which he can credit to himself, not to another. In fine, if, so far as he is concerned, we wish to form a correct judgement, the conversation is not a conversation, but something that may mean anything at all.

2. Cato the censor therefore committed no wrong in falsely promising aid to his allies, nor did Flaccus, who said to others that a city of the enemy had been stormed by Aemilius, although in both cases the enemy was deceived. A similar ruse is told of Agesilaus by Plutarch. Nothing in fact was said to the enemy; the harm, moreover, which followed was something foreign to the statement, and of itself not unpermissible to desire or to accomplish.

To this category Chrysostom and Jerome refer Paul's speech, in which at Antioch he rebuked Peter for being too zealous a Jew. They think that Peter was well aware that this was not done in earnest; at the same time the weakness of those present was humoured.

XIV.—*It is permissible to say what is false when the conversation is directed to him who wishes to be deceived in this way*

1. The third inference is that, whenever it is certain that he to whom the conversation is addressed will not be annoyed at the infringement of his liberty in judging, or 'rather will be grateful therefor, because of some advantage which will follow, in this case also a falsehood in the strict sense, that is a harmful falsehood, is not perpetrated; just so a man does not commit theft who with the presumed consent of the owner uses up some trifling thing in order that he may thereby secure for the owner a great advantage.

In these matters which are so certain, a presumed wish is taken as one that is expressed. Besides, in such cases it is evident that no wrong is done to one who desires it. It seems, therefore, that he does not do wrong who comforts a sick friend by persuading him of what is not true, as Arria did by saying what was not true to Paetus after the death of their son; the story is told in the *Letters* of Pliny. Similar is the case of the man who brings courage by a false report to one who is wavering in battle, so that, encouraged thereby, he wins victory and safety for himself, and is thus 'beguiled but not betrayed', as Lucretius says.

2. Democritus says: 'We must speak the truth, wherever that is the better course.' Xenophon writes: 'It is right to deceive our friends, if it is for their good.' Clement of Alexandria concedes 'the use of lying as a curative measure'. Maximus of Tyre says: 'A physician deceives a sick man, a general deceives his army, and a pilot the sailors; and in such deception there is no wrong.' The reason is given by Proclus in commenting on Plato: 'For that which is good is better than the truth.'

To this class of untruths belong the statement reported by Xenophon, that the allies would presently arrive; that of Tullus Hostilius, that the army from Alba was making a flank movement by his order; what histories term the 'salutary lie' of the consul Quinctius, that the enemy were in flight on the other wing; and similar incidents found in abundance in the writings of the historians. However, it is to be observed that in this sort of falsehood the infringement upon the judgement is of less account because it is usually confined to the moment, and the truth is revealed a little later.

XV.—*It is permissible to say what is false when the speaker makes use of a superior right over one subject to himself*

1. A fourth inference, akin to the foregoing, applies to the case when one who has a right that is superior to all the rights of another makes use of this right either for his own or for the public good. This especially Plato seems to have had in mind when he conceded the right of saying what is false to those having authority. Since the same author seems now to grant this privilege to physicians, and again to deny it to them, apparently we ought to make the distinction that in the former passage he means physicians publicly appointed to this responsibility, and in the latter those who privately claim it for themselves. Yet Plato also rightly recognizes that falsehood is not becoming to deity, although deity has a supreme right over men, because it is a mark of weakness to take refuge in such devices.

2. An instance of blameless mendacity, of which even Philo approves, may perhaps be found in Joseph, who, when ruling in the king's stead, accused his brothers first of being spies, and then of being thieves, pretending, but not really believing, that they were such. Another instance is that of Solomon, who gave an example of wisdom inspired by God, when to the women who were disputing over the child he uttered the words which indicated his purpose to slay it, although his real intent was the furthest possible from such a course, and his desire was to assign to the true mother her own offspring. [434] There is a saying of Quintilian: 'Sometimes the common good requires that even falsehoods should be upheld.'

IMMANUEL KANT
ON A SUPPOSED RIGHT TO LIE FROM ALTRUISTIC MOTIVES

In the journal *France*, for 1797, Part VI, No. 1, page 123, in an article entitled "On Political Reactions" by Benjamin Constant, there appears the following passage:

From Immanuel Kant, *Critique of Practical Reason and Other Writings in Moral Philosophy*, ed. and trans. Lewis White Beck (Chicago: University of Chicago Press, 1949), pp. 346–50.

The moral principle, "It is a duty to tell the truth," would make any society impossible if it were taken singly and unconditionally. We have proof of this in the very direct consequences which a German philosopher has drawn from this principle. This philosopher goes so far as to assert that it would be a crime to lie to a murderer who has asked whether our friend who is pursued by him had taken refuge in our house.

The French philosopher on page 124 refutes this principle in the following manner:

> It is a duty to tell the truth. The concept of duty is inseparable from the concept of right. A duty is that which in one being corresponds to the rights of another. Where there are no rights, there are no duties. To tell the truth is thus a duty: but it is a duty only in respect to one who has a right to the truth. But no one has a right to a truth which injures others.

The πρῶτον ψεῦδος in this argument lies in the sentence: "To tell the truth is a duty, but it is a duty only toward one who has a right to the truth."

It must first be noted that the expression, "to have a right to truth" is without meaning. One must rather say, "Man has a right to his own truthfulness *(veracitas),*" i.e., to the subjective truth in his own person. For to have objectively a right to truth would mean that it is a question of one's will (as in questions of what belongs to individuals generally) whether a given sentence is to be true or false. This would certainly produce an extraordinary logic.

Now the first question is: Does a man, in cases where he cannot avoid answering "Yes" or "No," have a right to be untruthful? The second question is: Is he not in fact bound to tell an untruth, when he is unjustly compelled to make a statement, in order to protect himself or another from a threatened misdeed?

Truthfulness in statements which cannot be avoided is the formal duty of an individual to everyone, however great may be the disadvantage accruing to himself or to another. If, by telling an untruth, I do not wrong him who unjustly compels me to make a statement, nevertheless by this falsification, which must be called a lie (though not in a legal sense), I commit a wrong against duty generally in a most essential point. That is, so far as in me lies I cause that declarations should in general find no credence, and hence that all rights based on contracts should be void and lose their force, and this is a wrong done to mankind generally.

Thus the definition of a lie as merely an intentional untruthful declaration to another person does not require the additional condition that it must harm another, as jurists think proper in their definition (*mendacium est falsiloquium in praeiudicium alterius*). For a lie always harms another; if not some other particular man, still it harms mankind generally, for it vitiates the source of law itself.

This benevolent lie, however, can become punishable under civil law through an accident (*casus*), and that which escapes liability to punishment only by accident can also be condemned as wrong even by external laws. For instance, if by telling a lie you have prevented murder, you have made yourself legally responsible for all the consequences; but if you have held rigorously to the truth, public justice can lay no hand on you, whatever the unforeseen consequences may be. After you have honestly answered the murderer's question as to whether this intended victim is at home, it may be that he has slipped out so that he does not come in the way of the murderer, and thus that the murder may not be committed. But if you had lied and said he was not at home when he had really gone out without your knowing it, and if the murderer had then met him as he went away and murdered him, you might justly be accused as the cause of his death. For if you had told the truth as far as you knew it, perhaps the murderer might have been apprehended by the neighbors while he searched the house and thus the deed might have been prevented. Therefore, whoever tells a lie, however well intentioned he might be, must answer for the consequences, however unforeseeable they were, and pay the penalty for them even in a civil tribunal. This is because truthfulness is a duty which must be regarded as the ground of all duties based on contract, and the laws of these duties would be rendered uncertain and useless if even the least exception to them were admitted.

To be truthful (honest) in all declarations, therefore, is a sacred and absolutely commanding decree of reason, limited by no expediency.

Mr. Constant makes a thoughtful and correct remark on

decrying principles so strict that they are alleged to lose themselves in such impracticable ideas that they are to be rejected. He says, on page 23, "In every case where a principle which has been proved to be true appears to be inapplicable, the reason is that we do not know the middle principle which contains the means of its application." He adduces (p. 121) the doctrine of equality as the first link of the social chain, saying (p. 122):

> No man can be bound by any laws except to the formulation of which he has contributed. In a very limited society this principle can be applied directly and needs no mediating principle in order to become a common principle. But in a society consisting of very many persons, another principle must be added to this one we have stated. This mediating principle is: the individuals can participate in the formulation of laws either in their own person or through their representatives. Whoever wished to apply the former principle to a large society without making use of the mediating principle would invariably bring about the destruction of the society. But this circumstance, which would only show the ignorance or the incompetence of the legislator, proves nothing against the principle.

He concludes (p. 125) that "a principle acknowledged to be true must never be abandoned, however obviously danger seems to be involved in it." (And yet the good man himself abandoned the unconditional principle of truthfulness on account of the danger which it involved for society. He did so because he could find no mediating principle which could serve to prevent this danger; and, in fact, there is no principle to be interpolated here.)

If we wish to preserve the names of the persons as they have been cited here, the "French philosopher" confuses the action by which someone does harm *(nocet)* to another in telling the truth when he cannot avoid making a statement, with the action whereby he does the other a wrong *(laedit)*. It was only an accident *(casus)* that the truth of the statement harmed the occupant of the house; it was not a free act (in a juristic sense). For to demand of another that he should lie to one's own advantage would be a claim opposed to all lawfulness. Each man has not only a right but even the strict duty to be truthful in statements he cannot avoid making, whether they harm himself or others. In so doing, he does not do harm to him who suffers as a consequence; accident causes this harm. For one is not at all free to choose in such a case, since truthfulness (if he must speak) is an unconditional duty.

The "German philosopher" will not take as one of his principles the proposition (p. 124): "To tell the truth is a duty, but only to him who has a right to the truth." He will not do so, first, because of the ambiguous formulation of this proposition, for truth is not a possession the right to which can be granted to one and denied to another. But he will not do so chiefly because the duty of truthfulness (which is the only thing in question here) makes no distinction between persons to whom one has this duty and to whom one can exempt himself from this duty; rather, it is an unconditional duty which holds in all circumstances.

Now in order to proceed from a metaphysics of law (which abstracts from all empirical conditions) to a principle of politics (which applies these concepts to cases met with in experience), and by means of this to achieve the solution of a problem of politics in accord with the universal principle of law, the philosopher will enunciate three notions. The first is an axiom, i.e., an apodictically certain proposition which springs directly from the definition of external law (the harmony of the freedom of each with the freedom of all others according to a universal law). The second is a postulate of external public law (the will of all united according to the principle of equality, without which no one would have any freedom). Third, there is the problem of how it is to be arranged that, in a society however large, harmony may be maintained in accordance with principles of freedom and equality (namely, by means of a representative system). The latter will then become a principle of politics, the organization and establishment of which will entail decrees drawn from the practical knowledge of men, which will have in view only the mechanism of the administration of justice and how this may be suitably carried out. Law must never be accommodated to politics but politics always accommodated to law.

The author says, "A principle recognized as true (I add, recognized as an a priori and hence apodictic principle) must never be abandoned, however obviously danger seems to be involved in it." But one must only understand the danger not as a danger of accidentally doing a harm but only as a danger of doing a wrong. This would happen if I made the duty of being truthful, which is unconditional and the supreme juridical condition in testimony, into a conditional duty subordinate to other considerations. Although in telling a certain lie I do not actually do anyone a wrong, I formally but not materially violate the principle of right with respect to all unavoidably necessary utterances. And this is much worse than to do injustice to any particular person, because such a deed against an individual does not always presuppose the existence of a principle in the subject which produces such an act.

If one is asked whether he intends to speak truthfully in a statement that he is about to make and does not receive the question with indignation at the suspicion it expressed that he might be a liar, but rather asks permission to consider possible exceptions, that person is already potentially a liar. That is because he shows that he does not acknowledge truthfulness as an intrinsic duty but makes reservations with respect to a rule which does not permit any exception, inasmuch as any exception would directly contradict itself.

All practical principles of right must contain rigorous truth, and the so-called "mediating principles" can contain only the more accurate definition of their application to actual cases (according to rules of policy), but they can never contain exceptions from the former. Such exceptions would nullify their universality, and that is precisely the reason that they are called principles.

H. SIDGWICK
THE CLASSIFICATION OF DUTIES—VERACITY

§ 2. In the first place, it does not seem clearly agreed whether Veracity is an absolute and independent duty, or a special application of some higher principle. We find (e.g.) that Kant regards it as a duty owed to oneself to speak the truth, because 'a lie is an abandonment or, as it were, annihilation of the dignity of man.' And this seems to be the view in which lying is prohibited by the code of honour, except that it is not thought (by men of

---

From H. Sidgwick, *The Methods of Ethics*, 7th ed. (London: Macmillan & Co., 1907).

honour as such) that the dignity of man is impaired by *any* lying: but only that lying for selfish ends, especially under the influence of fear, is mean and base. In fact there seems to be circumstances under which the code of honour prescribes lying. Here, however, it may be said to be plainly divergent from the morality of Common Sense. Still, the latter does not seem to decide clearly whether truth-speaking is absolutely a duty, needing no further justification: or whether it is merely a general right of each man to have truth spoken to him by his fellows, which right however may be forfeited or suspended under certain circumstances. Just as each man is thought to have a natural right to personal security generally, but not if he is himself attempting to injure others in life and property: so if we may even kill in defence of ourselves and others, it seems strange if we may not lie, if lying will defend us better against a palpable invasion of our rights: and Common Sense does not seem to prohibit this decisively. And again, just as the orderly and systematic slaughter which we call war is thought perfectly right under certain circumstances, though painful and revolting: so in the word-contests of the law-courts, the lawyer is commonly held to be justified in untruthfulness within strict rules and limits: for an advocate is thought to be over-scrupulous who refuses to say what he knows to be false, if he is instructed to say it. Again, where deception is designed to benefit the person deceived, Common Sense seems to concede that it may sometimes be right: for example, most persons would not hesitate to speak falsely to an invalid, if this seemed the only way of concealing facts that might produce a dangerous shock: nor do I perceive that any one shrinks from telling fictions to children, on matters upon which it is thought well that they should not know the truth. But if the lawfulness of benevolent deception in any case be admitted, I do not see how we can decide when and how far it is admissible, except by considerations of expediency; that is, by weighing the gain of any particular deception against the imperilment of mutual confidence involved in all violation of truth.

The much argued question of religious deception ('pious fraud') naturally suggests itself here. It seems clear, however, that Common Sense now pronounces against the broad rule, that falsehoods may rightly be told in the interests of religion.

But there is a subtler form in which the same principle is still maintained by moral persons. It is sometimes said that the most important truths of religion cannot be conveyed into the minds of ordinary men, except by being enclosed, as it were, in a shell of fiction; so that by relating such fictions as if they were facts, we are really performing an act of substantial veracity. Reflecting upon this argument, we see that it is not after all so clear wherein Veracity consists. For from the beliefs immediately communicated by any set of affirmations inferences are naturally drawn, and we may clearly foresee that they will be drawn. And though commonly we intend that both the beliefs immediately communicated and the inferences drawn from them should be true, and a person who always aims at this is praised as candid and sincere: still we find relaxation of the rule prescribing this intention claimed in two different ways by at least respectable sections of opinion. For first, as was just now observed, it is sometimes held that if a conclusion is true and important, and cannot be satisfactorily communicated otherwise, we may lead the mind of the hearer to it by means of fictitious premises. But the exact reverse of this is perhaps a commoner view: viz. that it is only an absolute duty to make our actual affirmations true: for it is said that though the ideal condition of human converse involves perfect sincerity and candour, and we ought to rejoice in exhibiting these virtues where we can, still in our actual world concealment is frequently necessary to the well-being of society, and may be legitimately effected by any means short of actual falsehood. Thus it is not uncommonly said that in defence of a secret we may not indeed *lie, i.e.* produce directly beliefs contrary to fact; but we may "turn a question aside," *i.e.* produce indirectly, by natural inference from our answer, a negatively false belief; or "throw the inquirer on a wrong scent," *i.e.* produce similarly a positively false belief. These two methods of concealment are known respectively as *suppressio veri* and *suggestio falsi*, and many think them legitimate under certain circumstances: while others say that if deception is to be practised at all, it is mere formalism to object to any one mode of effecting it more than another.

On the whole, then, reflection seems to show that the rule of Veracity, as commonly accepted, cannot be elevated into a definite moral axiom: for there is no real agreement as to how far we are bound to impart true beliefs to others: and while it is contrary to Common Sense to exact absolute candour under all circumstances, we yet find no self-evident secondary principle, clearly defining when it is not to be exacted.

R. F. HARROD
UTILITARIANISM REVISED

. . . The Utilitarian says "always choose that action which will contribute to the greatest happiness". Such a maxim is general enough. Its fault is that it is on too high a plane of generality. It is necessary to look in greater detail into human arrangements. Take the case of the lie. The Utilitarian, it would seem, should say, always lie when the probable consequences including the speaker's loss of credit and the possible general loss of confidence in the spoken word involve more happiness than those produced by the truth. If everyone lied in those circumstances and in those circumstances only, all would apparently go well. But as a matter of fact this is not the case.

Communication by language is a notable invention of man for the furtherance of his ends. It is of great importance that communications should be reliable for their truthfulness. Now if the Utilitarian rule of life in its crude form, as set out above, were adopted, they would become markedly less reliable and great consequential damage might ensue. But it might be pleaded that the loss of confidence is allowed for in the crude Utilitarian maxim—and *some* loss of confidence *is* allowed for. The plea nevertheless is fallacious.

If this plea were correct the consequences indicated by the crude utilitarian principle would always be identical with the consequences deduced by the application of Kant's principle. The consequences of the act considered in and by itself would not be different from the consequences of such an act when always performed in precisely similar relevant circumstances. This brings us to the essence of the matter. *There are certain acts which when performed on* n *similar occasions have consequences more than* n *times as great as those resulting from one performance.* And it

From R. F. Harrod, "Utilitarianism Revised," *Mind* 45 (1936): 137–56.

is in this class of cases that obligations arise. It is in this class of cases that generalizing the act yields a different balance of advantage from the sum of the balances of advantage issuing from each individual act. For example, it may well happen that the loss of confidence due to a million lies uttered within certain limits of time and space is much more than a million times as great as the loss due to any one in particular. Consequently, even if on each and every occasion taken separately it can be shown that there is a gain of advantage (the avoidance of direct pain, let us say, exceeding the disadvantages due to the consequential loss of confidence), yet in the sum of all cases the disadvantage due to the aggregate loss of confidence might be far greater than the sum of pain caused by truth-telling.

He who wishes people so to act that the ends of sentient beings should be best served, must wish them to act in accordance with the Kantian and not the crude utilitarian principle. He will find it necessary to refine the crude utilitarian principle by applying the process of generalization in all relevant cases, that is in all cases where the consequences of n similar acts exceed n times the consequences of any one.

In constructing a system of morality, it is necessary, then, to choose between the crude Utilitarian principle and the Kantian principle, between the lie of expediency and the obligation of truthfulness. A more refined Utilitarianism will decide in favour of the obligation, owing to the greater loss of advantage when the lie is generalised. Of course this may not be true in the case of the particular illustration given: the loss of confidence due to the universal lie of expediency may not be so great as the gain of advantage. This is a question of fact. The experience of generations, crystallised in moral consciousness, appears to be against the lie. But whichever side is right in the case of the lie, the point of principle has been established that an act which is expedient in the circumstances but would be inexpedient when done by all in precisely similar relevant circumstances must be judged to be wrong by a more refined utilitarian system. Thus the Kantian principle is embodied in utilitarian philosophy.

It should be noted in passing that what I call the Kantian principle does not condemn all lies. A lie is justified when the balance of pain or loss of pleasure is such that, if a lie was told in all circumstances when there was no less a balance of pain or loss of pleasure, the harm due to the total loss of confidence did not exceed the sum of harm due to truthfulness in every case. This doctrine, which I believe to be conformable to the common moral consciousness, puts the human interlocutor into a much stricter strait-jacket with regard to truthfulness than the crude utilitarian principle quoted at the outset.

Along with lies must be reckoned breaches of promises, of the law, of many, though not all, current standards of morality. The test is always—Would this action if done by all in similar relevant circumstances lead to the breakdown of some established method of society for securing its ends? I believe it will be found that this principle lies at the root of all so-called obligations. Their rigidity is precisely due to the fact that the relevant considerations are not the consequences of the particular act, but the consequences of the act when generalised.

I believe that whereas Kant was wrong in supposing his principle to be at the basis of all morality, it is the basis of those particular moral acts which are usually thought of as obligations. If the act is of a sort to which the Kantian principle is applicable, it is much more likely that there will turn out to be a balance of advantage in its favour. Hence the rigidity with which we regard those acts commonly called obligations. If there is a question of helping some one, this and that consideration are taken into account, and it is quite likely to turn out on balance even from a purely moral point of view to be not worth doing. But if it is a question of speaking the truth, it is considered very improbable that this should not be done—and this, even though the positive advantage that flows from this particular piece of truthfulness is not greater than that which flows from the particular act of kindness. The difference is due to the fact that in one case the Kantian principle does and in the other does not make a difference to the crude utilitarian principle.

This account explains the *prima facie* view that there is something in the recognised nature of an obligation that conflicts with any philosophy of ends. The conflict, we have seen, is apparent only. It also accounts for the fact that the quasi-instinctive emotions of disgust, which such actions evoke, often seem unreasonably strong. Only those societies could attain stability in which they were strong, because it is precisely in the case of these actions that the individual not understanding the Kantian principle might, if left unmolested, be most tempted to say—"well, why on earth should I?" One may even add that it is the subtlety and difficulty of the principle, which cannot be explained to the average man, that has made an arbitrary and authoritarian element in the moral sphere necessary to the evolution of stable society. This enlightened age has its dangers. Perhaps the philosophers of indefinable obligation still have their part to play, and it may be inexpedient that they should be put to public shame by the votaries of expedience.

It is interesting to notice that the system of free competition does not allow for the application of the Kantian principle in the purely economic or katallactic field. And it is precisely the phenomena of "Increasing Returns"—analogous to those requiring the application of the Kantian principle in everyday conduct—which have given one of the strongest arguments in justification of the demand for "economic planning."

Now it is not to be expected that the humble man in the street will be quick to jump spontaneously to what I for brevity call the Kantian point of view. Pessimism about him should not indeed be overdone. "Well, if everyone behaved in that sort of way" is a familiar phrase of condemnation. It will be found, however, that it is most frequently used for breaches of established conventions. It is owing to this weakness of the average man that types of act to which the Kantian principle is applicable are often associated with *recognised practices and institutions*. In the process by which stable society—temporarily stable society at least!—has evolved, those systems have survived which have established recognised practices and institutions giving effect to the Kantian principle, and allowing members to reap the additional advantages which adherence to it can yield. I am thinking of codes of honour, truthfulness, honesty, discharge of debt, performance of promises, etc., and of states with systems of law and recognised obligations of loyalty.

First consider *practices*. The Kantian principle is applicable if the loss due to n infringements is greater than n times the loss due to one. But suppose that in fact it is generally infringed. Suppose that I live in a society in which the spoken word is seldom to be relied on or men go about in constant fear of their lives. The community is not in fact reaping the benefit which could be reaped by the application of the Kantian principle. What is my obligation? It appears to be doubtful whether it is appropriate in these circumstances to apply the refining process to the crude utilitarian principle. Of course the example of an upright or peacefully minded man may be potent. But the direct effect of example is, it will be remembered, allowed for in the crude utilitarian principle. I think the common moral consciousness would judge the refining process to be inappropriate.

But it ought to be possible to put a finer point upon the argument. The common moral consciousness having endorsed the doctrine of common interest, it ought to be a question of fact whether the application of the refining process will in any case subserve it. Now when the process is applied there will be loss of advantage in particular instances; but there is a gain if it is applied in a large number of instances. The Utilitarian must wish it applied widely. I believe that, where the practice is not general, a second refining process is required. Will the gain due to its application by all conscientious, *i.e.*, moral, people *only* be sufficient to offset the loss which the crude utilitarian principle registers? It may be objected to this that there are no moral people, but only more or less moral people. To meet this, for the word moral in the second refining principle, say people sufficiently moral to act disinterestedly in this kind of case. It may be noticed that the second refining principle introduces some complicated mathematics into moral philosophy. This must not be held as an objection, if the facts demand it! It is needless to say that in practice the calculation will only be implicit and the roughest approximations possible. The game of refined calculation would not be worth the candle, and, anyhow, precise data are lacking.

The point is this. The double set of considerations are interlocked. When the practice is not generally observed, the conscientious man has to take into account not only the amount of crude utilitarian loss due to his particular act but also the amount of conquest of counteracting impulse which observance of the practice in his type of case entails. He may not observe the practice *either* because the direct loss is too severe or because the temptation to do the opposite in this case is so great that there would not be sufficient upright men overcoming it in similar circumstances to secure a net gain through wider performance of the practice. He has not only to write down a function showing in the case of various contingencies the relation of gross gain when the action is generalised to the amount of crude loss, but also one for a different but overlapping variety of contingencies showing the relation of the number of people prepared to overcome temptation (and the consequent net gain) to the intensity of the temptation, and he has to study the interaction of the functions. I will refrain from pursuing this line of thought further, and only state my belief that implicit calculations of this kind are actually carried out in the most ordinary affairs of everyday life by moral men.

It may be of greater interest to draw attention to the fact that a properly conceived utilitarianism does involve that the obligatoriness of a certain practice depends on the degree to which it is observed by others, and that that in turn partly depends on the prevalence of sanctions embodied in the moral sentiment of disapprobation. Hobbes was substantially right when he held that there are no obligations in a state of nature, *i.e.*, when none of these practices are generally observed, and in the reasons which he gave for that proposition. He was probably right in holding that without sanctions of force one cannot proceed far in getting practices sufficiently widely established to make, in my language, the two refining principles taken together yield much result. But he was wrong to hold that there can be no morality in a state of nature. For even then the crude utilitarian principle is applicable and will be applied by virtuous people.

Before leaving the topic of practices, I may refer to a principle which occupies a central position in the common moral consciousness, which I will call the Principle of Publicity. It has been seen that the obligatoriness of certain acts depends on a (reasonably) wide observance of the practice in question. In a large class of cases the gain of advantage is due to the maintenance of confidence, *e.g.*, in the reliability of informative utterance for truthfulness, of promises for being kept, etc. It might appear that if defalcation could be kept secret, as in the case of lies which could never be discovered, then, since no loss of confidence could ensue, the obligation would lapse and certain gain should not be sacrificed in the interest of truthfulness. Yet in fact common moral consciousness regards secret as more rather than less odious than public defalcations—and rightly. For if it can be shown that undiscovered lies are wrong, severer blame is required to overcome the greater temptation to commit those that will probably be undiscovered, and is therefore justified.

Take the case when the lie can never be discovered. The liar then has no debit due to loss of confidence to set against the interests served by the lie. If, in every case when there was a general balance of advantage and the lie could never be discovered, lies were told, there would be a sensible loss of confidence. Not, it will again be pleaded, if the lies are always to be kept secret. But what is this secrecy? If virtuous men are known to be acting on the crude utilitarian principle when secrecy is possible in the particular case, then it will be known that lies in this case will be told even by the most conscientious and there will be loss of confidence. What presumably is required is that all men should utterly forswear the crude utilitarian principle and at the same time act upon it when secrecy can be maintained. What doctrine is to be preached? The crude utilitarian principle because it is desired that all men should act upon it. Some anti-utilitarian principle because it is desired that all men should believe that no one is acting upon it. To such a system it almost seems that Kant was right to apply the much-abused expression, self-contradictory.

It may be that the common interest would in fact be best served by each man acting on the principle of crude expediency himself and believing that others were following certain arbitrary rules. Such a system would certainly be an interesting one. But it is not one which the word morality is used to denote. This may seem to be an appeal to brute fact. Such an appeal is highly salutary. The words moral obligation have always been used and can conveniently be used to apply to a system of behaviour which is commonly recognised by the participants. Now the system just outlined could not of its nature be commonly recognised. Moreover for a system of moral obligations to be workable—and this is an appeal to a different kind of brute fact—it is necessary that it should be closely connected with the emotion and expression of approbation and disapprobation. This again would be impossible. Thus the utilitarian who wishes the advantages yielded by embodying the Kantian principle in publicly recognised practices to be reaped, must wish them observed whether or not defalcation can be kept secret.

DIETRICH BONHOEFFER
WHAT IS MEANT BY "TELLING THE TRUTH"?

From the moment in our lives at which we learn to speak we are taught that what we say must be true. What does this mean? What is meant by "telling the truth"? What does it demand of us?

It is clear that in the first place it is our parents who regulate our relation to themselves by this demand for truthfulness; consequently, in the sense in which our parents intend it, this demand applies strictly only within the family circle. It is also to be noted that the relation which is expressed in this demand cannot simply be reversed. The truthfulness of a child towards his parents is essentially different from that of the parents towards their child. The life of the small child lies open before the parents, and what the child says should reveal to them everything that is hidden and secret, but in the converse relationship this cannot possibly be the case. Consequently, in the matter of truthfulness, the parents' claim on the child is different from the child's claim on the parents.

From this it emerges already that "telling the truth" means something different according to the particular situation in which one stands. Account must be taken of one's relationships at each particular time. The question must be asked whether and in what way a man is entitled to demand truthful speech of others. Speech between parents and children is, in the nature of the case, different from speech between man and wife, between friends, between teacher and pupil, government and subject, friend and foe, and in each case the truth which this speech conveys is also different.

It will at once be objected that one does not owe truthful speech to this or that individual man, but solely to God. This

From Dietrich Bonhoeffer, "What Is Meant by 'Telling the Truth'?," *Ethics*, ed. Eberhard Bethge (New York: Macmillan Co., 1965), pp. 363–72.

objection is correct so long as it is not forgotten that God is not a general principle, but the living God who has set me in a living life and who demands service of me within this living life. If one speaks of God one must not simply disregard the actual given world in which one lives; for if one does that one is not speaking of the God who entered into the world in Jesus Christ, but rather of some metaphysical idol. And it is precisely this which is determined by the way in which, in my actual concrete life with all its manifold relationships, I give effect to the truthfulness which I owe to God. The truthfulness which we owe to God must assume a concrete form in the world. Our speech must be truthful, not in principle but concretely. A truthfulness which is not concrete is not truthful before God.

"Telling the truth," therefore, is not solely a matter of moral character; it is also a matter of correct appreciation of real situations and of serious reflection upon them. The more complex the actual situations of a man's life, the more responsible and the more difficult will be his task of "telling the truth." The child stands in only one vital relationship, his relationship to his parents, and he, therefore, still has nothing to consider and weigh up. The next environment in which he is placed, his school, already brings with it the first difficulty. From the educational point of view it is, therefore, of the very greatest importance that parents, in some way which we cannot discuss here, should make their children understand the differences between these various circles in which they are to live and the differences in their responsibilities.

Telling the truth is, therefore, something which must be learnt. This will sound very shocking to anyone who thinks that it must all depend on moral character and that if this is blameless the rest is child's play. But the simple fact is that the ethical cannot be detached from reality, and consequently continual progress in learning to appreciate reality is a necessary ingredient in ethical action. In the question with which we are now concerned, action consists of speaking. The real is to be expressed in words. That is what constitutes truthful speech. And this inevitably raises the question of the "how?" of these words. It is a question of knowing the right word on each occasion. Finding this word is a matter of long, earnest and ever more advanced effort on the basis of experience and knowledge of the real. If one is to say how a thing really is, *i.e.* if one is to speak truthfully, one's gaze and one's thought must be directed towards the way in which the real exists in God and through God and for God.

To restrict this problem of truthful speech to certain particular cases of conflict is superficial. Every word I utter is subject to the requirement that it shall be true. Quite apart from the veracity of its contents, the relation between myself and another man which is expressed in it is in itself either true or untrue. I speak flatteringly or presumptuously or hypocritically without uttering a material untruth; yet my words are nevertheless untrue, because I am disrupting and destroying the reality of the relationship between man and wife, superior and subordinate, etc. An individual utterance is always part of a total reality which seeks expression in this utterance. If my utterance is to be truthful it must in each case be different according to whom I am addressing, who is questioning me, and what I am speaking about. The truthful word is not in itself constant; it is as much alive as life itself. If it is detached from life and from its reference to the concrete other man, if "the truth is told" without taking into account to whom it is addressed, then this truth has only the appearance of truth, but it lacks its essential character.

It is only the cynic who claims "to speak the truth" at all times and in all places to all men in the same way, but who, in fact, displays nothing but a lifeless image of the truth. He dons the halo of the fanatical devotee of truth who can make no allowance for human weaknesses; but, in fact, he is destroying the living truth between men. He wounds shame, desecrates mystery, breaks confidence, betrays the community in which he lives, and laughs arrogantly at the devastation he has wrought and at the human weakness which "cannot bear the truth." He says truth is destructive and demands its victims, and he feels like a god above these feeble creatures and does not know that he is serving Satan.

There is a truth which is of Satan. Its essence is that under the semblance of truth it denies everything that is real. It lives upon hatred of the real and of the world which is created and loved by God. It pretends to be executing the judgment of God upon the fall of the real. God's truth judges created things out of love, and Satan's truth judges them out of envy and hatred. God's truth has become flesh in the world and is alive in the real, but Satan's truth is the death of all reality.

The concept of living truth is dangerous, and it gives rise to the suspicion that the truth can and may be adapted to each particular situation in a way which completely destroys the idea of truth and narrows the gap between truth and falsehood, so that the two become indistinguishable. Moreover, what we are saying about the necessity for discerning the real may be mistakenly understood as meaning that it is by adopting a calculating or school-masterly attitude towards the other man that I shall decide what proportion of the truth I am prepared to tell him. It is important that this danger should be kept in view. Yet the only possible way of countering it is by means of attentive discernment of the particular contents and limits which the real itself imposes on one's utterance in order to make it a truthful one. The dangers which are involved in the concept of living truth must never impel one to abandon this concept in favour of the formal and cynical concept of truth. We must try to make this clear. Every utterance or word lives and has its home in a particular environment. The word in the family is different from the word in business or public. The word which has come to life in the warmth of personal relationship is frozen to death in the cold air of public existence. The word of command, which has its habitat in public service, would sever the bonds of mutual confidence if it were spoken in the family. Each word must have its own place and keep to it. It is a consequence of the wide diffusion of the public word through the newspapers and the wireless that the essential character and the limits of the various different words are no longer clearly felt and that, for example, the special quality of the personal word is almost entirely destroyed. Genuine words are replaced by idle chatter. Words no longer possess any weight. There is too much talk. And when the limits of the various words are obliterated, when words become rootless and homeless, then the word loses truth, and then indeed there must almost inevitably be lying.

When the various orders of life no longer respect one another, words become untrue. For example, a teacher asks a child in front of the class whether it is true that his father often comes home drunk. It is true, but the child denies it. The teacher's question has placed him in a situation for which he is not yet prepared. He feels only that what is taking place is an unjustified interference in the order of the family and that he must oppose it. What goes on in the family is not for the ears of the class in school. The family has its own secret and must preserve it. The teacher has failed to respect the reality of this institution. The child ought now to find a way of answering which would comply with both the rule of the family and the rule of the school. But he is not yet able to do this. He lacks experience, knowledge, and the ability to express himself in the right way. As a simple no to the teacher's question the child's answer is certainly untrue; yet at the same time it nevertheless gives expression to the truth that the family is an institution *sui generis* and that the teacher had no right to interfere in it. The child's answer can indeed be called a lie; yet this lie contains more truth, that is to say, it is more in accordance with reality than would have been the case if the child had betrayed his father's weakness in front of the class. According to the measure of his knowledge, the child acted correctly. The blame for the lie falls back entirely upon the teacher. An experienced man in the same position as the child would have been able to correct his questioner's error while at the same time avoiding a formal untruth in his answer, and he would thus have found the "right word." The lies of children, and of inexperienced people in general, are often to be ascribed to the fact that these people are faced with situations which they do not fully understand. Consequently, since the term lie is quite properly understood as meaning something which is quite simply and utterly wrong, it is perhaps unwise to generalize and extend the use of this term so that it can be applied to every statement which is formally untrue. Indeed here already it becomes apparent how very difficult it is to say what actually constitutes a lie. . . .

G. J. WARNOCK
THE OBJECT OF MORALITY

If we consider the situation of a person, somewhat prone by nature to an exclusive concern with his own, or with some limited range of, interests and needs and wants, living among other persons more or less similarly constituted, we see that there is one device in particular, very often remarkably easy to employ, by which he may be naturally more or less inclined to, so to speak, carve out his egoistical way to his own, and if necessary at the expense of other, ends; and that is *deception*. It is possible for a person, and often very easy, by doing things, and especially in the form of saying things, to lead other persons to the belief that this or that is the case; and one of the simplest and most seductive ways of manipulating and maneuvring other persons for the sake of one's own ends is that of thus operating self-interestedly upon their beliefs. Clearly this is not, necessarily, directly damaging. We all hold from time to time an immense range and variety of false beliefs, and very often are none the worse for doing so; we are the worse for it only if, as is often not the case, our false belief leads or partly leads us actually to act to our detriment in some way. Thus, I do not necessarily do you any harm at all if, by deed or word, I induce you to believe what is not in fact the case; I may even do you good, possibly by way, for example, of consolation or flattery. Nevertheless, though deception is thus not necessarily directly damaging, it is easy to see how crucially important it is that the natural inclination to have recourse to it should be counteracted. It is, one might say, not the implanting of false beliefs that is damaging, but rather the generation of the suspicion that they may be being implanted. For this undermines trust; and, to the extent that trust is undermined, all co-operative undertakings, in which what one person can do or has reason to do is dependent on what others have done, are doing, or are going to do, must tend to break down. I cannot reasonably be expected

---

From G. J. Warnock, *The Object of Morality* (London: Methuen & Co., 1971), chap. 6.

to go over the edge of a cliff on a rope, for however vital an object, if I cannot trust you to keep hold of the other end of it; there is no sense in my asking you for your opinion on some point, if I do not suppose that your answer will actually express your opinion. (Verbal communication is doubtless the most important of all our co-operative undertakings.) The crucial difficulty is precisely, I think, that deception is so easy. Deliberately saying, for instance, what I do not believe to be true is just as easy as saying what I do believe to be true, and may not be discriminable from it by even the most practised and expert of observers; thus, uncertainty as to the credentials of *any* of my performances in this respect is inherently liable to infect *all* my performances—there are, so to speak, no 'natural signs', or there may be none, by which the untrustworthy can be distinguished from the veracious, so that, if any may be deceptive, all may be. Nor, obviously, would it be any use merely to devise some special formula for the purpose of explicitly signalling non-deceptive performance; for, if the performance may be deceptive, so also might be the employment of any such formula—it is easy to say 'I really mean it', not really meaning it, and hence to say 'I really mean it' without thereby securing belief. Even *looking* sincere and ingenuous, though perhaps slightly more difficult than simply saying that one is, is an art that can be learned. In practice, of course, though there may be very few persons indeed whom we take to be non-deceptive on all occasions, we do manage, and rightly, to trust quite a lot of the people quite a lot of the time; but this depends on the supposition that, while sometimes they may have special reasons, which with luck and experience and judgment we may come to understand, for resorting to deceptive performance on some occasions, they do not do so simply *whenever* it suits their book.

NOTES

Introduction

1. See "The Ethics of Giving Placebos," *Scientific American* 231 (1974): 17–23; and Chapter V of this book.

2. *Cambridge Survey Research*, 1975, 1976.

3. The Harris Survey, March 1976. (The 1977 figures are up somewhat for the above categories and up dramatically, from 11% to 31%, for the White House.)

4. Paul Edwards, ed., *Encyclopedia of Philosophy*, 8 vols. (New York: Macmillan Co. and Free Press, 1967). "Truthfulness," "trust," and "veracity" are also absent from the Index.

CHAPTER I: Is the "Whole Truth" Attainable?

1. See E. H. Gombrich, *Art and Illusion* (New York: Pantheon, 1960), p. 93. And Plato's remarks, in the last book of *The Republic*, on art as "thrice-removed" from nature and truth, must be seen as in part a commentary upon and a reaction against the earlier view of "truth." See also M. Détienne, *Les maîtres de la vérité dans la Grèce archaïque* (Paris: François Maspero, 1967).

2. See, for example, J. L. Austin, *Philosophical Papers* (Oxford: Clarendon Press, 1961); William James, *The Meaning of Truth* (Cambridge, Mass., and London: Harvard University Press, 1975); W. F. Quine, *The Ways of Paradox and Other Essays* (Cambridge, Mass., and London: Harvard University Press, 1976); Bertrand Russell, *An Inquiry into Meaning and Truth* (London: Allen and Unwin, 1940); Alfred Tarski, *Logic, Semantics, Mathematics* (Oxford: Clarendon Press, 1956); Alan White, *Truth* (New York: Doubleday, 1970).

3. Consider, for example, the following statement by Sören Kierkegaard: "The passion of the infinite is the truth. But the passion of the

infinite is precisely subjectivity and thus subjectivity becomes the truth" (*Concluding Unscientific Postscript*, in *A Kierkegaard Anthology*, ed. Robert Bretall [Princeton, N.J.: Princeton University Press, 1946], p. 214).

4. I shall use "falsehood" in its usual sense of "intentional falsity." For a similar distinction, see Nicolai Hartmann, *Ethics*, vol. 2 (Atlantic Highlands, N.J.: Humanities Press, 1967), p. 283.

5. Dietrich Bonhoeffer, *Ethics*, trans. Neville H. Smith (New York: Macmillan Co., 1955), p. 369.

6. Friedrich Nietzsche, *The Will to Power*, ed. Walter Kaufmann (New York: Random House, 1967), p. 451.

7. Diogenes Laertius, "Pyrrho," in *Lives of Eminent Philosophers*, trans. R. D. Hicks (London: William Heinemann, and Cambridge, Mass.: Harvard University Press, 1925), bk. 9, chap. 11 (pp. 475–519).

8. For a discussion of the many parallels between epistemology and ethics, see R. B. Brandt, "Epistemology and Ethics, Parallel Between," in Paul Edwards, ed., *The Encyclopedia of Philosophy*, 3:6–8. For a refutation of the priority of epistemology over ethics, see John Rawls, "The Independence of Moral Theory," *Proceedings and Addresses of The American Philosophical Association*, 1974–75, pp. 5–22.

9. See David Hume, "Of the Academic or Skeptical Philosophy," *An Inquiry Concerning Human Understanding*, ed. Charles W. Hendel (Indianapolis and New York: Bobbs-Merrill Company, 1955), sec. 12, pt. 2 (pp. 158–64).

10. But some carried their beliefs into their lives. Thus Pyrrho is said to have led a life "going out of his way for nothing, taking no precaution, but facing all risks as they came, whether carts, precipices, dogs or what not . . . but he was kept out of harm's way by his friends who . . . used to follow close after him" (Diogenes Laertius, "Pyrrho," 62, p. 475).

11. Epictetus, *The Encheiridion*, trans. W. A. Oldfather (Cambridge, Mass.: Harvard University Press, 1928), p. 536. (I have altered the translation in this edition so as to make it accord more closely to the text.)

12. Lawrence Henderson, "Physician and Patient as a Social System," *New England Journal of Medicine* 212 (1935): 819–23.

13. See selection in Appendix. See also Roderick Chisholm and Thomas D. Feehan, "The Intent to Deceive," *The Journal of Philosophy* 74 (1977): 143–59; Nicolai Hartmann, *Ethics*, vol. 2 (chap. 25), pp. 281–85; A. Isenberg, "Deontology and the Ethics of Lying," in Judith J. Thomson and Gerald Dworkin, *Ethics* (New York: Harper & Row, 1968); John Henry Cardinal Newman, *Apologia Pro Vita Sua*

(London: Longmans, Green, and Co., 1880), pp. 274–83, 348–63; Frederick A. Siegler, "Lying," *American Philosophical Quarterly* 3 (1966): 128–236; George Steiner, *After Babel* (New York and London: Oxford University Press, 1975).

14. Hugo Grotius, *On the Law of War and Peace*, trans. F. W. Kelsey and others (Indianapolis: Bobbs-Merrill Company, 1925), bk. 3, chap. 1.

15. See notes, Chapter III.

16. Self-deception offers difficult problems of definition. Is it deception or not? Intentional or not? Is there even communication or not? If a person appears to deceive himself, there are not two different human beings of whom one intends to mislead the other. Yet, arguably, two "parts" of this person are involved in a deceptive relationship. Are there times when the right hand does not know what the left hand is doing? And times when the left hand is in fact deceiving the right hand? New research on brain function may show that there is then not so much a deceiver and a deceived, but rather two different processes coordinated by the brain. Whether these processes should properly be called deception is a question discussed since Plato, and taken up anew by contemporary philosophers. See R. Demos, "Lying to Oneself," *Journal of Philosophy* 57 (1960): 588–94; and H. Fingarette, *Self-Deception* (Atlantic Highlands, N.J.: Humanities Press, 1969). For a recent discussion of the psychology of self-deception, see Guy Durandin, "Les Fondements du mensonge," pp. 273–598.

17. See Gordon W. Allport and Leo Postman, *Psychology of Rumor* (New York: Henry Holt & Co., 1947). The authors set forth a "basic law of rumor": the amount of rumor in circulation will vary with the importance of the subjects to the individuals concerned *times* the ambiguity of the evidence pertaining to the topic at issue. If either ambiguity or importance is zero, likelihood of rumor is nil.

Chapter II: Truthfulness, Deceit, and Trust

1. See quotation on p. 43, where Dante characterizes force and fraud as the two forms of malice aiming at injustice. See also Northrop Frye, *The Secular Scripture: A Study of the Structure of Romance* (Cambridge, Mass.: Harvard University Press, 1976), chap. 3.

2. Samuel Johnson, *The Adventurer* 50 (28 April 1753), in *Selected Essays from The Rambler, Adventurer, and Idler*, ed. W. J. Bate (New Haven and London: Yale University Press, 1968).

3. Nicolai Hartmann, *Ethics*, 2: 282.

4. The discussion that follows draws upon the framework provided by decision theory for thinking about choice and decision-making. This framework includes the *objectives* as they are seen by the decision maker, the *alternatives* available for reaching them, an estimate of *costs and benefits* associated with both, and a *choice rule* for weighing these.

5. Aristotle, *Nicomachean Ethics*, trans. H. Rackham (London: William Heinemann, and Cambridge, Mass.: Harvard University Press, 1934), bk. 4, chap. 7. For a discussion of Aristotle's concept of "truth," see Paul Wilpert, "Zum Aristotelischen Wahrheitsbegriff," *Phil. Jahrbuch der Görresgesellschaft*, Band 53, 1940, pp. 3–16.

6. See Michel de Montaigne, "Des Menteurs," in *Essais*, vol. 1, chap. 9 (pp. 30–35); and *What Luther Says: An Anthology*, comp. Ewald M. Plass (St. Louis, Mo.: Concordia Press, 1959), p. 871.

7. For a discussion of bias and "opportunistically distorted beliefs," see Gunnar Myrdal, *Objectivity in Social Research* (New York: Pantheon, 1968).

8. "Dogs" is taken to mean "heathens" or "sodomites"; and John Noonan, Jr., argues, in *The Morality of Abortion* (Cambridge, Mass.: Harvard University Press, 1970), p. 9, that the word *pharmakoi*, here translated as "medicine-men," referred to those who procured abortions and prescribed abortifacient drugs..

9. W. Montgomery Watt, *The Faith and Practice of Al-Ghazali* (London: George Allen and Unwin, 1953), p. 133. Al-Ghazali allowed, however, lies for necessary and praiseworthy goals where no truthful alternatives exist. See Nikki Keddie, "Sincerity and Symbol in Islam," *Studia Islamica* 19 (1963): 45.

10. Homer, *Odyssey*, trans. Robert Fitzgerald (Garden City, N.Y.: Doubleday & Company, Anchor Books, 1961), p. 251. Compare Nietzsche, *The Will to Power*, p. 293: "A thousandfold craftiness belongs to the essence of the enhancement of man. . . ."; and "On Truth and Lie in an Extra-Moral Sense," *Nietzsche*, trans. Walter Kaufmann (New York: Viking Press, 1954), pp. 42–47.

11. While such a principle is not as frequently stressed as others, it has been vigorously defended. Cicero stated, "The foundation of justice, moreover, is good faith—that is truth and fidelity to promises and agreements" (*De officiis* 1. 7. 23, trans. Walter Miller [Cambridge, Mass.: Harvard University Press, and London: William Heinemann, 1913], p. 25). Francis Hutcheson stated the "general law of veracity" in his *System of Moral Philosophy*, bk. 2, p. 32, published posthumously in 1755 (New York: Augustus M. Kelley, 1968). Richard Price, *A Review of the Principal Question of Ethics*, 1758, ed. Daiches Raphael (Oxford: Clarendon Press,

1948), pp. 153–57, takes veracity to be one of the sources of duty. Hastings Rashdall mentions a "Principle of Veracity" in his *Theory of Good and Evil*, 2d ed. (London: Oxford University Press, 1924), bk. 1, p. 192. W. D. Ross emphasized "duties of fidelity," which include an undertaking not to lie, in *The Right and the Good* (Oxford: Clarendon Press, 1930), pp. 19–22. And G. J. Warnock, in his recent book, *The Object of Morality* (London: Methuen & Co., 1971), pp. 83–86, stresses the need for a principle of nondeception.

For some, the principle is supported by religious evidence, while for others intuition supports it, and for still others, the weight of past experience.

12. Compare Robert Nozick, "Moral Complications and Moral Structures," *Natural Law Forum* 13 (1968): 1–50. See also Richard McCormick, *Ambiguity in Moral Choice* (Milwaukee: Marquette University Press, 1973), and the discussions of Pareto optimality: the state of affairs when there does not exist an alternative action which is at least as acceptable to all and definitely preferred by some.

Chapter III: Never to Lie?

1. Augustine, "On Lying," "Against Lying," *Treatises on Various Subjects* and *Enchiridion*. For discussions of earlier views, see Hugo Grotius, *On the Law of War and Peace*, and John Henry Cardinal Newman, *Apologia Pro Vita Sua*.

2. "On Lying," chap. 3. It is important to realize that Augustine *did* include the intention to deceive in his definition, as shown in the quotation from the *Enchiridion* at the head of this chapter and in chap. 3 of "On Lying." In the latter, the intention to deceive is stressed a few sentences after what appears to be the definition of lying, and is thus not always understood to be part of it.

3. "On Lying," chap. 14. Once more, Augustine returns in greater simplicity to this distinction in the *Enchiridion*: "For the sin of a man who tells a lie to help another is not so heinous as that of the man who tells a lie to injure another; and the man who by his lying puts a traveller on the wrong road does not do so much harm as the man who by false or misleading representations distorts the whole course of a life" (chap. 18, p. 21).

4. *Enchiridion*, chap. 22, p. 29.

5. For the Penitentials, see "Bigotial Penitential" (sixth and seventh centuries), III, 5; in Ludwig Bieler, ed. *The Irish Penitentials* (Dublin:

Institute for Advanced Studies, 1963); and John McNeill and Helena M. Gamer, eds., *Medieval Handbooks of Penance* (New York: Columbia University Press, 1938).

In the twelfth century the major systematic compilation dealing with lying, and a standard textbook for many centuries, was the *Sententiarum Libri Quattuor,* by Peter Lombard, *Patrologia Latina,* vol. 192, ed. J. P. Migne (Paris, 1880), bk. 3, distinction 38. It adopts definitions, categories of analysis, and moral judgments from Augustine entirely. Thomas Aquinas, in his *Summa Theologica,* works to reconcile Augustine with Aristotle and others, in 2. 2. ques. 110.

A monumental fifteenth-century work on moral theology, the *Summa Theologica* of Antoninus of Florence (reprint of Verona 1740 edition [Graz: 1959]), bk. 2, pt. 10, chap. 1, incorporates the entire body of medieval thought on the subject of lying, showing once again how the basic terms of the discussion derive from Augustine.

6. Aquinas contributed to this development by distinguishing very clearly between intent to say what is false and intent to deceive, and adding that only the former is part of the essential notion of a lie. *Summa Theologica* 2. 2. ques. 110, art. 1. (See Appendix.)

7. See, for example, J. P. Gury, *Compendium Theologiae Moralis,* ed. A. Sabetti and T. Barrett (Rome, New York, and Cincinnati: Ratisbon, 1902), pp. 221–23. See also the discussion by Bernard Häring in *The Law of Christ,* pp. 556–76, and the conflicts described by Cardinal Newman in his *Apologia Pro Vita Sua,* pp. 269–74, 348–61.

8. Blaise Pascal, *Provincial Letters,* in *Pensées, Provincial Letters,* trans. W. F. Trotter (New York: Modern Library, 1941), Letter 9, p. 443. (I have altered the translation in a few places to correspond more closely to the French.)

9. John Maguire et al., "Truthfulness," in *Cases and Materials on Evidence,* 6th ed. (Mineola, New York: The Foundation Press, 1973), pp. 248–52.

10. John Calvin, "Petit Traicté Monstrant Que C'est Que Doit Faire un Homme Cognoissant la Vérité de L'Evangile Quand Il Est Entre les Papistes," *Opera Omnia VI* (Geneva, 1617), pp. 541–88. In a later letter Calvin argued that the borrowing of the name of Nicodemus, who had followed Jesus in secret, did a great wrong to this holy personage, since Nicodemus abandoned his secrecy to claim Jesus's body publicly, whereas the Nicodemites continued their "idolatry" without such public admission. See John Calvin, *Three French Treatises,* ed. Francis M. Higman (London: Athlone Press, 1970), pp. 133–45.

11. Charles J. McFadden, *Medical Ethics* (Philadelphia: F. A. Davis, 1967), p. 391.

12. Grotius, *On the Law of War and Peace*, vol. 3, chaps. I, II.

13. Thomas Percival, for example, in *Medical Ethics*, 3d ed. (Oxford: John Henry Parker, 1849), cites Grotius and says, "A lie is always understood to consist in a *criminal* breach of truth, and therefore under no circumstances can be justified" (p. 135).

14. The textbook used by Kant was Alexander Gottlieb Baumgarten's *Ethica Philosophica*, 3d ed. (Magdeburg, 1763). Its conclusions on lying were quite strict (pars. 343, 344).

15. Paul Menzer reconstructed and published these student notes in 1924, calling them *Lectures on Ethics* (trans. Louis Infield [London: Methuen & Co., 1930]). He especially cautioned against drawing conclusions about Kant's moral philosophy merely from these notes, since the students taking them were quite unschooled. Kant, moreover, gave these lectures while he was working on his *Critique of Pure Reason*. He never published them. This has to be remembered in reading the growing number of references to the notes as "Kant's Lectures on Ethics." And it is especially important when it comes to judging Kant's views on lying. He was extremely stern on this subject in all his published writings. His Pietist upbringing and his schooling in the Collegium Fridericianum, run by the strict theologian and philosopher F. A. Schultz, support this rigid view. Yet in the *Lectures on Ethics* Kant is reported to set forth circumstances where false speech is not lying and therefore not reprehensible. Some have assumed that these flexible views are Kant's own; many have argued that what he actually later wrote on lying was so unnecessarily harsh that it had to be due to his old age. (See, for example, W. I. Matson, "Kant as Casuist," *Journal of Philosophy* 51 [1954]:855–60.) Such a view is based on nothing that Kant ever published himself. I believe that the flexibility to be found in the student lecture notes, insofar as they can be trusted as evidence, is more likely to show that Kant, at a time when he had not yet written on ethics, was willing at least to entertain in teaching the exceptions to a prohibition on lying which were commonly stated.

16. Two places where Kant takes up lying in detail are: "On a Supposed Right to Lie from Altruistic Motives," (reprinted in the Appendix to this book), and *The Doctrine of Virtue*, trans. Mary J. Gregor (New York: Harper & Row, 1964), pp. 92–96.

17. Kant, "On a Supposed Right to Lie."

18. *Ibid.*

19. Kant, *The Doctrine of Virtue*, p. 93.

20. In "On a Supposed Right to Lie," Kant takes up this view as expressed by Benjamin Constant, in "Des réactions politiques," *France,*

1797, 6: 123. Kant claims that the expression "to have a right to truth" is without meaning.

In *The Doctrine of Virtue*, p. 92, Kant argues, "In the doctrine of Law an intentional untruth is called a lie only if it infringes on another's right. But it is clear of itself that in ethics, which derives no moral title to an action from its harmlessness [to others], every deliberate untruth in the expression of one's thoughts deserves this harsh name."

21. Kant, "Introduction to the Metaphysic of Morals," *The Doctrine of Virtue*, p. 23.

22. Kant, "On a Supposed Right to Lie."

23. Cardinal Newman's *Apologia Pro Vita Sua*, pp. 274, 361. His book is a passionate defense of his life as a convert to Catholicism, wherein the subtleties of the long tradition of taking up cases of lying are upheld against Protestant critics. See also J. L. Altholz, "Truth and Equivocation: Liguri's Moral Theory and Newman's *Apologia,*" *Church History* 44 (1975):73–84.

24. Compare James Martineau, *Types of Ethical Theory* (Oxford: Clarendon Press, 1875), 2:241: "Must the enemy, the murderer, the madman, be able to wreak his will upon his victim by our agency in putting him on the right track?"

25. See selection from Kant in Appendix. See also the Introduction to "The Metaphysic of Morals" in *The Doctrine of Virtue*: "The good or bad effects of a due action . . . cannot be imputed to the subject" (p. 28).

26. See the quotation from John Wesley at the head of this chapter, taken from *Works*, vol. 7 (London: Wesleyan Conference Office, 1878). Wesley was preaching a sermon on "Behold an Israelite indeed, in whom there is no guile," holding that for such a person, "as there is no guile lodged in his heart, so there is none found on his lips." The first thing implied herein, for Wesley, is *"veracity—the speaking the truth from his heart,—the putting away all willful lying, in every kind and degree."* He then defines lying so as to rule out both "mental reservations" and claims that certain intentional untruths are not lies.

27. Paul, First Epistle to Timothy, 1:9–10. Compare with this passage from *The Didache, or Teaching of the Twelve Apostles*, in *The Apostolic Fathers*, trans. Kirsopp Lake, vol. 1 (Cambridge, Mass.: Harvard University Press, and London: William Heinemann, 1912), a second-century manual of Church instructions: "Thou shalt do no murder; thou shalt not commit adultery; . . . thou shalt not steal; thou shalt not use magic; . . . thou shalt not commit perjury; thou shalt not bear false witness; thou shalt not speak evil; thou shalt not bear malice. Thou

shalt not be double-minded or double-tongued, for to be double-tongued is the snare of death . . ." (pp. 311, 313).

28. Dante, *The Divine Comedy: Inferno*, trans. Charles S. Singleton (Princeton, N.J.: Princeton University Press, 1940), canto 11, p. 111.

29. Kant, *Critique of Practical Reason*, p. 129.

30. Augustine, "On Lying," p. 66. He based his view that a lie kills the soul on Wisdom 1:11, in the Old Testament, "A lying mouth deals death to the soul," and contrasted that statement with Matthew 10:28: "Do not be afraid of those who kill the body but cannot kill the soul; fear him rather who can destroy both body and soul in hell."

31. Richard F. Gombrich, *Precept and Practice* (Oxford: Clarendon Press, 1971), pp. 64–65, 255.

32. See Lewis Jacobs, *Jewish Values* (London: Vallentine, Mitchell, 1960), pp. 145–54. For views on lying and dissimulation in Islam, see Nikki Keddie, "Symbol and Sincerity in Islam."

CHAPTER IV: Weighing the Consequences

1. Erasmus, *Responsio ad Albertum Pium, Opera Omnia*, vol. 9 (Leiden, 1706; reprinted Hildesheim, 1962), cols. 1194–96.

2. H. Sidgwick, "The Classification of Duties. Veracity," p. 316 (see Appendix). See also Hastings Rashdall, *The Theory of Good and Evil*, 2d ed. (New York and London: Oxford University Press, 1924), bk. 1, pp. 192–93.

3. Laurence Tribe, in "Policy Science: Analysis or Ideology?," *Philosophy and Public Affairs* 2 (1972):66–110, criticizes the tendency in much modern philosophy including utilitarianism to focus on end results only rather than taking also into account "the *procedures* that shape individual and social activity." At root, I believe, the failure to discount for lying reveals such an attitude. See also R. Nozick, *Anarchy, State and Utopia* (New York: Basic Books, 1968), chap. 7.

4. That part of the negative weight which stems from harm to the integrity of the liar, however, would be hard for Bentham to accept, so long as no *pain* is involved. Mill would not find this so difficult.

5. D. H. Hodgson has shown, in *Consequences of Utilitarianism* (London: Oxford University Press, 1967), how a utilitarian approach to lying and truth-telling must cause trust in communication to deterio-

rate. (See reply by D. K. Lewis, "Utilitarianism and Truthfulness," *Australian Journal of Philosophy* 50 [1972]:17–19.)

6. See, for example, Sidgwick, *Methods of Ethics*, p. 316, and Rashdall, *The Theory of Good and Evil*, p. 193.

7. See J. J. C. Smart and Bernard Williams, *Utilitarianism, For and Against* (London: Cambridge University Press, 1973), p. 62.

8. Thus F. H. Bradley claimed, in *Ethical Studies* (New York and London: Oxford University Press, 1927), p. 193, that "there cannot be a moral philosophy which will tell us what in particular we are to do and . . . it is not the business of philosophy to do so."

See also C. D. Broad, in *The Philosophy of C. D. Broad*, ed. P. Schilpp (New York: Tudor Publishing Co., 1959), p. 285, and R. M. Hare, *Essays on Philosophical Method* (Berkeley and Los Angeles: University of California Press, 1972), pp. 1–18.

9. In *A Theory of Justice* (Cambridge, Mass.: Harvard University Press, Belknap Press, 1971), p. 34, John Rawls classifies as "intuitionists" those who hold that there is a plurality of principles that may conflict, and who also deny that there is an explicit priority rule or method for resolving such conflicts. They are therefore reduced to a resort to "intuition" for answers to such conflicts. It is true that I believe that one can work usefully with a number of principles and that I have not found a workable priority rule for resolving difficult conflicts of principle. But I would still like to reject the label of "intuitionist." I do believe that methods of practical moral reasoning exist which are superior to the use of "intuition" and which permit the resolution of a number of conflicts. A direct resort to "intuition" tends to short-circuit such reasoning, and never more than where lies are at stake. Intuitions, as advocated for distinguishing between when it is all right to lie and when it is not, are often transparently self-serving, as in the remark attributed to Disraeli: "A gentleman is one who knows when to tell the truth and when not to."

10. That it should be so difficult to root out torture in *practice* is a matter that cannot be attributed, needless to say, to any failure of systems of ethics.

11. The same is true of two methods of moral reasoning worked out in theological ethics: Situation Ethics, and the Principle of Double Effect (Joseph Fletcher, *Situation Ethics: The New Morality* [Philadelphia: Westminster Press, 1966], and Richard A. McCormick, *Ambiguity in Moral Choice* [Milwaukee: Marquette University Press, 1973]). These methods have large utilitarian components. They can be expanded, like utilitarianism, to "account for" much that seems to be beyond an immediate calculus.

12. For a discussion of the conflicting positions on suicide and on voluntary euthanasia that can be derived within each system of moral philosophy, see my "Voluntary Euthanasia," Harvard University, unpublished dissertation, 1970, chaps. 1 and 2.

13. This kind of tradition is often referred to as one of casuistry. See L. Edelstein, *The Meaning of Stoicism* (Cambridge, Mass.: Harvard University Press, 1966), pp. 71–98; K. E. Kirk, *Conscience and Its Problems* (London: Longmans, Green and Company, 1927), pp. 106–212; R. Thamin, *Un Probleme Moral dans l'Antiquité* (Paris: Hachette et Cie, 1884); W. Whewell, "Note" on casuistry, in *Lectures on the History of Moral Philosophy in England* (London: John W. Parker and Son, 1852).

Chapter V: White Lies

1. See Appendix.

2. Aristotle, in *Nicomachean Ethics* (pp. 239–45), contrasts these as "boasting" and "irony." He sees them as extremes between which the preferable mean of truthfulness is located.

3. This discussion draws on my two articles, "Paternalistic Deception in Medicine, and Rational Choice: The Use of Placebos," in Max Black, ed., *Problems of Choice and Decision* (Ithaca, N.Y.: Cornell University Program on Science, Technology and Society, 1975), pp. 73–107; and "The Ethics of Giving Placebos," *Scientific American* 231 (1974):17–23.

4. O. H. Pepper, "A Note on the Placebo," *American Journal of Pharmacy* 117 (1945):409–12.

5. J. Sice, "Letter to the Editor," *The Lancet* 2 (1972):651.

6. I am grateful to Dr. Melvin Levine for the permission to reproduce this case, used in the Ethics Rounds at the Children's Hospital in Boston.

7. C. M. Kunin, T. Tupasi, and W. Craig, "Use of Antibiotics," *Annals of Internal Medicine* 79 (October 1973):555–60.

8. In a sample of nineteen recent, commonly used textbooks, in medicine, pediatrics, surgery, anesthesia, obstetrics, and gynecology, only three even mention placebos, and none detail either medical or ethical dilemmas they pose. Four out of six textbooks on pharmacology mention them; only one mentions such problems. Only four out of eight textbooks on psychiatry even mention placebos; none takes up ethical problems. For references, see Bok, "Paternalistic Deception in Medicine and Rational Choice."

9. Form DA 67–7, 1 January 1973, U.S. Army Officer Evaluation Report.

Chapter VI: Excuses

1. John McNeill and Helena M. Gamer, trans., *Medieval Handbooks of Penance* (New York: Columbia University Press, 1938), p. 163.

2. William Shakespeare, *Othello*, act 1, scenes 1 and 3.

3. *Othello*, act 1, scene 3.

4. To disguise oneself, on the other hand, so as to gain unfair advantage is, of course, not an excuse, though, again, a common situation.

5. Insofar as the protection of confidentiality is based on a promise, there is also an indirect appeal to veracity—to making one's promise a true one.

6. For a discussion of the differences between such rights and more general human rights, see H. L. A. Hart, "Are There Any Natural Rights?," in Anthony Quinton, ed., *Political Philosophy* (London: Oxford University Press, 1967), pp. 53–66.

7. The question of competence is, of course, crucial in such circumstances. Merely to say that subjects have accepted experimental deception in advance is not sufficient if there is doubt as to their ability to give informed consent. In addition, both competence *and* consent are insufficient when the experiment presents risks to which reasonable persons would object. See Jay Katz, *Experimentation with Human Beings* (New York: Russell Sage Foundation, 1972).

8. See Ilmar Waldner, "Comments," in Max Black, ed., *Problems of Choice and Decision*, (Ithaca, N.Y.: Cornell University Program on Science, Technology and Society, 1975), pp. 118–19, for an example of such a lie.

9. Compare Hastings Rashdall, *The Theory of Good and Evil*, 2d ed. (New York and London: Oxford University Press, 1924), bk. 1, p. 194: "There are even cases in which a lie has to be told in the interests of Truth itself; a statement literally untrue must be made that a higher truth may be taught or real liberty of thought and speech advanced."

10. Shakespeare, *Othello*, act 1, scene 3.

Chapter VII: Justification

1. David Hume, *An Enquiry Concerning the Principles of Morals*, "Conclusion," in *Hume's Moral and Political Philosophy*, ed. Henry D. Aiken (New York: Macmillan Co., Hafner Press, 1948), p. 252.

2. Ludwig Wittgenstein, *Philosophical Investigations*, ed. G. E. M. Anscombe (New York: Macmillan Co., 1953), par. 265 (p. 93e).

3. John Rawls, *A Theory of Justice* (Cambridge, Mass: Harvard University Press, Belknap Press, 1971), p. 133. Compare Kurt Baier, *The Moral Point of View: A Rational Basis of Ethics* (Ithaca, N.Y.: Cornell University Press, 1958): " 'Esoteric morality' is a contradiction in terms," p. 196.

4. An interesting contemporary demonstration of such a development is to be found on the ethics committees that meet to evaluate experiments on human beings in hospitals. No one who has participated in the work of such a committee, provided it take its work seriously, will deny the powerful impact upon members of having to consider with care one moral choice after another.

5. Seneca, *Moral Epistles*, trans. Richard M. Gummere (Cambridge, Mass.: Harvard University Press, and London: William Heinemann, 1917), vol. 1, p. 185.

6. Irving L. Janis, *Victims of Groupthink* (Boston: Houghton Mifflin, 1972), p. 204.

7. See, for example, The National Commission for the Protection of Human Subjects of Biomedical and Behavioral Research, *Report and Recommendations, Research on the Fetus* (U.S. Department of Health, Education and Welfare, Publication No. [OS] 76–128, 1975).

8. Needless to say, such a process of weighing can effectively take place only against a background of rights and liberties already protected by law.

9. See Appendix.

Chapter VIII: Lies in a Crisis

1. In the absence of an acknowledged obligation such as that of captains of ships in distress, or the more general precept of "women and children first."

2. George Steiner, *After Babel*, p. 224.

3. *United States* v. *Holmes*, 26 Fed. Cas. 360 (C.C.E.D. PA 1842). See also James Childress, "Who Shall Live When Not All Can Live?," in

Thomas A. Shannon, ed., *Bioethics* (New York: Paulist Press, 1976), pp. 397–411.

4. Plutarch, "Lycurgus," *Lives of the Noble Greeks*, ed. Edmund Fuller (New York: Dell Publishing Co., 1959), p. 42.

5. See K. Donaldson, *Insanity Inside Out* (New York: Crown, 1976), for an account of his struggle to be released from involuntary confinement in a Florida State Hospital. He was released after fifteen years, in 1971. In 1975, the United States Supreme Court upheld his appeal (*O'Connor* v. *Donaldson*, 422 U.S. 563).

6. I am indebted to Dr. Melvin Levine for the use of this case.

CHAPTER IX: Lying to Liars

1. It is a sign of the neglect of these debates in recent centuries that so widely read a writer as Hannah Arendt could claim, in "Truth and Politics," that, except for Zoroastrianism, none of the major religions included lying as such in its catalogue of grave sins, and that lies only came to be considered as serious offenses with the rise of puritan morality (in Peter Laslett and W. G. Runciman, eds., *Philosophy, Politics and Society*, 3d ser. [New York: Barnes and Noble, 1967], p. 108).

2. Augustine, "Against Lying," p. 125–26.

3. Compare Benjamin Spock, *Baby and Child Care* (New York: Pocket Books, 1976), p. 355.

4. See Marcel Mauss, *The Gift* (New York: W. W. Norton & Company, 1967), for a discussion of the complex rituals of gift-giving and reciprocation.

5. Augustine, "Against Lying," chap. 2.

6. Christopher Ricks discusses the "lie/lie pun" so common in the English language in "Lies," *Critical Inquiry*, Autumn 1975, pp. 121–42.

7. Steven N. Brenner and Earl A. Molander, "Is the Ethics of Business Changing?," *Harvard Business Review* 55 (January-February 1977): 57–71.

CHAPTER X: Lying to Enemies

1. Machiavelli, *The Prince* (New York: Random House, 1950), chap. 18 (p. 64).

2. James Martineau, *Types of Ethical Theory* (Oxford: Clarendon Press, 1875), 2:242,244.

3. For an account of the widespread resort to torture, see the literature of Amnesty International, an organization working for the release of political prisoners who have not used or advocated violence. The increasing participation of medical personnel in torture is discussed in "Medical Ethics and Torture," by Leonard A. Sagan and Albert Jonsen, in the *New England Journal of Medicine* 294 (1976): 1427–30.

4. Francis Hutcheson, in *A System of Moral Philosophy*, bk. 2, chap. 10 (p. 34), puts the case as follows, in discussing an exception to the law of veracity: "when promises or narrations are extorted by the avowedly unjust violence of men who in their course of life renounce all the law of nature; as 'tis alleged that they have forfeited all those rights of mankind, the maintaining of which in them would fortify or encourage them, or give them advantages in their wicked courses."

5. Hannah Arendt, "Truth and Politics," p. 128.

6. See Ernst Kris and Nathan Leites, "Trends in Twentieth Century Propaganda," in Bernard Berelson and Morris Janowitz, eds., *Reader in Public Opinion and Communication* (New York: Free Press, 1950), pp. 278–88. See also J. A. C. Brown, *Techniques of Persuasion: Propaganda to Brainwashing* (Baltimore: Penguin Books, 1963), for an account of the many ways of affecting opinions.

7. Though forms of deception contrary to the law would, needless to say, be ruled out with respect to both.

8. See Alva Myrdal, *The Game of Disarmament* (New York: Pantheon Books, 1976).

CHAPTER XI: Lies Protecting Peers and Clients

1. Prince Albert Morrow, *Social Diseases and Marriage* (New York and Philadelphia: Lea Brothers & Co., 1904), p. 51.

2. Marcel Eck, *Lies and Truth* (New York: Macmillan Co., 1970), p. 183.

3. Bernard Häring, *The Law of Christ*, 3:575.

4. See, for example, Harvey Kuschner et al., "The Homosexual Husband and Physician Confidentiality," *Hastings Center Report*, April 1977, pp. 15–17.

5. See, for an empirical study of teen loyalty, Esther R. Greenglass, "Effects of Age and Prior Help on 'Altruistic Lying,'" *The Journal of Genetic Psychology* 121 (1972): 303–13. Twelve-year-olds were found more willing to lie for a peer who previously helped them than eight-year-olds. No differences were found between the eight-year-olds and twelve-year-olds who had been refused help by a peer.

6. Dietrich Bonhoeffer, *Ethics*, p. 367.

7. American Medical Association, *Principles of Medical Ethics*, reprinted in Stanley Joel Reiser, Arthur J. Dyck, and William J. Curran, eds., *Ethics in Medicine* (Cambridge, Mass., and London: MIT Press, 1977), pp. 38–39.

8. Boyce Rensberger, "Unfit Doctors Create Worry in Profession," *New York Times*, 26 January 1976. (Naturally, much higher or lower statistics can be provided, depending on what one means by "incompetent." But all would have to take into account those physicians who are addicted to alcohol or other drugs.)

9. *Hoffman* v. *Lindquist*, 37 Cal. 2d (1951) (J. Carter, dissenting): "But regardless of the merits of the plaintiff's case, physicians who are members of medical societies flock to the defense of their fellow member charged with malpractice and the plaintiff is relegated, for his expert testimony, to the occasional lone wolf or heroic soul, who, for the sake of truth and justice, has the courage to run the risk of ostracism by his fellow practitioners and the cancellation of his public liability insurance policy."

See also *Agnew* v. *Parks*, 172 Cal. App. 2d 756, 343, p. 2d 118 (1959), and *L'Orange* v. *Medical Protective Company*, 394 F. 2d 57 (6th Cir. 1968).

10. *Boston Sunday Globe*, editorial, 24 August 1975.

11. For a sociological view of the theme of mistakes and failure in human work, see Everett Hughes, "Mistakes at Work," in *The Sociological Eye* (Chicago and New York: Aldine-Atherton, 1971), pp. 316–25.

12. Charles Curtis, "The Ethics of Advocacy," *Stanford Law Review* 4 (1951): 3; Henry Drinker, "Some Remarks on Mr. Curtis' 'The Ethics of Advocacy,'" *Stanford Law Review* 4 (1952): 349, 350; Marvin Frankel, "The Search for Truth: An Umpireal View," *University of Pennsylvania Law Review* 123 (1975): 1031.

13. Monroe H. Freedman, *Lawyers' Ethics in an Adversary System* (Indianapolis and New York: Bobbs-Merrill Co., 1975), pp. 40–41.

14. "The Penitential of Cummean," in James McNeill and Helena M. Gamer, *Handbooks of Penance* (New York: Columbia University Press, 1938), p. 106.

15. For a criticism of this position, see John Noonan, "The Purposes of Advocacy and the Limits of Confidentiality," *Michigan Law Review* 64: 1485.

16. *Code of Professional Responsibility*, Canon 7, reproduced in Andrew Kaufman, *Problems in Professional Responsibility* (Boston: Little, Brown and Co. 1976), p. 669.

17. David Mellinkoff, *Lawyers and the System of Justice* (St. Paul, Minn.: West Publishing Company, 1976), p. 441. See also Lloyd L. Weinreb, *Denial of Justice* (New York: Free Press, and London: Collier Macmillan Publishers, 1977).

18. Hugo Grotius, *On the Law of War and Peace*, bk. 3, chap. 1; Samuel Pufendorf, *Of the Law of Nature and Nations*, trans. Basil Kennett (London, 1710), vol. 2.

19. Thomas D. Morgan and Ronald D. Rotunda, *Problems and Materials on Professional Responsibility* (Mineola, N.Y.: Foundation Press, 1976), p. 2.

20. Lawyers are not at all alone in such an intuitive view of decision. See, for example, Nicolai Hartmann, *Ethics*, 2:285: "What a man ought to do, when he is confronted with a serious conflict that is fraught with responsibility, is this: to decide according to his best conscience; that is according to his own living sense of the relative height of the respective values, and to take upon himself the consequences, external as well as inward, ultimately the guilt involved in the one value."

21. Frankel, "The Search for Truth," pp. 203–4.

CHAPTER XII: Lies for the Public Good

1. The *gennaion pseudos* has generated much controversy. Some have translated it as "pious fraud" and debated whether such fraud can be perpetrated. Thus Hastings Rashdall, in *The Theory of Good and Evil*, 2d ed. (New York and London: Oxford University Press, 1924), bk. 1, p. 195, argued that such frauds would be justifiable "if (when *all* their consequences are considered) they were socially beneficial." Other translations are: "royal lie" (Jowett), and "bold flight of the imagination" (Cornford). The latter represents an effort to see Plato as advocating not lies by the government but stories, and possible errors; an interpretation that is difficult to uphold in view of the other contexts in the *Republic* where lying is discussed, such as 389b: "The rulers of the city may, if anybody, fitly lie on account of enemies or citizens for the

benefit of the state." For Plato to have endorsed lying by the state is very significant, as truth for him was opposed, not just to falsehood, but to unreality.

2. Arthur Sylvester, "The Government Has the Right to Lie," *Saturday Evening Post*, 18 November 1967, p. 10.

3. Erasmus, *Responsio ad Albertum Pium*, *Opera Omnia*, vol. 9 (Leiden, 1706; reprinted Hildesheim, 1962).

4. The Senator Gravel Edition, *The Pentagon Papers* (Boston: Beacon Press, 1971), 3:556–59.

5. As early as March 1964, Lyndon Johnson knew that such a hard choice might have to be made. See telephone transcript cited by Doris Kearns in *Lyndon Johnson and the American Dream* (New York: Harper & Row, 1976), p. 197.

6. Theodore H. White, *The Making of the President 1964* (New York: Atheneum, 1965), p. 373.

7. *Cambridge Survey Research*, 1975, 1976.

8. *The Public Papers and Addresses of Franklin D. Roosevelt*, 1940, vol. 8, p. 517 (October 30, 1940).

9. See Arthur M. Schlesinger, Jr., *The Imperial Presidency* (Boston: Houghton Mifflin, 1973), p. 356: "The power to withhold and the power to leak led on inexorably to the power to lie . . . uncontrolled secrecy made it easy for lying to become routine." See also David Wise, *The Politics of Lying* (New York: Random House, 1973)

10. For discussions of lying and moral choice in politics, see Plato, *The Republic*; Machiavelli, *The Prince*; Grotius, *On the Law of War and Peace*; Werner Krauss, ed., *Est-il utile de tromper le peuple?*, a fascinating compilation of answers by Condorcet and others in a contest sponsored by Frederick II in 1780 (Berlin: Akademie-Verlag, 1966); Max Weber, "Politics as a Vocation," in *Essays in Sociology*, trans. H. H. Gerth and C. Wright Mills (New York: Oxford University Press, 1946), pp. 77–128; and Michael Walzer, "Political Action: The Problem of Dirty Hands," *Philosophy and Public Affairs* 2 (Winter 1973): 160–80.

CHAPTER XIII: Deceptive Social Science Research

1. Stanley Milgram, "Some Conditions of Obedience and Disobedience to Authority," *Human Relations* 18 (1965): 57–75; and "Problems of Ethics in Research," in Stanley Milgram, *Obedience to Authority* (New York: Harper & Row, 1974), app. 1 (pp. 193–202).

2. Jay Katz, *Experimentation with Human Beings* (New York: Russell Sage Foundation, 1972); and Henry K. Beecher, *Research and the Individual* (Boston: Little, Brown and Company, 1970).

3. DHEW *Code of Federal Regulations*, Title 45, revised as of Nov. 6, 1975, pars. 46.101, 102, 103.

4. Revised Ethical Standards of Psychologists, Principle 9, d, g, *APA Monitor*, March 1977, pp. 22–23.

5. Elliot Aronson, "Experimentation in Social Psychology," in *The Handbook of Social Psychology*, ed. Gardner Lindzey and Elliot Aronson, vol. 2 (Reading, Mass., Addison-Wesley, 1968), p. 26.

6. Herbert Kelman, "Human Use of Human Subjects: The Problem of Deception in Social Psychological Experiments," *Psychological Bulletin* 67 (1967): 1–11.

7. Francis Bacon, "Of Truth." (See Appendix.)

8. Charles McClintock, *Experimental Social Psychology* (New York: Holt, Rinehart and Winston, 1972), p. 62.

9. *Ethical Standards*, Principle 9, h.

10. Herbert Kelman, "Research, behavioral," *Encyclopedia of Bioethics* (New York: Free Press, 1978).

11. Kai Erikson voices similar concerns with respect to "disguised observation" in "A Comment on Disguised Observation in Psychology," *Social Problems*, 1967, pp. 366–73. He holds that: "This particular research strategy can injure persons in ways we can neither anticipate in advance nor compensate for afterwards" (p. 367).

12. DHEW *Code* (see note 3 above).

13. See Judith Jarvis Thomson, "The Right to Privacy," *Philosophy and Public Affairs* 4 (1975): 295–322, for examples of such invasions and a discussion of what is at the root of our concern about them.

14. Donald Warwick, "Social Scientists Ought to Stop Lying," *Psychology Today* 8 (February 1975): 38–49, 105–6.

15. Stuart Sutherland, "The Case of the Pseudo-patient," *Times Literary Supplement*, 4 February 1977, p. 125.

16. David Rosenhan, "On Being Sane in Insane Places," *Science* 179 (1973): 250–58.

17. Allan Owen and Robin Winkler, "General Practitioners and Psychosocial Problems: An Evaluation Using Pseudo-patients," *Medical Journal of Australia* 2 (1974): 393–98.

18. *The New York Times*, 30 August 1976.

19. Owen and Winkler, "General Practitioners and Psychosocial Problems," p. 398.

CHAPTER XIV: Paternalistic Lies

1. Thomas Hobbes, *De Corpore Politico*, in *Body, Man, and Citizen: Selections from Thomas Hobbes*, ed. Richard Peters (New York: Collier Books, 1962), p. 330.

2. Homer, *Odyssey* 12. 226.

3. See John Stuart Mill, "On Liberty," in *The Philosophy of John Stuart Mill*, ed. Marshall Cohen, pp. 185–319, and Gerald Dworkin, "Paternalism," in R. Wasserstrom, ed., *Morality and the Law* (Belmont, Cal.: Wadsworth Publishing Company, 1971), pp. 107–126, for discussions of the problems of paternalism.

4. See Leona Baumgartner and Elizabeth Mapelsden Ramsey, "Johann Peter Frank and His 'System einer vollständigen medizinischen Polizei," *Annals of Medical History* n.s. 5 (1933): 525–32, and n.s. 6: 69–90.

5. Erik Erikson, *Toys and Reasons* (New York: W. W. Norton & Co., 1977), p. 17.

For lying in childhood and children's views of lying, see Sigmund Freud, "Infantile Mental Life: Two Lies Told by Children," *Collected Papers*, ed. James Strachey (London: Hogarth Press, 1950), pp. 144–49; Jean Piaget, "Lying," *The Moral Judgment of the Child* (New York: Collier Books, 1962), pp. 139–96; Durandin, *Les fondements du mensonge*. For a developmental theory of the growth of moral judgment in children, see Lawrence Kohlberg, "The Development of Children's Orientations Toward a Moral Order: I. Sequence in the Development of Moral Thought," *Vita Humana* 6 (1963): 11–33, and subsequent writings.

6. Edmund Gosse, *Father and Son* (New York: Charles Scribner's Sons, 1908), pp. 22, 24.

For a discussion of the role of fairy tales in child development, see Bruno Bettelheim, *The Uses of Enchantment* (New York: Alfred A. Knopf, 1976).

7. Milton's list of obvious targets for deception, as quoted by Cardinal Newman in *Apologia Pro Vita Sua*, p. 274, also included "enemies, men in error, and thieves." See also Erasmus, *Responsio ad Albertum Pium*, *Opera Omnia*, vol. 9 (Leiden, 1706; reprinted Hildesheim, 1962); Hugo Grotius, *On the Law of War and Peace* (see Appendix); H. Sidgwick, *The Methods of Ethics*, p. 316, "nor do I perceive that any one

shrinks from telling fictions to children on matters upon which it is thought well that they should not know the truth."

8. Renée C. Fox and Judith P. Swazey, *The Courage to Fail: A Social View of Organ Transplants and Dialysis* (Chicago and London: University of Chicago Press, 1974), p. 15.

9. Martin Luther: see quotation, p. 48, passages cited in *What Luther Says* (St. Louis, Mo.: Concordia Publishing House, 1959), 2:870–72; and *Saemmtliche Schriften*, vol. 1 (St. Louis, Mo.: Concordia Publishing House, 1892), pp. 787–88.

10. Daniel Pekarski, in "Manipulation and Education" (Ph. D. diss., Harvard University, 1976), discusses such choices as they arise in education.

11. See Dworkin, "Paternalism," and John Rawls, *A Theory of Justice* (Cambridge, Mass.: Harvard University Press, Belknap Press, 1971), pp. 209, 249, for mentions of this form of implied consent in paternalistic contexts. See also Grotius in the Appendix.

12. Mill, "On Liberty," pp. 197–98.

Chapter XV: Lies to the Sick and the Dying

1. Plato, *The Republic*, 389 b.

2. B. C. Meyer, "Truth and the Physician," *Bulletin of the New York Academy of Medicine* 45 (1969): 59–71. See, too, the quotation from Dr. Henderson in Chapter I of this book (p. 12).

3. W. H. S. Jones, trans, *Hippocrates*, Loeb Classical Library (Cambridge, Mass.: Harvard University Press, 1923), p. 164.

4. Reprinted in M. B. Etziony, *The Physician's Creed: An Anthology of Medical Prayers, Oaths and Codes of Ethics* (Springfield, Ill.: Charles C Thomas, 1973), pp. 15–18.

5. See Harry Friedenwald, "The Ethics of the Practice of Medicine from the Jewish Point of View," *Johns Hopkins Hospital Bulletin*, no. 318 (August 1917), pp. 256–61.

6. "Ten Principles of Medical Ethics," *Journal of the American Medical Association* 164 (1957): 1119–20.

7. Mary Barrett, letter, *Boston Globe*, 16 November 1976, p. 1.

8. Though a minority of physicians have struggled to bring them to our attention. See Thomas Percival, *Medical Ethics*, 3d ed. (Oxford: John Henry Parker, 1849), pp. 132–41; Worthington Hooker, *Physician and Patient* (New York: Baker and Scribner, 1849), pp. 357–82; Richard

C. Cabot, "Teamwork of Doctor and Patient Through the Annihilation of Lying," in *Social Service and the Art of Healing* (New York: Moffat, Yard & Co., 1909), pp. 116–70; Charles C. Lund, "The Doctor, the Patient, and the Truth," *Annals of Internal Medicine* 24 (1946): 955; Edmund Davies, "The Patient's Right to Know the Truth," *Proceedings of the Royal Society of Medicine* 66 (1973): 533–36.

9. Lawrence Henderson, "Physician and Patient as a Social System," *New England Journal of Medicine* 212 (1955).

10. Nicholas Demy, Letter to the Editor, *Journal of the American Medical Association* 217 (1971): 696–97.

11. For the views of physicians, see Donald Oken, "What to Tell Cancer Patients," *Journal of the American Medical Association* 175 (1961): 1120–28; and tabulations in Robert Veatch, *Death, Dying, and the Biological Revolution* (New Haven and London: Yale University Press, 1976), pp. 229–38. For the view of patients, see Veatch, *ibid.*; Jean Aitken-Swan and E. C. Easson, "Reactions of Cancer Patients on Being Told Their Diagnosis," *British Medical Journal*, 1959, pp. 779–83; Jim McIntosh, "Patients' Awareness and Desire for Information About Diagnosed but Undisclosed Malignant Disease," *The Lancet* 7 (1976): 300–303; William D. Kelly and Stanley R. Friesen, "Do Cancer Patients Want to Be Told?," *Surgery* 27 (1950): 822–26.

12. See Avery Weisman, *On Dying and Denying* (New York: Behavioral Publications, 1972); Elisabeth Kübler-Ross, *On Death and Dying* (New York: The Macmillan Co., 1969); Ernest Becker, *The Denial of Death* (New York: Free Press, 1973); Philippe Ariès, *Western Attitudes Toward Death*, trans. Patricia M. Ranum (Baltimore and London: Johns Hopkins University Press, 1974); and Sigmund Freud, "Negation," *Collected Papers*, ed. James Strachey (London: Hogarth Press, 1950), 5:181–85.

13. Kübler-Ross, *On Death and Dying*, p. 34.

14. Michel de Montaigne, *Essays*, bk. 1, chap. 20.

15. It is in literature that these questions are most directly raised. Two recent works where they are taken up with striking beauty and simplicity are May Sarton, *As We Are Now* (New York: W. W. Norton & Co., 1973); and Freya Stark, *A Peak in Darien* (London: John Murray, 1976).

16. Herman Feifel et al., "Physicians Consider Death," *Proceedings of the American Psychoanalytical Association*, 1967, pp. 201–2.

17. See Ivan Illich, *Medical Nemesis* (New York: Pantheon, 1976), for a critique of the iatrogenic tendencies of contemporary medical care in industrialized societies.

18. See, for example, "Statement on a Patient's Bill of Rights," reprinted in Stanley Joel Reiser, Arthur J. Dyck, and William J. Curran *Ethics in Medicine* (Cambridge, Mass., and London: MIT Press, 1977), p. 148.

19. See Ralph Aphidi, "Informed Consent: A Study of Patient Reaction," *Journal of the American Medical Association* 216 (1971): 1325–29.

20. See Steven R. Kaplan, Richard A. Greenwald, and Arvey I. Rogers, Letter to the Editor, *New England Journal of Medicine* 296 (1977): 1127.

21. Oken, "What to Tell Cancer Patients"; Veatch, *Death, Dying, and the Biological Revolution;* Weisman, *On Dying and Denying.*

22. Norman L. Cantor, "A Patient's Decision to Decline Life-Saving Treatment: Bodily Integrity Versus the Preservation of Life," *Rutgers Law Review* 26: 228–64; Danielle Gourevitch, "Suicide Among the Sick in Classical Antiquity," *Bulletin of the History of Medicine* 18 (1969): 501–18; for bibliography, see Bok, "Voluntary Euthanasia."

23. Lewis Thomas, "A Meliorist View of Disease and Dying," *The Journal of Medicine and Philosophy* 1 (1976): 212–21.

24. Claude Lévi-Strauss, *Structural Anthropology* (New York: Basic Books, 1963), p. 167; See also Eric Cassell, "Permission to Die," in John Behnke and Sissela Bok, eds., *The Dilemmas of Euthanasia* (New York: Doubleday, Anchor Press, 1975), pp. 121–31.

25. Ariès, *Western Attitudes Toward Death,* p. 11.

26. See Charles Fried, *Medical Experimentation: Personal Integrity and Social Policy* (Amsterdam and Oxford: North Holland Publishing Co. 1974), pp. 20–24.

27. Cicely M. S. Saunders, "Telling Patients," in Reiser, Dyck, and Curran, *Ethics in Medicine,* pp. 238–40.

28. "Personal Directions for Care at the End of Life," Sissela Bok, *New England Journal of Medicine* 295 (1976): 367–69.

CHAPTER XVI: Conclusion

1. See "The Pressure to Compromise Personal Ethics," Special Report, *Business Week,* 31 January 1977, p. 107, and Steven N. Brenner and Earl A. Molander, "Is the Ethics of Business Changing?," *Harvard Business Review* 55 (January–February 1977): 57–71.

2. See Richard Austin Smith, "The Incredible Electrical Conspiracy," pt. 1, *Fortune,* April 1961, pp. 132–37, 170–80.

3. See Jerry R. Green and Jean-Jacques Laffont, *Incentives in Public Decision Making* (Amsterdam: North-Holland Publishing Co., 1978), and William Vickery, "Counterspeculation, Auctions, and Cooperative Sealed Tenders," *Journal of Finance* 16 (March 1961): 8–37. I am grateful to Howard Raiffa for bringing this new line of research to my attention.

4. See Derek Bok, "Can Ethics Be Taught?" *Change* 8 (October 1976): 26–30.

SELECT BIBLIOGRAPHY

I have found these works especially helpful in studying the ethics of lying and truthfulness. This list does not include all the works referred to in the footnotes, and a few are listed here though not mentioned in the footnotes.

Aquinas, Thomas. *Summa Theologica*, 2.2 ques. 109, 110. Literally translated by the Fathers of the English Dominican Province. London: Burns Oates & Washbourne Ltd, 1st ed. 1922.

Arendt, Hannah. "Truth and Politics." In Peter Laslett and W. G. Runciman, eds., *Philosophy, Politics and Society*, 3d series. New York: Barnes & Noble, 1967.

Aristotle. *Nicomachean Ethics*. Book IV, Ch. 7.

Augustine. "Lying," and "Against Lying." In *Treatises on Various Subjects*, vols. 14, 16. Edited by R. J. Deferrari. Fathers of the Church. New York: Catholic University of America Press, 1952.

Augustine. *Enchiridion*, on Faith, Hope and Love. Edited by Henry Paolucci. Chicago: Henry Regnery Company, 1961.

Bacon, Francis. "Of Truth." In *Essays Civil and Moral*. London: Ward, Lock & Co., 1910.

Bentham, Jeremy. *The Principles of Morals and Legislation*, chap. 16. New York: Macmillan Co., Hafner Press, reissued 1948.

Bonhoeffer, Dietrich. "What Is Meant by 'Telling the Truth'?" In *Ethics*, pp. 363–72. Edited by Eberhard Bethge. New York: Macmillan Co., 1965.

Chisholm, Roderick, and Feehan, Thomas D. "The Intent to Deceive." *The Journal of Philosophy* 74 (1977): 143–59.

Durandin, Guy. "Les Fondements du Mensonge." Thesis, Faculté des Lettres et Sciences Humaines, Paris, 1970. Service de reproduction des thèses de l'Université de Lille, 1971.

Grotius, Hugo. *On the Law of War and Peace*, bk. 3, chap. 1. Translated by Francis W. Kelsey. Indianapolis: Bobbs-Merrill Co., 1925.

Häring, Bernard. *The Law of Christ: Moral Theology for Priests and Laity*, vol. 3, pp. 556–76. Translated by Edwin G. Kaiser. Westminster, Md.: Newman Press, 1966.

Harrod, R. F. "Utilitarianism Revised." *Mind* 45, no. 178 (1936): 137–56.

Hartmann, Nicolai. "Truthfulness and Uprightness." *Ethics*, vol. 2, pp. 281–85.

Hutcheson, Francis. *A System of Moral Philosophy*, bk. 2, pp. 31–35. New York: Augustus M. Kelley, 1968.

Isenberg, Arnold. "Deontology and the Ethics of Lying." In J. Thomson and Gerald Dworkin, eds., *Ethics*, pp. 163–85. New York: Harper & Row, 1968.

Jacobs, Lewis. "Truth." In *Jewish Values*, pp. 145–54. London: Valentine, Mitchell, 1960.

Kant, Immanuel. "On a Supposed Right to Lie from Benevolent Motives." In *The Critique of Practical Reason and Other Writings in Moral Philosophy*, pp. 346–50. Edited and translated by Lewis White Beck. Chicago: University of Chicago Press, 1949.

Kant, Immanuel. "The Doctrine of Virtue," pt. 2 of *The Metaphysic Morals*. Translated by Mary Gregor. New York: Harper & Row, 1964.

Montaigne, Michel de. "Des Menteurs." [On Liars.] *Essais*. Edited by Maurice Rat. Paris: Éditions Garnier Frères, 1952.

Newman, John Henry Cardinal. *Apologia Pro Vita Sua: Being a History of His Religious Opinions*. London: Longmans, Green & Co., 1880.

Piaget, Jean. *The Moral Judgment of the Child*, chap. 2. New York: Collier Books, 1952.

Plato. *Hippias Minor*.

Plato. *Republic*.

Rousseau, J. J. "Les Rêveries d'un Promeneur Solitaire" (Reveries of a Solitary). 4ème Promenade. *Oeuvres Complètes*, vol. 1. Paris: N. R. F. Gallimard 1959. Trans. John Gould Fletcher. New York: B. Franklin, 1971.

Sidgwick, H. "Classification of Duties—Veracity." In *The Methods of Ethics*. 7th ed. London: Macmillan & Co., 1907.

Steiner, George. *After Babel*, pp. 205–35. New York and London: Oxford University Press, 1975.

Taylor, Jeremy. *Doctor Dubitandum or the Rule of Conscience*, bk. 3. London, 1660.

Warnock, G. J. *The Object of Morality*, chap. 6. London: Methuen & Co., 1971.

INDEX

lies to, 4, 48, 61, 84–5, 102, 125, 128, 206–10, 214, 216, 218–19; placebos for, 66

choice, xx–xxi; abandonment of, 20; effects of lying on, 18–22; requisites of, 22; in survival situations, 110–13; for terminally ill, 221–2, 231–2. *See also* moral choice

Christian philosophy, xx, 55, 78–9. *See also* Calvinism; Catholics and Catholicism

clients, 88, 158–64. *See also* confidentiality; professions

clergy, 82, 151, 152, 158

coercion, xxii, 41, 204; deception as, 18–22, 29; labeled paternalism, 215. *See also* force-deception analogy; violence

Coleridge, Samuel Taylor, 207; *Biographia Literaria*, 207n

colleagues: consultation with, 96–7; fidelity to, 148, 153–8. *See also* confidentiality; justification; professions

common sense, 48, 57, 59

communication, 4; distortions of, 8n; filters, 15–16

compact, 129–30

competition, 120, 244

Concept of Law, The (Hart), 111n

confessor, 147, 151. *See also* clergy

confidentiality, 82–3, 146–64, 166; arguments supporting, 149–52; between colleagues, 153–8; clergy and, 82, 151, 152, 158; doctor-patient, 147–8, 224; perjury and, 158–64; protecting client's, 81, 158–64

conflicts of duty, 39–42

Confucius, 93n

Congress, 27, 98, 174, 179

Conrad, Joseph: *Lord Jim*, 112

conscience, 94, 113n

consent, 98; to government deception, 175–81; implied, 214–17, 218; to paternalistic lying, 214–17; suspension of disbelief as, 207n. *See also* informed consent

Consentius, 123–5, 128

consequences, 46, 48–56. *See also* utilitarians and utilitarianism

contraceptives, 151; placebos given for, 67

contract, 81, 88. *See also* compact

corruption, 23, 83, 115, 118

counterfeiters, 144

court proceedings, 36. *See also* law; lawyers; oaths

Cratylus, 9

credibility, 24, 26, 178, 219

criminals, 159

crisis and crisis lies, 107–22, 127, 150, 166, 213–14, 215; acute, 108–10; chronic, 110–13; imposed by an enemy, 140–5; liars' perception of, 113, 118; line-drawing in, 113–19; political, 172, 179–80; word, 108n

Curtis, Charles, 158; "The Ethics of Advocacy," 146

cynicism, 142

Dante: *Inferno*, 43

death, 61, 219, 228, 229; denial of, 229–30; "dying response," 235–7; fears of, 232–3; preparation for, 236–7. *See also* terminally ill

Death of Ivan Ilych, The (Tolstoy), 220

debriefing, 187, 190–3

deceit. *See* deception and deceptive practices; lies and lying

deceived person(s): consent of, 83, 88, 98, 100, 129–33; effect of lying on, 50; enemies as, 138, 139; liar's view of, 167, 168; power of, 19, 22; relationship to liar, 88. *See also* children; patients; perspective of the deceived; perspective of the liar

deception and deceptive practices, xix, 60, 79, 118; as coercion, xxii, 18–22, 29, 103, 126, 205, 213–14; confused with fiction, 207n; consent to, 83, 88, 103, 175–81, 214–17; contemporary debate about, xvi, 5; defined, 13–16; expected, 144; among family members and friends, 205–19; government, xvii, 27, 95, 97, 98, 99, 125, 142–3, 167–81; legal profession, 158–64; legitimate uses of, 18, 31, 41, 45, 71, 103, 109, 130–1, 141, 177, 181; medical profession, 61–8, 153–8, 220–41; mutual, 129–33; in research and experimentation, 80, 83, 182–202; spread of, 104–5, 109, 112, 115, 119–22, 127, 169, 176, 180, 195; taught, 196, 247; therapeutic, 221–6; violence parallel, 18, 29, 43, 103–4, 109, 126, 130n, 145, 205, 213–14; ways of discouraging,

fiction: and deception, 206–7

flattery, 58, 71n, 210

force-deception analogy, 18, 29, 41, 103–4, 109, 126, 130n, 205, 213–14. *See also* coercion

foreign policy, 97, 99, 170–3, 179–81

forgery, 207n

Fox, Renée, 211

Frank, Johann Peter, 204–5

Frankel, Marvin E., 164

fraud, 43, 85, 149, 244

Freedman, Monroe, 158–9

freedom, 21, 230

fugitives, 40–1

"Game Theory and the Study of Ethical Problems" (Schelling), 17

Gandhi, Mahatma: *Defense Against Charge of Sedition*, 134

General Electric, 245–6

Golden Rule, 28–9, 93; negative form, 93n

Goldwater, Barry, 171

Gospels, 7. *See also* Bible

Gosse, Edmund: *Father and Son*, 207

gossip, 72

government: giving information to, 132, 150

government lies and deception, xvii, 167–81, 244; consent to, 12, 175–81; examples, xviii, 21, 27, 97, 125, 170–4, 176–9; excuses for, 12, 97, 125, 143, 166–70; foreign policy, 97, 99, 142; justifiable, 178, 181; as paternalism, 167, 205; publicity test, 95, 98, 99, 175–81; public trust and, xviii, 27, 142–3, 178. *See also* political lies and deception; Watergate

government research, 186

gratitude, 58

Greek philosophy: Aristotle, 22, 30, 81n; Plato, 5, 165, 167, 168, 207n; pre-Socratic, 5

Grotius, Hugo, 14, 37, 161, 209; on the character of falsehood, 263–7; *Law of War and Peace, The*, 203

Groundwork of the Metaphysic of Morals, The (Kant), 95n

harm, 21, 24–8, 45–6, 50, 52, 104, 126, 127, 195; of deceptive research, 191, 193–7; lying to avert, 39–42, 76–9, 80, 109, 135, 149–50, 167, 187, 200, 223; of lying

to enemies, 140–3; of paternalistic lies, 214; of placebo-giving, 62–8; residual, 191; of truth-telling, 234–7; of white lies, 60–72

Harrod, R. F.: "Utilitarianism Revised," 275–82

Hart, H. L. A.: *The Concept of Law*, 111n

Hartmann, Nicolai, 19

health professionals. *See* medical profession

Held, Virginia, 91n

hero, 29

Hillel, Rabbi, 93n

Hippocratic Oath, 153, 223

Hitler, Adolf: *Mein Kampf*, 134

Hofstra Law School, 158

Holmes, Oliver Wendell: *Medical Essays*, 220

honesty, 60, 87, 138; incentives for, 247. *See also* truth; truthfulness

Hulka, Barbara S., 237n

Hume, David, 91, 111; *An Enquiry Concerning the Principles of Morals*, 111n, 134

Hutcheson, Francis: *A System of Moral Philosophy*, 17, 107

hypocrites and hypocrisy, 84

hysterectomy, unnecessary, 63

identity: denial of, 79

incompetent persons: lying to, 209, 218

individualism, 244

informed consent: of experimental subjects, 67, 185–7, 189, 194; as justification element, 103; of sick and dying, 228, 233, 234–5, 236. *See also* consent

injustice, 81. *See also* fairness; justice

innocence, 113

integrity, 24–5, 45, 249; bodily, 115; derivation of word, 25n; lawyers', 163

intelligence operators, xvii, 27, 120

intention, 33, 34, 81; to mislead, 6–9, 15, 35, 58, 74, 87, 207n. *See also* excuses

invalids. *See* medical lies and deception; patients; terminally ill

Jacobs, Lewis: "Truth," 74

Janis, Irving, 97

Jewish texts, 45, 55, 73–4

Jewish Values, 74
Johnson, Lyndon B.: political lies of, 170–3, 179, 180
Johnson, Samuel, 18–19, 40
journalism and journalists, xvii; Watergate and, 120–1
judges, 85, 163, 210
juries, 163–4
justice, 8in, 139, 149; adversary system of, 161, 164; Hume on, 111. *See also* fairness
justification, 74–5n, 89, 90–106; appeal to conscience, 94–5; appeal to reasonable persons, 92–3; consultation with chosen peers, 96–7; crisis as, 107–22; by faith, 91; of government lies, 167–70, 178, 181; to imaginary public, 95; of lying to enemies, 134–45, 139; of lying to liars, 124–33; paternalistic, 204; test of publicity, 90–4. *See also* excuses; publicity test
"Justification, Legal and Political" (Held), 91n

Kansas, 233
Kant, Immanuel, 37–9, 46, 49, 60, 108; on altruistic lies, 267–72; answers to, 39–42; Categorical Imperative, 52; *Critique of Practical Reason.* . . . 267–72; *Doctrine of Virtue,* 32, 43n; *The Groundwork of the Metaphysic of Morals,* 95n; religious parallels to, 43
Kelman, Herbert, 182
kidnappers, 144
knowledge, 21–2
Kübler-Ross, Elisabeth, 229–30

Laertius, Diogenes: *Lives of Eminent Philosophers,* 232
Lancet, 62
law, xvii, 27, 91n, 149, 247; corrupt, 114–15, 117–18; divorce, 117, 245; encouraging deception, 245; enforcement, 244–5. *See also* government lies and deception; lawyers
Law of War and Peace, The (Grotius), 203
lawyers, xvii, 120, 148, 222; arguments for lying in court, 85, 151, 159–64; relationship with client, 81, 147, 151, 152, 158–64. *See also* professions

letters of recommendation, 68–70, 71
Lévi-Strauss, Claude, 236
liar(s), 84, 90; effect of lying on, 24–6, 38, 50, 52, 60, 117, 139, 195, 209; as enemy, 133, 135; excuses of, 74–89; free-rider status, 23, 26; lying to, 123–33; in myth, 112; pathological, 126; power of, 19, 22, 23, 26; relationship to deceived, 88; risk-benefit scale of, 44, 50–1. *See also* perspective of the liar
lie-detector tests, 151
lies and lying: absolutist position, 32–46, 118; alternatives to, 88, 103, 108, 112, 117–19, 121, 138; to avoid harm, 39–42, 77–80, 109, 135, 149–50, 167, 187, 200, 223; Catholic theologians on, 32–5, 39–40; to children, 48, 61, 84–5, 102, 206–10, 214, 216, 218–19; choice and, 18–22, 29; confused with error, 6–7n; in court, 158–64; in a crisis, 107–22, 135, 140; defined, 13–16, 33, 49; distinctions, 33, 34, 49, 78–9, 132, 250–1; to enemies, 134–45, 179; *gennaion,* 167; harmful results of, 21, 24–8, 104, 172–4; justification of, 75–89, 90–106, 213–19; to liars, 123–33; negative presumption on, 30–1, 50, 75; pact on, 129–33; pardonable, 33, 34, 89; paternalistic, 81, 203–19; perspective of the deceived, 20–3, 28–9; perspective of the liar, 22, 23–30; philosophical neglect of, xix–xxi, 10–11; power-distribution effects, 19, 20, 22, 23, 26; to produce benefits, 79–81, 165–81; to protect confidentiality, 24, 146–64; for the public good, 81, 165–81; punishment for, 43–4, 73; religious, 7, 14, 86; for sake of truth, 84–6, 161; to save life, 22, 43–4, 80, 91, 104, 108, 109, 214; to the sick and dying, 88, 97, 130, 219, 220–41; as survival strategy, 23, 135; trivial, 21, 57–61; utilitarian view, 47–52, 53; white, 4, 25, 57–72, 80, 127, 175, 176, 214, 217, 218. *See also* deceived person(s); deception and deceptive practices; deceptive research; excuses; liar(s); medical lies and deception; professions
Lives of Eminent Philosophers (Diogenes Laertius), xixn, 232n
logic and logicians, 5, 54n

110, 120–2; deceptive practices, xv–xviii, 79, 99, 100, 119–22; effect of deceptive research on, 195–7; ethics and ethical codes, xvi, xvii, 11, 154, 185–6, 189–90, 192, 223–4, 245–6; monitoring of, 201. *See also* clergy; government; journalists; lawyers; medical profession

promises and promise-breaking, 51, 81, 151–2

propaganda, 61, 207n

Protestants, 14, 36

pseudonyms, 82

pseudo-patient studies, 197–202

psychiatrists, xvii. *See also* medical profession

psychologists: ethical standards, 185–6, 189–90, 192. *See also* social sciences

psychosurgery, 98

public: government view of, 167–78

public confidence, xviii, 26–8, 95, 97, 142, 176. *See also* social trust

publicity, 90–2

publicity test, 92–106; for crisis lies, 109, 115, 117, 119; for deceptive research and experimentation, 188; for government lies, 175–81; for lies to enemies, 139, 140, 143–5; for lies to protect confidentiality, 162–4; limitations of, 100–2; for lying to liars, 127; for paternalistic lies, 218

public justification. *See* justification; publicity test

Pufendorf, Samuel, 161

punishment, 73

Pyrrho, 9

radical skeptics, 9

ratings: inflated, 68–72

Rawls, John, 92; *A Theory of Justice*, 90, 111n

reasonable persons, 101–6, 138, 176, 218

reciprocity, 128, 129–30

recommendations, 96; inflated, 59, 68–72

religion, 55, 91n, 150; concealment of, 36, 124; denial of, 79

religious lies, 7, 86; definition problems, 14

religious persecution, 111, 124

religious truth, 6–7

Republic, The (Plato), 165, 207n

research and experimentation, 12, 182–202; biomedical, 67, 83, 185, 187, 189, 193; ethical codes for, 185–6, 195–6; fairness in, 83; Federal regulations, 185; fetal, 98; informed consent of subjects, 67, 185–7, 189, 194; review committees, 193–5; social sciences, 182–202. *See also* deceptive research

Reveries of a Solitary (Rousseau), 57

revolution, 53

rights, 177; to coerce and manipulate, 204; of criminals, 159; to know, 37, 38, 209, 233; of subjects of experimentation, 192. *See also* privacy; self-defense

Roman Stoics, 55

Roosevelt, Franklin D., 179

Rosenhan, D. L.: "On Being Sane in Insane Places," 197

Rosenthal, Robert, 183

Ross, William David, 152n

Rousseau, Jean-Jacques, 59; *Reveries of a Solitary*, 57

rulers, 167, 168

St. Christopher's Hospice (England), 239

salesmanship and selling, 66, 131–2, 244–6

Sartre, Jean-Paul: *Dirty Hands*, 165–6

Saunders, Cicely, 239

Schelling, Thomas: "Game Theory and the Study of Ethical Problems," 17

Scholastics, 39

scientific lies, 80, 85. *See also* deceptive research

secrets. *See* confidentiality

secret-service agents, 120

Segretti, Donald, 120

self-deception, 8, 15, 54, 84; of physician, 62. *See also* perspective of the liar

self-defense, 41, 79, 80, 104, 113, 115, 135, 137, 140, 141, 142, 145

sentimentality, 84

Sermon (Wesley), 32

sex discrimination, 200

sexual preferences, 79

Shakespeare, William, 123, 129

shock, 236

sick people. *See* medical lies and deception; patients

ing, 104. *See also* coercion; force-deception analogy

war, 53, 135, 137, 141, 144, 179–80. *See also* Vietnam; World War II
Warnock, G. J.: *The Object of Morality*, 47, 76n, 287–8
Watergate, xviii, 61, 107, 120–1, 173
welfare system, 245
Wesley, John, 42, 44n; *Sermon*, 32
white lies, 4, 57–72, 127, 214, 217; alternatives to, 71–2; author's definition, 58; excuses for, 58, 80; harm of, 24, 60–72, 217; inflated ratings and recommendations, 68–70, 71; placebos as, 59, 60, 61–8, 71; polite expressions, 58; political, 175, 176; types of, 59
whole truth, 3–16
Will to Power, The (Nietzsche), 17
Wilson, Menahem, 7
Wittgenstein, Ludwig, 92
Woodward, Bob: *All the President's Men*, 107
World Health Organization (WHO), 153
World Medical Association, 224
World War II, 116, 135, 141, 179–80

Yale, 183

ABOUT THE AUTHOR

Sissela Bok was born in Sweden and educated in Switzerland, France, and the United States. She received a Ph.D. in philosophy from Harvard University in 1970. She has taught philosophy at Brandeis University since 1985 and earlier taught courses in ethics and decision-making at Harvard Medical School and the John F. Kennedy School of Government. She is the author of numerous articles on ethics, literature, and biography, and of *Secrets: On the Ethics of Concealment and Revelation* (1982), and *A Strategy for Peace* (1989), as well as of a biography of her mother, Alva Myrdal, published in Sweden, to appear in the United States in 1990.